THE PSYCHOLOGY OF GAMBLING

Edited by Jon Halliday
and Peter Fuller

 HARPER COLOPHON BOOKS
Harper & Row, Publishers
New York, Evanston, San Francisco, London

This book was originally published in Great Britain in 1974 by
Allen Lane.

THE PSYCHOLOGY OF GAMBLING Copyright ©1974 by Jon Halliday and Peter Fuller. All rights reserved. Printed in the United
States of America. No part of this book may be used or reproduced in any manner without written permission except in the
case of brief quotations embodied in critical articles and reviews.
For information address Harper & Row, Publishers, Inc., 10 East
53d Street, New York, N.Y. 10022. Published simultaneously in
Canada by Fitzhenry & Whiteside Limited, Toronto.

First HARPER COLOPHON edition published 1975

LIBRARY OF CONGRESS CATALOG CARD NUMBER: 75–548

STANDARD BOOK NUMBER: 06–090418–6

75 76 77 78 79 80 10 9 8 7 6 5 4 3 2 1

Contents

Acknowledgements

We would like to thank Vickie Hamilton, Fred Halliday and Alexander Cockburn who read the introduction and made numerous useful suggestions, and Tom Nairn who translated Elvio Fachinelli's 'Anal Money-time'.

J. H. and P. F.

I would like to add my thanks to the following: David Cooper, in particular for his observations on gambling with life, James Greene, and Cindy Klein who helped me with the original research. I also wish to express my thanks to the many friends, almost all of them gamblers of one kind or another, who discussed their own and others' experiences at the track and round the green baize, especially Josephine Winham and Michael Best. Good luck to you all.

J. H.

Editor's Note

The texts in this volume have been chosen because they represent the development of psychological thinking on gambling. Several of the texts contain passages which we consider to be racist and sexist. Inclusion of these texts in no way constitutes endorsement of their contents.

Methodist ministers, according to Lord Soper on the B.B.C., are more likely to be moral than a bunch of bookmakers.

Whatever gave him that idea?

I don't want to offend anyone's religious susceptibilities, but my experience of both is that they are much of a muchness, like the rest of us. Both rely on uncertainties. Both cater for humanity's search for security in this world or the next. Both count, among their number, men with redeeming vices.

From a long experience of the two, I don't think there is much to choose between them where compassion is concerned. But since bookmakers usually pitch their claims lower and certainly suffer less from the sin of spiritual pride, I would rather lay odds on the average bookmaker troubling St Peter at the pearly gates than the average Methodist minister.

JACK LOGAN, 'Friday commentary', *Sporting Life*, 1 June 1973

Sitting here contemplating a load of bills from various bookmakers, I can suddenly remember what made me fall in love with horse-racing. There was a boy at school with a name like Tosh who got twelve strokes of the cane and expelled for making a book. Anything you could get that lot for, I thought, can't be bad.

JEFFREY BERNARD, 'A Year at the Races', *New Statesman*, 1 June 1973

I must be a character out of Krafft-Ebing. My fetish is chips. Someday I'll graduate to where they must be poured on my face and chest and genitals for the ultimate orgasm.

ABEN KANDEL, *The Strip*, a popular novel about the phantasies of a Las Vegas gambler

Gambling: A Secular 'Religion' for the Obsessional Neurotic

When the seventeenth-century gambler Le Chevalier de Méré ran into problems playing at dice he turned to Blaise Pascal, the mathematician and theologian, for guidance. As a result, Pascal became fascinated by the problems involved in gambling. He is reputed to have invented the first roulette wheel while experimenting on perpetual-motion devices in a monastic retreat. While there is no real evidence to support this rumour, it is true that Pascal's involvement with Le Chevalier's irrational pursuit of gambling drove him to discover the Laws of Chance. His ruminations on the subject did not stop there; the very language of gambling provided the terms in which he articulated his own irrationality, his superstitious belief in Christianity.

If God existed, he reasoned, faith would be rewarded with eternal life. If he did not, then nothing stood to be lost on its account except, perhaps, a little time. If, however, one did not profess faith, one could never be sure. If God did not exist, fair enough, nothing was lost by agnosticism, but if He did, then the price the faithless man had to pay was the eternal damnation of his soul. Faith, even for the expert mathematician, constituted a good, safe bet.

The inextricably intertwined psychodynamics of gamblers and Christians continue to entail similar metaphysical calculations. Their respective 'faiths' are quasi-rational insurance policies against what they do not know for certain, but they also involve all the mechanisms of the individual's psychological politics. This makes the study of the gambling neurosis very complex: it has a cultural moment as well as a private, psychosexual significance.

In this introduction we will try to trace the diverse elements of that neurosis, and study the way in which they interact, using the discoveries of Freudian psychoanalysis, although applying them to material on which they have been but little used in the past. Freud encountered similar difficulties in much of his later work. Many of his investigations into culture and religion he himself characterized as hypothetical. Some of the arguments we present have a similar status. Psychoanalysis can help us to arrive at a limited, scientific explanation of why individual men gamble. It can do this by uncovering causality in infantile experiences. But in studying the interrelation of gambling, religion and culture, using Freudian theory, we will find that, though we reach interesting and enlightening conclusions, they will remain quite tentative.

We start with an examination of a specific case of gambling neurosis, which exemplifies many of the phenomena which we will encounter throughout this investigation. We then define the terms we are using in the analysis, and review the psychoanalytic literature, significant examples of which form the body of the book. Next we trace the relationships of gambling to social and political formations; then we discuss the attitude of the Church to the practice, both historically and today. This reveals a crucial link between the forces involved in the Reformation, capitalism, Protestant attitudes to money and the Christian moralistic approach to gambling. This link leads us to an understanding of the historic role of anality and its continuing relevance to the gambler. Our theory, at this point, will have reached its most controversial stage. But what are the alternative theories that have been produced to explain the dynamics of gambling? Contemporary sociologists and behavioural 'scientists' have presented their explanations. These are reviewed, and found wanting. We argue that the behavioural approach is positively dangerous in its therapeutic applications to gamblers. Finally, we engage in some speculative extensions of Freud's link between gambling and masturbation, and conclude with a tentative model for the psychoanalytic approach to the gambler.

A clear case of 'gambling sickness'

Gamblers Anonymous (*G.A.*) is a valuable source book for students of gambling psychology. Produced by the G.A. Publishing Company in Los Angeles, it contains several true-life accounts of gambling experiences. Gamblers Anonymous, a self-help, therapeutic organization closely modelled on Alcoholics Anonymous, remains unsophisticated about the neurosis, openly scorning psychoanalytic interpretations and all kinds of psychiatric intervention. A structured attitude towards motivational Oedipal forces, and their relevance to the neurosis, can usually be discounted. 'Gambling Sickness',[1] which is contained within this collection, is longer, fuller and less iconized than most. Its author is intent on grappling with the entirety of his experience, and does not confine his comments to the facts of his gambling and its 'cure'. His story is told with a florid, pantheistic religiosity, characterized by a search to 'know God' (become a love-object for the father).

It is dangerous to try to interpret a text psychoanalytically without listening to the free associations of the author. In this case, however, we feel justified in making cautious observations on account of the transparency of the symbolism, and the persistence of the Oedipal themes.

'Gambling Sickness' begins on the rocks above the sea. Watching the waves crashing below him, the author finds 'irresistibly my mind carried me back to the time of my youth'. His romantic memories of the landscapes he saw then are highly sexualized.

I thought of the times I climbed great mountains and stood upon high peaks. The rugged canyons plunged downward and swept into long green valleys. The blue waters of the Snake River wound among the gorges, cut across the lowlands and disappeared into the distant horizon. I turned and scanned the towering mountains to the north, and came to understand, in some part, the vastness of creation.

These pantheistic experiences, with their insistence on phallic ('great mountains', 'high peaks', 'Snake River') and anal–vaginal ('rugged canyons', 'long green valleys', 'gorges') imagery, characterize this account. They are arresting because of their apparent dissociation from the main theme of the text. But they are significant because the author associates them with a particular emotional state. After the description quoted above, he wrote, 'Lying on my back, I searched the blue sky and became aware of the phenomenon of endless space. A growing hunger to know God rose within me.' All the accounts of his religious emotions are distinguished by the particular variation of the Oedipus complex which Freud designated as characteristic of the gambler: its most prominent feature is the desire of the male child to turn himself into a love-object for the father. These sentences characterize the condition precisely: the subject is in a prone position; he uses the words 'growing hunger' and 'desire to know', and employs the verb 'rose' which can only be seen as a sexualized usage in this context. God becomes the archetypal father surrogate.

He also idolizes his infant memories of his mother: 'At home I heard the sweet clear voice of our mother raised in song. She, too, was filled with the joy of spring, and because she lived close to God she gave expression in the words of the melody. They fell softly upon my ears, "Count your many blessings, name them one by one, and it will surprise you what the Lord hath done." ' The author is jealous of his mother; he envies her intimate relationship with the father–God, and while he comprehends, no doubt with painful surprise, 'what the Lord hath done' to her, he himself experiences only 'a growing hunger for God'. The stage is set for a momentous neurotic resurgence of a particular variation of the Oedipal conflict, a variation whose essential dynamics are quite distinct. The child is searching, desperately struggling to know the father–God, first through nature, and later through gambling and religion. But, unconsciously, he knows that his mother has a special relationship with Him. He fears both his exclusion and his desires. In early childhood the wish to become a love-object for the father is invariably repressed when the child learns that the price which has to be paid is castration.

Soon he gets married. 'I came to understand the blessings which only a woman brings into the world.' But this idyllic state did not last long, despite the arrival of his 'infant son'. His attitude to the birth is significant. The use of the biblical formulation for the child suggests that he sees it as a Christ-child, born of his wife–mother, conceived through union with God. Commenting about his experiences when holding the baby in his arms, he writes, 'Humbleness welled up in my heart. I looked down at the face of my wife who had been the channel of this unfoldment of life. The smile on her lips, and the light in her eyes, told me that we thought as one.'

Despite the torrid humility of this passage, a degree of dissociation from his own role in the reproductive process and the retention of elements of masochistic thought, it appears that by participation in the act of creating a child through the 'channel' of the mother–wife, he had effected a temporary reconciliation with the father (by momentarily becoming him). This is emphasized by the paradoxically active experience of 'humbleness' which 'welled up', one might almost say with uncharacteristically assertive pride. However, if such a psychological reconciliation took place, it was short-lived.

Clearly, the arrival of the child had a strong emotional significance for him, because immediately afterwards we find him at Santa Anita race-track, in Arcadia, about to engage in his first gambling bout. The events of 'that black day' are worth quoting at length.

I stood in front of the paddocks entranced by the sleek thoroughbreds as the grooms lashed the tiny saddles upon their backs. I sensed the excitement of the crowd as it surged around me. We moved toward the grandstand. I bounded up the high stairs two steps at a time. My body felt as if it were devoid of gravity, and then I turned and looked out at the beautiful spread below. My eyes followed the contour of the track as it swept round in a great oval. Then I beheld the masses of color that covered the infield. The clear-cut pattern of the vivid flowers formed a design as through [*sic*] it were stamped there by the hand of God, and beyond this I saw the gentle rise of the oak covered knolls as they swept toward the base of the rugged mountains silhouetted against the blue sky to the north.

The horses were on the track and the starter lined them up in the iron stalls. My hand gripped the tickets that I had bought on the horse of my choice. The faint ring of the bell, the lunge of the horses and riders, and the race was under way. I jumped to my feet, searching for my horse among the pack that moved swiftly up the back stretch. The roar of the crowd was deafening. I was frantic, for I could not see my number among the leaders as they moved into the far turn. Suddenly the voice of the announcer penetrated the din . . . 'On the outside – here comes Captain Cal – it is Captain Cal now taking command.' A tremendous exhilaration swelled within me. A wild shout burst from my lips. People turned and stared at me, but I rushed to join the winning line that formed in front of the cashier's window . . .

The landscape is characteristically sexualized; right in the centre of the course is this ominous sign of the hand of God. The race is orgasmically described, 'hands gripped', 'lunge of the horses', 'penetrated', and its effects on the new gambler were climactic. 'I was frantic,' he told us, with this 'tremendous exhilaration' swelling within him, and this 'wild shout' bursting from his mouth. Freud believed that gambling closely paralleled masturbation, and this account appears to verify his argument. Traces of the masturbator's conscious guilt are also present. As soon as the incident is over, he believes that people are turning and staring at him, though, with his shouts and excitement, he is only behaving in the usual way for a winning racegoer.

Anyway, he does not realize immediately that in the day's events were 'the seeds of an all-consuming passion' which was to become his 'way of life'. But, 'In the weeks and months that followed, the gambling fever took possession of me. I was carried on the crest of a great wave that engulfed my every waking moment.' For a time, he wins, but eventually 'my luck changed', and at the same moment, 'my conscience came to life, bringing confusion and gloom.'

There follows a sequence of events characteristic of many gamblers' histories. Attempts to abandon betting prove abortive; he leaves behind 'a long trail of broken promises that brought me face to face with the sickening realization that I could not stop gambling'. His wife and family suffer, though his moralistic masochism probably makes him exaggerate the extent of the damage his betting did to them.

The nature of the gambling itself moves progressively further away from that first, comparatively light-hearted, experience. 'My mind became a battlefield for terrible guilt and the obsession to gamble. Little by little, I retreated into a hideous, lonely world. Gambling no longer brought visions of large sums of money but was simply a dark monster that shadowed my every move.'

We should expect to find a very active sense of guilt in a man in whom a vigorously developed super-ego clashes so violently with repressed infantile and aggressive wishes. In the gambler, this guilt is often of a specific kind. First, as we have seen, the ego remains in a passive – that is, invariably masochistic – relationship to the super-ego. That is, at one level, because the wish to kill the father, which is primal and inevitable, is frequently confused by the desire to become a love-object for the father. Gambling emerges as a means of self-punishment, through loss, and also a questioning of fate as to whether the individual's wishes are strong enough to kill his father or not. Any answer is intolerable.

As we shall see, these are among the most striking of Freud's observations on Dostoyevsky's gambling.[2] They also form the centre of this gambling confession. Up until this point in the story, although we have heard about his mother, his siblings, his wife and his son, the writer has neither mentioned nor referred to his father overtly at all. The dynamics of his relationship with God have been pursued so exclusively that the vexed relationship with his father has been forced right out of consciousness. The first time that he is mentioned, and it follows immediately the description of the writer's undefined 'terrible guilt', is on the day of his father's death.

A day came when I stood at the foot of a white bed in St Luke's Hospital in Pasadena, California, gazing at my dying father. Helpless grief made my head swim, and a wave of nausea swept through me at the thought of my failure as a son. There was a terrible hurt in my heart. I closed my eyes and whispered a few words of prayer for my beloved dad. When I again looked at him, he had lifted his head and was frantically searching the room. Then his eyes came to rest upon my face. Slowly his head dropped back to his pillow. A faint smile crossed his lips and I saw again the look of affection he had for me always. I moved softly to the head of the bed and picked up the limp hand and pressed it to my body. Never again would I hear his voice or feel the touch of his kindly hand upon my shoulder. I dropped to my knees and put my head against the still-warm body and the sounds of my grief passed into the silence of the still room.

I sat beside the casket in the mortuary and the only sound in the dim light was the beating of my own heart. I dwelt on my wasted life. A shiver of cold fear moved into [*sic*] haunt me. A thousand times I had promised or sworn that I would never gamble again, but always it was there to claim me, and each time a little of me died with my broken promise. Rising I moved to the casket and looked down upon the quiet face. This was my last chance. If only in this great loss could I find the strength! The sounds of my whispered words seemed to fill the silent room. 'I promise you, Dad, that I will never gamble again, so help me God!'

We laid his body to rest beneath a sturdy pine in the Rose Hills Cemetery. In the days that followed, like a man in a dream I moved quietly about my work, fearful that any sudden movement might break the spell and chase away the peace and serenity that, like a timid dove, had come to rest in my mind. The terrible churning of my gambling compulsion was stilled, but I lived with a feeling of unreality. If only I could find again the feeling of God around me. Each day I lived with my prayer in my heart.

The cessation of gambling on his father's death is particularly interesting. It appears that the 'timid dove' flutters into life when the writer receives, for the first time, an unequivocal reply to the life-long question 'Are my feelings strong enough to kill my father?' By irrationally assuming the guilt for his father's death, and emphasizing his 'failure as a son', the gambler temporarily relieves himself of the need to question fate. The absence of the being 'beneath a sturdy pine' and the continued, fateful separation from 'God around me' became punishment enough in themselves.

But the ambiguities of parricide cannot be resolved so simplistically. Eventually the unconscious guilt about both the incestuous and murderous elements in the relationship with the father will re-assert themselves, and may be expected to do so with an added vengefulness where the dread act of parricide appears, in the mind of the gambler, to have been committed.

Soon he was back at the track, and even added card clubs to his repertoire. The decision to enter a race-course again followed a peculiarly vivid phantasy: 'I could see the thoroughbreds streaking around the track, and the piles of money seemed so close I could touch them. It was all there for the taking.' This image inevitably relates directly to the anal element in gambling. The piles of money, following the thoroughbreds, are faeces. The gambler's desire to reach out and touch them relates to the desire of the infant to play with his stool, a wish that is repressed in the toilet-training process. This daydream 'seemed the answer to all my problems and the fulfillment of the secret hopes that poured into my mind again. Like a cyclone, my obsession swept all before it.'

The 'post-parricidal' phase of his gambling leads him to be overwhelmed by oceans of guilt and anxiety. He writes of 'a parade of thoughts, born of the sickness in my soul'.

'My conscience felt like a bloody mass. A world of desolation closed in on me, "Oh, God," I whispered, "was I born for this? Why will you not break the shackles and set me free? Why, dear God, why?"'

On one particularly bad day he finds himself in a gambling club in Gardena. 'Impending doom has placed a clutching hand upon my heart,' he writes, ominously. He watches a pregnant woman play, and notes, 'Even the unborn infant cannot escape the stigma of this terrible sickness.' He leaves the club, and starts the long drive home. 'The awful guilt that has become such a painful living part of my world up through the years spawns, as always, a haunting urgency that I must get to her [his wife] at all costs . . .' and so he drives so fast that he crashes.

He wakes up in the hospital. 'The pain in my soul far over-shadows the hurt in my body, for I have come to the sickening realization that, added to all my other sins, I am now a menace upon the highways,' he writes, not missing an excellent opportunity for pounding his masochistic ego again.

He survives, but his masochism is now reaching a more consciously suicidal phase. Driving along one day, 'I pass again the scene of my wreck and it rises to haunt me. Now the highway joins the seashore and I slowly bring my car to a halt and climb upon the rocks above the sea. Now – this is the end.' But, remembering that his wife (mother) still loves him, despite his catastrophic, father–God relationship, he goes back home.

I reached home and stood for a moment looking upon the dim light in the window that awaited my return always. I climbed the stairs, and like a wounded animal crawled into the sanctuary beside her and I knew she was crying. I stared into the darkness. Suddenly my mind began to whirl. It became a thing that shrieked through the endless darkness of hell. It swelled into a bulging mass of stark fear, and with the speed of light it plunged in all directions, but . . . there . . . was . . . no . . . escape. And then the quivering mass was stilled, and I seemed to be floating up from the depths of a chasm, and again my mind came into focus. My body was chilled from cold sweat and I knew that my sanity hung by a tiny thread. What was I to do now? Where could I turn for help? *Was* there any help – anywhere?

The writer is at least partially right in his analysis of his situation. His unconscious neurotic conflicts had reached such a crescendo, and were so violent in their forms of expression, that he had either to confront them and work them through or to find a far more meaningful compromise than those he had attempted before. He chose the latter course, and made contact with Gamblers Anonymous. During his first meeting he starts thinking again:

> In the time of my own deep suffering and despair, my soul had cried out to comprehend the mystery of life, but the only certainty I could understand was that I live for a short time, in the very center of an eternity that had already passed, and an eternity that would never end. How could a man cast away his chance to share, with those he loved, this miracle of life, in the full expression of love, hope, peace, joy and beauty, in the brief time they were really together, living upon the earth? Yet still – I COULD NOT STOP GAMBLING. If only they could give me medicine, or a doctor could open my body and cut away the awful obsession and set me free.

Gradually, during the meeting, he realizes that there are others in the group just like him. His life is about to appear to change.

> I think of the hundreds of thousands of homes scattered across our beloved America that are filled with desolation and misery from gambling sickness. I know that there are millions of little children, and other millions yet unborn, who must look to Gamblers Anonymous if they are to have the fruits of their golden years.

The story ends with the narrator once again climbing by the seashore, but not, this time, contemplating death. 'At long last I have found peace in freedom from my obsession. I now walk in dignity and usefulness among my fellow men. There is love, trust and harmony in my home.'

He finishes with a long and revealing pantheistic eulogy about how he has found God in the clouds, the squirrels and the earth – that is, become united with the father–God figure – and in 'the love of a mother', his wife. 'Even though I face eternity in the very center of infinity, I have no fear, for I have come to live with a deep conviction that I no longer walk alone.'

We have quoted this case at length because, with its own florid vividness, and thinly veiled symbolism, it illustrates almost to excess the main points which we wish to argue theoretically in this introduction. It contains themes either all or most of which emerge again and again in the histories of gamblers: the mobilized guilt which the subject cannot specify, the crushing weight of neuroses readily traceable to Oedipal conflicts, but Oedipal conflicts which vary significantly from the usual pattern, undercurrents of infantile parricidal and incestuous desire and, above all, the neurotic fusion of masochistic religious and gambling solutions. The conflicts, of course, are partially resolved through contact with Gamblers Anonymous. Gamblers Anonymous allows him to become, at last, the love-object of the father–God figure, to unite himself in a quasi-sexual union with 'the Power Greater than Ourselves' to which all members of Gamblers Anonymous turn for deliverance. The apparent separation of this new Power from the father diminishes incestuous guilt: the ambiguous religiosity of the group allows for a continuation of the underlying Oedipal masochism, by transferring it, largely unchanged, into a socially acceptable format. Step Three of the Twelve-Stage Recovery Programme, to which we will return later, is 'Made a decision to turn our will and our lives over to the care of this Power of our own understanding.' Any superior being, up there, will do as long as we can subject ourselves to it. 'I promise you, Dad, that I will never gamble again, so help me God!'

While the underlying conflict, which informed the gambling practice, remains unaltered in the transference to this quasi-religious mode of behaviour, it would appear that there are certain qualitative differences in the mode of displaced resolution which is sought after – and that they relate to the comparative emotional tranquillity commonly reported after the change has been effected.

The father–God–Power-Greater-than-Ourselves is elevated to such an extent in the quasi-religious group that the need to compete (to win or lose) is dramatically reduced. This may result in a more satisfactory object-relationship with the mother–wife; the process of becoming the father is then able to proceed. There is a lessening of violence in the ego–super-ego relationship; the commands of the super-ego are consequently experienced as being more compatible with the desires and ambitions of the ego. This no doubt accounts for the tendency within Gamblers Anonymous – and other similarly based groups – to emphasize and over-value conventional bourgeois preoccupations ('Even though I still have this urge to gamble, which I must fight against the whole time, I have stopped betting, and I have bought a new fridge and TV, and next year I will take the wife on holiday for the first time . . .').

Introduction

We can see that the concept of sickness – of the 'compulsive gambler' as a diseased man within a group sharing the same disease – begins to take on a comparable role to that of 'original sin' in Christian sects. The price which is paid for this qualitative change is the apparent cessation of interest in the aggressive aspect of the struggle against the father – the punitive super-ego is able to consolidate its claim on the personality, with all the resultant ossification which this entails.

Defining the terms

Before we can go on to review the psychoanalytic literature, we must define gambling, outline the procedural elements shared by all the different forms and propose a typology of gamblers.

Other writers have always found it difficult to agree on an adequate definition of what gambling is, but for our purposes a gamble may tentatively be defined as a re-allocation of wealth, on the basis of deliberate risk, involving gain to one party and loss to another, usually without the introduction of productive work on either side. The determining process always involves an element of chance, and may be only chance.

One writer has tried to categorize the four kinds of play which predominate in industrial societies.[3] They are: gaming, or the exchange of money in a game in which chance plays a part (roulette); betting, or the staking of money on a future event, or any event, the issue of which is doubtful or unknown to the participants in the wager (horse-race gambling); lotteries, or the distribution of a mutually contributed prize by lot (football pools); and speculation, which covers gambling activities conducted on any of the established exchange markets (commodity speculation).

Erving Goffman, an American social psychologist, has tried to document the four phases which are common to every completed gambling transaction. First, there is 'squaring off', which entails the agreement to engage in risk, a decision as to the method of settlement and the fixing of the amount of the wager (placing a bet at a roulette table). Next comes 'determination', when 'relevant causal forces actively and determinatively produce the outcome' (the spinning of the wheel). Then follows the 'disclosive phase', or announcement of the result (calling of the numbers) and the 'settlement phase', when losses are paid and gains collected.[4]

Types of gambler

These definitions do not mean much when taken on their own. Gambling has served different cultural functions in different societies, and may fulfil different needs for separate individuals within the same society. This has led to attempts to classify gamblers, and to suggest that some engage in the activity for rational or secondary cultural reasons, whereas others are trapped by neurotic symptoms.

Most writers accept a distinction between the 'punter', or occasional gambler, and the 'gambler' proper, who stakes regularly and for whom gambling constitutes a significant feature of his life.[5] Investigators at Colgate University have tried to show that, in a group of students who gambled, about half conformed to approximately uniform psychoneurotic tendencies, in addition to their common interest in gambling, but the other half did not.[6]

More recently E. Moran, honorary consultant psychiatrist to the British branch of Gamblers Anonymous, has categorized what he terms 'varieties of pathological gambling'.[7] He listed five types:

'Subcultural variety': in which he related gambling to the incidence of the practice in the individual's social setting while conceding that, although 'social pressures were paramount', individual characteristics 'in part also determined the fact that the gambling became pathological'.

'Neurotic variety': described as neurotic gambling related to 'some stressful situation'. Gambling merely provided relief for this underlying tension. It was 'with money rather than for money'.

'Impulsive variety': 'Here the gambling was associated with loss of control and ambivalence to the activity, so that while being longed for, it was also dreaded, since it had become irresistible.'

'Psychopathic variety': 'In this case the basic abnormality was that of psychopathy. The pathological gambling was therefore only part of the global disturbance that characterized this disorder.'

'Symptomatic variety': 'Here the pathological gambling was associated with mental illness which appeared to be the primary disorder. The gambling was therefore only one among many other symptoms characteristic of the particular illness.'

Moran's conclusions were based on a clinical study of fifty patients for whom 'pathological gambling' was a problem, and who were referred for psychiatric help. All the patients were male, aged twenty to fifty-eight, with 72 per cent aged twenty to thirty-nine. Moran commented, 'Obviously these five categories were not mutually exclusive. If a particular patient showed characteristics of more than one variety, the most prominent features in his gambling problem determined into which category he was placed.' Of the patients he treated, Moran classified 14 per cent subcultural, 34 per cent neurotic, 18 per cent impulsive, 24 per cent psychopathic and 10 per cent symptomatic. He argued that each group required different kinds of 'help'.

If Moran accepted the psychoanalytical interpretation of neurosis, which he does not, an overall description of the activities he describes as 'neurotic' would not appear to be excluded. His divisions are not satisfactory. The 'subcultural variety' appears to have only a tenuous and dubious basis as a distinct entity. The difference between 'psychopathic' and 'symptomatic' gambling must be hard to define in a clinical situation.

As we might expect, Freudians are most insistent on their assertion of the universality of the neurotic elements in gambling. Rejecting empirical, symptomatic classifications, they emphasize that the gambler is motivated by his repressed Oedipal conflicts, and regard cultural analysis as secondary. Edmund Bergler,[8] the psychoanalyst who has done the most work on the subject, argues that all gamblers, without exception, gamble because of 'psychic masochism'. He does stress, however, that not everyone who makes a bet is necessarily a gambler. He also recognizes a typology of gamblers, consisting of four groupings. He described the 'classical' gambler, who conforms closely to the expected psychoanalytic model, like the gambler in our opening case study; the gambler who identifies with his mother, and for whom the process of being overwhelmed by loss has a special significance; the aggressive, extraverted gambler who is seeking to hide his feminine identification; and finally what he calls the 'fictitious' poker-faced practitioner, whose passions and conflicts are there, but are quite invisible on the surface. Bergler's categorization stresses that differences in gambling behaviour derive from differences in infantile experience.

Existential psychologists reject all these attempts to 'label' people. David Cooper has written:

> No person should ever be called a gambler because all labelling of people is lethal. If you are called an alcoholic, a schizophrenic, a psychopath, that is an act of violence done against you. And the same thing applies to the labelling of a gambler. There is just gambling but no gamblers. We have to abolish 'gamblers' and then work out the problem of gambling.[9]

In the case of gambling, Cooper's approach is valuable. As we shall argue, the gambling impulse is close to the religious impulse, both in its exterior forms and in the comparable psychological dynamics of those involved. Freud was unequivocal in his statement that religious ideas are 'illusions, fulfilments of the oldest, strongest, and most urgent wishes of mankind . . .'[10] He wrote, 'One might venture to regard obsessional neurosis as a pathological counterpart of the formation of a religion, and to describe that neurosis as an individual religiosity and religion as a universal obsessional neurosis.'[11] The evidence indicates that gambling is a secular counterpart of that 'universal obsessional neurosis' called religion.

Whether one prayer, or one bet, is more or less rationally motivated than a series of prayers or bets, or whether a given individual says enough prayers to be called a Christian, or makes enough bets to be labelled a gambler, are diversions when compared with the real issue: men and women have always prayed and gambled, yet why do they bother to do either at all?

Freud and the Freudians

A body of psychoanalytical literature has grown up about the gambling neurosis. But it is not as extensive or as comprehensive as the scale and universality of gambling might lead us to expect.

The first paper which began to suggest an explanation was a study of anal erotism by Hans von Hattingberg, published in 1914.[12] He noted that the fear inherent in the risks taken by gamblers was eroticized. He perceptively linked that fear, which he called '*Angstlust*', with infantile urethral–anal strivings, and the attempt of outside agencies to deny the child pleasure in them. He related this 'pleasure in fear' to masochism. The importance of von Hattingberg's paper is that it stresses the intimate association between infantile anality and gambling, an aspect which was not explored satisfactorily by many subsequent writers.

What von Hattingberg lacked, however, was an understanding of the Oedipal conflicts involved in gambling. But six years later Ernst Simmel[13] made the necessary connection, while retaining the crux of the anality theory. His paper was based largely on a single case study. He saw the gambler as a man regressing constantly to the anal level of libidinal development. He reported that his patient was subject to 'many active pregenital anal-sadistic impulses . . . Gambling satisfied narcissistic bisexual impulses and provided autoerotic gratification.' Simmel equated gambling with forepleasure, winning with orgasm, losing with ejaculation, defecation and castration. Gambling satisfies the 'bisexual ideal which the Narcissus finds in himself . . . the Narcissus rejected by father becomes Herostratus'. Simmel believed that 'on the developmental path of mankind, games of chance are a reservoir for the anal-sadistic impulses held in a state of repression'.

It should be emphasized that 'the developmental path of mankind' is no longer seen in quite the perspective on which Simmel insists. Simmel, following Freud, is referring to an ordered progression through three phases of narcissistic, autoerotic, pre-Oedipal development: the oral, anal and phallic.

Freud assumed that in each of these developmental phases the mouth, the anus and the penis, respectively, became the centres of sexual interest, and that the child was motivated by a desire to seek instinctual, autoerotic gratification. This outline of libidinal development, which relies on a disputed concept of infantile narcissism, has been increasingly challenged by recent discoveries and subsequent developments in psychoanalytic theory. Several analysts, including Fairbairn, Klein and Winnicott, have stressed the importance of the infant's earliest relationship with objects, in particular the mother and her breast, and have cast increasing doubt over the concept of primary narcissistic libidinal impulses. While these new theoretical developments continue to make use of the concepts of oral and anal phases (though not of the phallic phase in the way which Freud proposed it) their attitude to manifestations commonly associated with those phases is significantly different. For example, doubt is immediately cast on concepts such as 'anal-sadism', of which Simmel makes use.

If the infant is regarded as seeking relationships with objects, and not as searching for autoerotic gratification of specific zones, the characteristic components of aggressiveness and sadism manifest when interest in the anal functions is at its height may be seen as responses to the object's attitude towards the child's faeces and eliminative functions, and not as inherent elements of this phase of libidinal development as defined by classical theory.

While these recent discoveries represent a genuine extension of theory, it should be emphasized that object theory as such is sometimes associated with a wholesale restructuring of the dynamics of the Oedipal conflict – a product of its important revaluation of the child's early object relationship with the mother. This has led some analysts to devalue excessively the importance of the father relationship in the formation of neurosis.

Significantly, Simmel thought that should a patient's gambling cause him to engage in criminal activities, the dominance of Oedipal factors in the neurosis should be assumed. The patient, he argued, was then looking for the punishment of the avenging father, or a convenient father-substitute, such as that provided by the condemning judge. In adding this concept, Simmel was relying on Freud's account of the Oedipal role in recidivism.[14] Freud had discovered a masochistic dynamic in persistent criminality. Unconscious guilt was mobilized, yet rationalized when the recidivist was repeatedly punished for present offences. In fact, Simmel need not have looked outside the gambling neurosis itself for this structure. The inevitable loss which the gambler faces is punishment enough in itself. Like the intractable criminal, he appears to be unable to learn by his past experiences. The wheel, the croupier or the bookie can become the avenging father.

It was Freud himself who consolidated on these tentative beginnings. When invited to write an introduction to the post-humously collected sketches and drafts for Dostoyevsky's *Brothers Karamazov*, he produced 'Dostoevsky and Parricide' in 1928.[15] Although this essay is largely concerned with the Russian writer's neurosis as it manifested itself in his 'epilepsy', it is the almost incidental analysis of his relationship to roulette which is of particular interest for our purposes.

But before we examine Freud's evidence, we must declare a difference of emphasis. Freud clearly does not regard gambling itself as an obsessional neurosis. On the only occasion on which he gives it a label he calls it an 'addiction' and, linking it with what he considers to be comparable addictions to morphine and alcohol, traces its descent from the 'primal addiction': mastur-bation. While in no way seeking to deny that phallic and masturbatory elements are invariably operative in gambling, we go on to argue later in this introduction that anal factors are dominant.

Freud nowhere discusses the phenomenon of gambling as an entity at any length, and it would be foolish to hypothesize on what he might have written, had he done so. But it is worth noting that his categorization of it has had far-reaching effects. The fact that he designated it an 'addiction' in part accounts for the comparative poverty of psychoanalytic writing on the subject, and the particular deficiency of the clinical literature. In terms of psychiatric diagnosis, the 'addictions' have latterly been treated as one of the 'behaviour disorders'. These condi-tions, which include so-called 'psychopathy' and the perver-sions, have in common the fact that they meet with societal disapproval. Although the subject may complain of his condi-tion, and may, on certain occasions, wish to be rid of it, the 'behaviour disorders' are complicated from the viewpoint of psychoanalysis by the fact that the yield of pleasure for the subject from the symptoms tends to outstrip the anxiety which they produce. As Charles Rycroft has written, 'Theoretically they can be regarded as the opposite of the neuroses, since they are characterized by deficiency not excess of inhibition. They are, in general, amenable to psychoanalytical explanation, but only infrequently to psychoanalytical treatment.'[16]

The whole question of the 'behaviour disorders' raises numerous theoretical questions for practising psychiatrists, not least among which is the apparently fictional status of mental 'illness'. But, in so far as psychoanalysis is concerned, what Rycroft calls the 'deficiency . . . of inhibition', and consequent inappropriateness for analytical treatment, usually leads to a poor prognosis when a potential patient with a 'behaviour disorder' presents himself for treatment. Selection for analysis tends to be made from subjects for whom the outlook is considered to be more favourable.

There are good reasons for questioning the validity of the concept 'behaviour disorders' in regard to psychoanalytic (as distinct from psychiatric) practice but, these apart, there appear to be even more compelling arguments for extricating gambling from this category altogether. Gambling is linked with the 'behaviour disorders' on the grounds that it is an addiction. From the viewpoint of psychoanalysis, this diagnosis rests on the exclusive emphasis of the masturbatory elements considered to be dominant in it. However, we maintain that beneath its masturbatory superstructure, gambling is an unsuccessful defence against an underlying anal-fixation, and that, as such, it more closely approaches the condition of obsessional neurosis, which Freud, incidentally, regarded as the most fruitful area for psychoanalytical research and practice.

Certainly, it is noticeable that those writers who insist that gambling is an 'addiction' tend to ignore many of its essential elements. In his paper Freud himself places very little stress on the handling of *money* (rather than just handling), relationships to value and time, attitudes to giving and taking, stubborn optimism and obsessive ritual, all of which are invariably of great importance to those who gamble and are strongly indicative of underlying anal factors. More recently, some psychiatrists have attempted to deal with gambling as if it were directly comparable to alcoholism or drug-addiction. Such approaches invariably fail because no physiological dependence is involved in gambling, and it is consequently quite impossible to say what it is that the gambler is addicted to. The argument is sometimes presented that he is addicted to the ritual of gambling – which would appear to be another way of saying that he is an obsessional neurotic. Nevertheless, it must be conceded that there are similarities between gambling and the 'addictions'. One of them resides in the presence of the masturbatory element, described by Freud in his study on Dostoyevsky. Even though this cannot be said to account for all the components of the practice, any analysis of gambling which failed to emphasize it would be quite unsatisfactory.

In this essay Freud put forward a crucial amplification of the Oedipus conflict. The normal process, he reminded his readers, was for the male child to have an ambivalent relationship with his father, in which tenderness mingled with parricidal impulses. The child both admires the father and wants to remove him as a rival. But he comes to understand that the attempt to do the latter would be punished by castration, so he abandons this course of action. However, the repressed parricidal impulses remain in the unconscious as the basis of guilt.

Freud stressed fixation on the Oedipus complex in the ontogenesis of neuroses. 'Orthodox' Freudians and the neo-Freudians still argue about the extent of his determinism, the degree to which he believed that the Oedipus conflict was unalterable biological fact or anthropological phenomenon. Few psychologists now accept that the Oedipus complex, in anything resembling the form in which Freud described it, is an invariable feature of every society. Japan, for example, appears to be a distinct case, which raises issues which do not seem to have been satisfactorily dealt with by any branch of psychoanalytic thinking. While parricidal preoccupations exist in forms comparable to those current in the West, male masturbation is a completely open and accepted practice, which parents teach to their sons, and which is openly discussed both inside and outside the family. No guilt, in any form, attaches to the practice. Japan clearly will not fit into the Western monotheistic pattern, either, and it would seem that the entire constellation of Oedipus-complex–parricide–masturbation-guilt–monotheistic-God must be queried for the Japanese case. Interestingly, however, gambling has been severely repressed in Japan in modern times: in a representative year, 1936, it figured as the number two 'crime', exceeded only by theft, and well ahead of fraud. In that year a total of 78,714 men were charged with offences under the rubric 'gambling', as well as 7,384 women (a ratio of over 10 to 1). And in 1897 the entire Japanese Supreme Court was arrested on gambling charges. But a 1972 report shows the prominence gambling now has in Japanese culture: total annual expenditure on it came to 630,000 million yen (nearly £1 billion). Gambling takes up 18 per cent of Japan's total annual recreational expenditure. Although the volume of illegal betting makes the comparable figure hard to estimate in America, it is usually given as between 2 and 3 per cent.[17]

But the validity of the Oedipus complex for males, in the Western Judeo–Christian tradition, has never been seriously contested – although psychoanalysts still argue about the developmental stage at which it first appears, and the degree to which it, rather than the preceding object relations with the mother, determines neurosis. Without space to enter into the anthropological–biological dispute, we can simply state that we agree with those writers who have argued that Freud's final position on the Oedipal question allowed for anthropological variations, and we consider this to be the more satisfactory thesis.

After Freud outlined the expected pattern of Oedipal conflicts in his study of Dostoyevsky, he went on to argue that the situation was quite different when there was a constitutional tendency towards bisexuality in the child. Many contemporary analysts might dispute the word 'constitutional' in this context, and argue that this tendency itself was determined by earlier experiences. However, Freud saw that in this instance the child wishes to put himself in the mother's place, to become the object of the father's love. But he added that this was no solution to the threat of castration. Castration becomes the price which has to be paid in the transformation into a love-object for the father. This is an intolerable self-sacrifice, which the child rejects. 'Thus', says Freud, 'a strong bisexual predisposition becomes one of the preconditions or reinforcements of neurosis.'

Freud then goes on to argue that, despite this, permanent identification with the father finds its place in the ego: this separate sector of the ego Freud designated as the 'super-ego'. In fact, the dynamic of super-ego formation which he describes here is far simpler than that contained in other writings, and certainly cannot be taken as being applicable in every case. In 'Dostoevsky and Parricide' he says that, if the father was hard and cruel, the child's super-ego would eventually manifest those characteristics, and the ego itself would revert to passivity in its relationship to the super-ego. So, the super-ego becomes sadistic; the ego the masochistic recipient.

But in 'Civilization and Its Discontents' he demonstrated

that even when the father was far from being hard and cruel, a sado-masochistic relationship could become established between the ego and super-ego of the son. In such cases the super-ego 'enters into possession of all the aggressiveness' which the child would have liked to have exercised against the father's authority, rather than simply that which the father really did mete out on the son. But, as Freud points out, these two descriptions of super-ego development 'do not contradict each other, and they even coincide at one point, for the child's revengeful aggressiveness will be in part determined by the amount of punitive aggression which he expects from his father'.[18] But, in striking contrast to the much over-simplified version in the study on Dostoyevsky, he continues in 'Civilization and Its Discontents',

> Experience shows, however, that the severity of the super-ego which a child develops in no way corresponds to the severity of treatment which he has himself met with. The severity of the former seems to be independent of that of the latter. A child who has been very leniently brought up can acquire a very strict conscience. But it would also be wrong to exaggerate this independence; it is not difficult to convince oneself that severity of upbringing does also exert a strong influence on the formation of the child's super-ego. What it amounts to is that in the formation of the super-ego and the emergence of a conscience innate constitutional factors and influences from the real environment act in combination.[19]

Returning to the study on Dostoyevsky, Freud claims that if a sado-masochistic relationship does become established between ego and super-ego (by whatever route) a resultant need for punishment soon manifests itself in the ego, 'which in part offers itself as a victim to fate, and in part finds satisfaction in ill-treatment by the super-ego'. Every punishment then becomes the fulfilment of the old, passive attitude towards the father. 'Even fate is, in the last resort, only a later father-projection.'

It is specifically against this important expansion of the expected politics of the Oedipal situation that Freud goes on to explain the intimate relationship between gambling and masturbation. The two parts of this essay cannot be separated; the detailed discussion of Oedipal processes is a necessary introduction to the masturbatory significance of the gambler's actions.

Freud paraphrases Stefan Zweig's short story about a gambler, which, he argues, epitomizes a boy's wish that his mother should initiate him into sexual life, so that he should be saved from the fearful and harmful effects of masturbation. 'The "vice" of masturbation is replaced by the mania for gambling.' Freud notes the importance of the hands in the gambling process – a feature constantly emphasized in Zweig's story. He points out that 'play' is used both for infantile handling of the genitals and for many forms of gambling activity. In English the word has even been dragged in to describe many forms of gambling where no apparent physical activity resembling non-masturbatory play takes place at all (e.g. 'playing the Stock Exchange' or 'playing the horses') thus giving added weight to Freud's derivation of this usage from nursery onanism.[20]

Freud stresses the irresistible nature of the temptation to masturbate, the solemn promises not to indulge again, invariably linked to the belief that it is a ruinous practice. All these characteristics remain unaltered when gambling comes to take its place – a fact which was poignantly illustrated in the case history with which we opened this introduction.

He uses these arguments to explain Dostoyevsky's gambling, within the overall context of his other symptoms. He emphasizes that there are no cases of severe neurosis in which early autoerotic satisfaction did not play its part, 'and the relation between efforts to suppress it and fear of the father are too well known to need more than a mention'.

The passages on gambling in this essay provided the key for the majority of the psychoanalytic studies which followed. They explained, for the first time, the paradox of the gambler's search for loss and the compulsive nature of his repetitive behaviour, and suggested powerful reasons for gambling's widespread appeal. But, as we have already noted, there were many things missing from Freud's account. Because he saw gambling as an 'addiction' rather than a manifestation of obsessional neurosis, he goes into no very great depth about the significance of money in the activity. By this time he was well aware of the relationship which exists between faeces and money – both he and his followers had already explored it in considerable depth. One can only regret that he never considered the implications of these discoveries for gambling itself.

Theodor Reik later criticized Freud's text and described it as an 'occasional piece'.[21] But Reik realized the importance of the essay for the understanding of both Dostoyevsky and the whole psychology of the gambler. He extended Freud's thesis by examining gambling's religious associations, and suggesting a link between Dostoyevsky's gambling and his Orthodox Church upbringing.

Throughout his life the great artist unconsciously stood in the heavy shadow of that unfortunate error which nineteen hundred years ago separated mankind into saints and sinners. The dominance of this view in his psyche explains the hypertrophy of his conscience and the radical swings between sin and repentance. We children of another age, which appears as a progressed one to simpler spirits, are no longer capable of fully understanding the psychology of the Russian people of this period. No one who has not undergone the profound influence of Christianity can project himself into the feelings of these people. Religious upbringing added a new, more refined form of gratification of the impulses to the old ways: the voluptuousness of giving oneself up for lost, of knowing that one was damned. It is very hard for us to comprehend emotionally the orgies of passion and suffering which were the psychological aftermath of this attitude.

During Dostoyevsky's atheistic period gambling became a precise, secular counterpart of the psychological processes implied and involved in the religious beliefs of his childhood and adolescence. When he abandoned the pleasures of Baden-Baden's casinos such was his masochistic craving for 'the voluptuousness of giving oneself up for lost', a situation to which he constantly returned throughout his life, that he threw himself wholeheartedly into the painful–pleasurable embraces of the Church again.

Reik sees this as the reason why the novelist eventually resolved his inner conflict by bowing completely 'before all secular and ecclesiastical authority'.

Finally, Reik discusses that section of Freud's essay specifically devoted to Dostoyevsky's gambling activities.

We may notice an abrupt transition between this section and the main theme. Perhaps our impression is that the author has turned arbitrarily to this new subject because it interests him and not because it has any special connection with the whole. And yet there is a very definite organic connection. What inspires the efforts to suppress the onanism is nothing else but fear of the father. This Freud intimates in a single word at the end of the section.

Unfortunately, Freud breaks off his analysis at this point. Had he continued, I believe he would have pointed out how the gambling passion later assumes a form whose psychic motivation and mechanisms are akin to certain obsessional symptoms. Gambling which never had as its end money or gain, becomes a kind of question addressed to destiny. It is a form of oracle which the modern psyche readily accepts, although this latent meaning does not become conscious. Now, recalling that destiny is the ultimate father surrogate, we see the significance in the unconscious of this questioning. Originally, it sought to discover whether or not expectation of evil was justified. In other words, would the threatened punishment for the trespass be carried out or would the angered father forgive the son's disobedience? Good or bad luck stands as a symbol of the answer. Observing the rules of the game is the psychological equivalent of obedience to the compulsive neurotic symptoms. Uncertainty plays the same role in gambling as it does in the compulsion complex. Take, for example, a game like patience. Here we can clearly see the oracular meaning, which is obscured in other games where new players may enter late and where the prime purpose seems to be gain.

Reik is implying that gambling is a characteristic neurotic mechanism involving the evolution of an untenable system of control; in this respect it strongly resembles the characteristic symptom-formations of obsessional neurosis. The actual play of the gambler – the questions he asks of destiny – is an attempt to exert control over a situation in which (as in the conflict with the father) he knows that in fact control lies elsewhere – with destiny, fate, luck, chance or what-have-you. It is, almost literally, 'in the lap of the gods'.

Gambling may be seen as an attempt to construct a defensive mechanism to deal with the anxiety originating from both 'bad' internal impulses, too strong to be coped with by less dramatic defences (e.g. unconscious incestuous or parricidal impulses), and what were once experienced as external threats, emanating from a potentially castrating father or his symbols, later becoming super-ego admonishments.

Because the 'bad' internal impulses cannot be discharged, they are mediated through the elaborate forms and rituals of gambling-as-defence-mechanism. But, as in obsessional neurosis, symptom-formation often seeks to express the very impulses against which it is such an elaborate control device. It can also cope with giving expression to contradictory impulses –

the product of an ambivalent relationship with an object. This provides the compulsive–destructive–repetitive dynamic – the inherent contradiction within all obsessional control systems – which makes them so unpleasant for those compelled to engage in them.

Reik's main contribution to the Freudian interpretation of gambling was to link the practice specifically with religious psychology and to add the interesting concept that gambling is a 'question asked of destiny', a reference back to ritualistic, divinatory origins and forward to Oedipal conflicts. With the development of the notion of destiny itself as avenging father-substitute comes the bridge between the understanding of gambling as both private and universal neurosis.

Most analysts writing after Freud on this subject have concentrated on the elaboration of aspects already raised but inadequately explored. René Laforgue,[22] for example, went back to von Hattingberg and argued that for many people fear and orgasm become completely fused in the unconscious. Developing the concept of the eroticization of fear, he argues that gamblers derive pleasure from pain; that they are invariably masochists. He proposes a sequence: fear and fore-pleasure; punishment and orgasm.

There is much evidence to support this, particularly in gamblers' accounts of their activities. Dostoyevsky himself described the tremulous excitement which losing afforded him, and pointed out that the punishment of total loss at the end of a losing run led to orgasm.

The relationship of games to the Oedipus complex and to parricide was taken up by Ernest Jones, the English Freudian, in 1930 with 'The Problem of Paul Morphy'.[23] While not strictly a study of gambling, this explored the career, neurosis and ultimate psychosis of a nineteenth-century chess master in terms of his parricidal sublimations, expressed through his enthusiasm to 'get the king', effect 'check-mate', or kill the father. Historically, chess emerged from a gambling game – the pieces were originally moved according to the dictates of dice – and it continues to emphasize the parricidal aspect which flourishes in all gambling, although, of course, the element of chance is now confined to which player has the white pieces and which the black.

Jones found that Morphy had created a father surrogate out

of Howard Staunton, a cantankerous English chess master and Shakespearean scholar. Staunton steadfastly refused to play Morphy, and constantly insulted him, accusing him of being motivated by money. This shattered the effective sublimation of Morphy's parricidal conflicts in chess, and unleashed a virulent psychosis leading to total insanity and early death. Staunton had exposed the apparently innocent offer of a challenge at chess as an aggressive assault against the father, symbolized at one level by the desire to take money off him (inherit his wealth). In the later stages of his short life Morphy became obsessed with his father's patrimony and the supposed attempts by others to rob him of it. After the Staunton débacle he refused to play international chess again.

This lucid psychograph deserves a place in any account of the development of the psychology of gambling. It opened up the whole of games theory with the new and significant concept of the game as an Oedipal battleground. Its relevance to this study was underlined by the centring of the sub-action on the theme of money, with its accentuation of aggressive monetary exchange. Freud's theory of roulette and Jones's account of chess have been amplified by a considerable body of later literature,[24] and similar studies have also uncovered the Oedipal symbolism of playing-cards.[25]

The psychoanalyst Edmund Bergler devoted much work to the study of gamblers,[26] and produced more material on them than did anyone else. He was a pupil of Freud and Assistant Director of the Psychoanalytic Freud Clinic in Vienna. He later emigrated to America.

Bergler developed the theme of 'psychic masochism'. He considered that gambling was invariably the result of a search for unjust treatment: confirmation of the gambler's belief that his parents were depriving him. He saw all gamblers as neurotics, motivated solely by this Oedipally derived masochism.

He noted the six characteristics of the gambler which all combined to reinforce his basic thesis. These were: a habitual predilection for risk-taking; the preclusion of all other interests; the invariable presence of an absurd optimism, which refused to be modified in the face of consistent defeat (this he specifically linked to the phenomenon of 'infantile omnipotence', a universal belief of early childhood in the effectual power of thoughts); the inability of the gambler to stop when winning; the inevitability with which he risks more than he can afford, although he tends to start with small sums; and the 'pleasurable–painful' tension, the main thrill of gambling, which arises between 'squaring off' and 'determination', to use Goffman's description.

The gambler, according to Bergler, launches aggressively into an attack on reality, epitomized by objective, logical probability. Exhibiting the unshakeable belief in the power of thoughts to change the external environment, which characterizes childhood, he seeks to dominate and control chance itself. This futile aggression leads to guilt. The consequent need for self-punishment is sexualized as psychic masochism.

Although many analysts were taking an interest in gambling in the 1930s,[27] Bergler carried out by far the most extensive clinical work on the phenomenon, and devoted considerable time to systematic description of his discoveries.

When Otto Fenichel came to write his great compendium on the interpretation of neurotic behaviour, *The Psychoanalytic Theory of Neurosis*,[28] published in 1946, he classified gambling under 'perversions and impulse neuroses'.

The excitement of the game corresponds to sexual excitement, that of winning to orgasm (and to killing); that of losing to punishment by castration (and by being killed). Just as compulsion neurotics invent various kinds of oracles in their intention to force God to permit masturbation and to free their guilt feeling (which as a rule fails) the gambler, too, tempts fate to declare whether it is in favour of his playing (masturbation) or whether it is going to castrate him. As in all conflicts around masturbation, here too, the activity serves as the scapegoat for the objectionable (hostile) phantasies of which it is the agent. The intensity of the conflicts around getting the 'supplies' again hints at an oral fixation; besides the anal element (the part played by money) also appears conspicuous.

There is an element of confusion among some analysts as to whether the gambler associates winning (Fenichel) or losing (Laforgue) with orgasm. Fenichel tended, in his categorical taxonomy, to cling to symptomatic descriptions of neurotic activity, perhaps oversimplifying complex procedures, such as gambling.

Like Fenichel, Ralph Greenson also classified gambling among the impulse neuroses. In 1947, he argued[29] that the need to gamble was derived from an infantile sense of impending danger. According to Greenson, it also resolves a whole plethora of distorted sexual and aggressive drives, ranging through latent homosexuality, anal-sadism and oral receptivity. Oral elements in gambling are also under-estimated in much of the literature. When he does win, the gambler's 'pay-out' may signify the maternal breast. A 'winning-streak' thus brings the same kind of conflicts and consolations as substitutive infantile masturbation.

Greenson's essay is interesting because, unlike many other analysts, he considers cultural and historical material to be relevant, while accepting the overriding importance of the Oedipal conflict. He is also the first analyst to make the point that there are vital differences in the psychodynamics of male and female gambling. Unfortunately, he is only able to provide a few tentative guesses on this sparsely examined subject.[30] Greenson was not optimistic about the beneficial effects of treatment on the neurosis. He repeatedly emphasizes that gamblers are motivated by an overwhelming desire to lose. Even Edmund Bergler, who gave so much of his time to trying to treat gambling patients, was pessimistic about their ability to sustain a course of analysis.

But Greenson was not the only Freudian interested in gambling's primitive cultural origins. In 1950 George Devereux, an anthropologist, followed with 'The Psychodynamics of Mohave Gambling'.[31] The importance of this text is that it shows how gambling served quite a different function in a society where oral and anal sexuality were less repressed than in our own. 'For the average Mohave,' Devereux writes, 'gambling represents a relatively innocuous temporary return of repressed omnipotent fantasies (sure to win) and of oral and anal elements, rather than a neurosis or an addiction in the strictest sense of the term.'

The bisexual element noted by Freud and others is, however, strongly present in the superstitions with which the Mohave surround their play. They consider transvestites to be lucky gamblers. Anality is also represented: 'If one dreams of picking up money in the "dirt" (i.e., in the dust, or from among clods) one will either be lucky in gambling or else find a well paid job.'[32]

Devereux comments:

The inveterate gambler's real losses are the penalties inherent in the possession of charms, the temporary forfeiting of genital pleasure for the sake of the thrill of gambling, and loss of social esteem. At the same time this temporary, and in many ways ancillary, interest in possessions (stakes) seems to represent a return of the repressed, i.e., in this case, of oral and also of anal interests, at the expense of genitality. This is not surprising, since not even the most lenient toilet-training can lead to as complete a lack of interest in possessions as Mohave ethics require.

Even so, Mohave gambling practices embody attitudes to money which would not be tolerated in advanced industrial societies: in the event of a dispute arising over a bet, the umpire burns the stakes of both sides.

If psychoanalytic orthodoxy was growing complacent in its definitions of gambling, Robert Lindner introduced important new concepts in a study of its psychodynamics published in 1950.[33] After a precise résumé of the existing literature, Lindner gave a detailed account of one of his patients, Paul, who suffered from uncontrollable gambling which had landed him in prison at the time of the analysis.

Lindner disputes Fenichel's description of gambling as one of the 'impulse' neuroses, on the grounds that it is always an ego-alien activity. 'The gambler is not a psychopath with a perversion, as the term "impulse neurotic" suggests; he is an obsessional neurotic engaged in what might be called the making of magic.'

These differences in the categorization of gambling are not just semantic exercises. Firstly the opposing positions throw some light on the unsatisfactory insistence in classical psycho-analytical literature that the perversions are the negative of the neuroses. This is based on Freud's thesis that what he calls the pervert discharges impulses which the neurotic is intent on repressing. But, in its simplified forms, it ignores the defensive function of the perversions – against anxiety produced by even more terrifying unconscious impulses – and the unsuccessful nature of neurotic repression, which often leads to the enactment of rituals which closely approximate the perversions themselves. It is not uncommon to find that perversions and obsessional neurotic defences co-exist in the same subject. Doubt is thus thrown on the concept of 'impulse neuroses' as an independent entity: frequently the perversions,

Introduction

at least, can be understood as exceptionally unsuccessful obsessive defences. With regard to gambling, one's categorization depends on how far one assumes that it is an activity in which impulses are discharged – thus providing pleasure – and how far one sees it as a ritualistic, obsessive response to anxiety, equatable with neurotic symptom-formation. Those who ignore the ritualistic (and anal) elements in the activity may not now use the unfashionable term 'impulse neurosis', but are likely to resort to describing gambling as an 'addiction' or 'behaviour disorder' – despite the unsatisfactory nature of these terms in general, and their inappropriateness for gambling in particular. The most extreme examples of this view are to be found in the writings of Moran[34] who has devoted a lot of space to the categorization of gambling. He writes,

Compulsions are the behavioural component of the obsessional state in which the subject finds his abnormal behaviour alien and attempts to resist it. If this element of resistance is not present the term compulsive should not be used no matter how strong the urge to indulge in the activity.

Excessive gambling which has produced deleterious effects is not usually associated with these characteristics. Some of these gamblers not only do not wish to stop gambling but also often openly admit that they enjoy it if only something could be done about the unfortunate side effects . . . Typically, the gambling is not felt to be alien as is invariably the reaction to the abnormality in the obsessive–compulsive state.

Moran's argument depends on a dubious distinction between 'gambling' and its 'unfortunate side effects'. But if these so-called 'side effects' are regarded as an indissoluble component of the whole gambling syndrome, his position falls down. He is attempting to treat gambling as if it was a substance, producing physiological effects, some of which were pleasurable and some of which were destructive, and assuming that it is the pleasurable physiological effects alone which the gambler is 'really' seeking. But the analogy collapses because gambling is not a drug; it is a ritualistic mode of behaviour. The reason that the gambler does not always experience the form of the gambling ritual as an ego-alien activity resides partly in the fact that, unlike the private rituals of many obsessionals, gambling, even in its most superstitious modes, is not widely regarded as an 'abnormality'. We will have occasion to return to this point

31

when we argue that in this respect it resembles religion, in being a form of universal neurosis.

Moran's distinction between gambling and obsessional neurosis also appears to ignore the fact that secondary gains are a characteristic product of even the most distressing 'obsessive–compulsive' states. In gambling symptoms the neurotic can convince himself that these secondary gains are potentially of considerable value – even though this is rarely the case. The conscious belief in the possibility of pulling off a large financial *coup* may appear to reduce the degree of alienation felt towards the rituals involved – but they remain obsessional none the less.

Part of the case for regarding the gambler as an obsessional neurotic is put in Lindner's important paper. He makes an interesting extension of the Reik–Bergler thesis that gambling is a masochistic testing of destiny, which appears as the ultimate father surrogate.

Lindner noticed that the gambler asked *two* questions of destiny: 'Did I kill my father (or if he is still alive, are my wishes powerful enough to cause the death of my father)?'; and 'Will I be punished or rewarded for my secret sexual desires (incest)?'

Lindner points out that if the gambler wins, the omnipotence of his wishes is proved and his incest condoned, but, of course, he is guilty on the parricidal tally. If he loses, he is not guilty of 'unconscious murder'; however his omnipotence is shattered, and he has to face the full penalty for his incest. Lindner calls this 'the great dilemma which literally chains the gambler to his place at the gaming table . . .' He acknowledges Bergler's 'trenchant paradox' that the gambler wants to lose, adding that he has made it comprehensible: 'It now appears that the gambler must *win and lose at the same time* for his sanity's sake, and this can never be done.'

In his *The Psychology of Gambling* Bergler published a note about other psychoanalytic contributions to the study of gambling.[35] He wrote,

Lindner's paper is the most informative among all the studies quoted above. I believe, however, that he deals with more superficial, though also repressed, mechanisms. Further clinical experience, I am sure, would have convinced Lindner (who died recently) that he had observed the second, not the first 'edition' of the subterranean conflict in gamblers.

He dismisses Lindner's case as 'an ingenious modification of my thesis that the gambler unconsciously wishes to lose'. He also criticizes Lindner for basing his entire thesis on a single case history, although it should be noted that Lindner takes note of the cultural implications of gambling and of its ontogenesis in religious ritual, aspects which Bergler consistently avoids.

Lindner is the first analyst to try to grapple with the specific role of money in the gambling equation. He describes the stakes of the gambler as attempts to bribe the Delphic Oracle, in a situation in which the gambler, himself, does not know which answer he would prefer. Somewhat cursorily, he also adds 'money unquestionably relates to the eliminative functions'.

Lindner was not the only analyst to be criticized by Bergler when venturing into this field. In 1951 Iago Galdston delivered a lecture on the relationship of gambling, alcoholism and superstition[36] in which he said,

I am rather persuaded to consider the gambler as one who has not successfully egressed out of the child's world of precausality . . . Those who have studied the gambler are in agreement about the principle of his psychological characteristics. Thus he does not gamble to gain money. Money may be the token of his favor but not the aim of his gambling. The neurotic gambler seldom if ever quits when he has made a 'killing'. The neurotic gambler stays until he loses and he seems to have a compulsion to lose. The neurotic gambler appears to know that he cannot win, but acts as if he might. The neurotic gambler behaves as if he were bent on soliciting and teasing Fortune into smiling benignantly upon him and granting him her favors. Neurotic gambling can thus be understood as a compulsion acting out of a plea to the surrogate figures, mother most likely, but father also, for a show of favor, for the affirmative response to the questions – 'Do you love me?' – 'Do you approve of me?' – 'Do you think I am good, and smart, and strong?' It were as if these questions, proper to the child, were for these children now grown, never answered in childhood adequately, and thus they remain fixated, and incapable of realizing that there are other means of eliciting an appropriate response; the testing of one's worth, for example, in the list of adult relations. The gambler is obsessive in his uncertainty – and compulsive in his need to pose the question – 'Is Lady Luck with me?' Since a definite and ultimately satisfactory, that is, reassuring for all time, answer to his query is impossible, the gambler will not 'quit' – until he is without the means to continue gambling. This will make understandable the gambler's *seeming* compulsion to lose, for the more he wins, the more means he has wherewith to gamble, and the more intensive becomes the gambling. Release is only to be found by losing.

Bergler commented:

Galdston's interesting deduction, in my opinion, places too much emphasis on the child's reality experiences, and disregards the masochistic elaboration. In his scheme, the masochistic wish to lose is but a by-product of the gambler's wish to elicit 'love'. I believe it is exactly the other way around: the masochistic wish to lose is covered up by the libidinous psuedoaim of pseudolove. Finally, 'precausal thinking' is but another way of stating that infantile megalomania is used: the technique and vehicle of infantile megalomania is – precausal thinking. Precausal thinking in adult neurotics is called – psychic masochism.

Since Galdston's lecture there has been surprisingly little psychoanalytic work on gambling, and even less which provides a genuine extension of the underlying Freudian thesis. When H. I. Harris reviewed the literature and reported on a single case in detail he observed, 'It becomes clear that only minor alterations are necessary to fit the hypotheses into the basic theoretical structure proposed by Freud. Most of the other comments are derivatives of this basic formulation which so often proves the case when we compare Freud's profound thinking with that of his followers.'[37]

Gambling and social formations

Gambling is a political as well as a psychological force.

Dr Johnson tersely dismissed it as 'the mode of transferring property without any intermediate good'. As always with Johnson, this is inadequate as a definition, but it does point towards one interesting aspect of gambling: the fact that although its medium is almost always money, it occupies a kind of limbo, or no-man's-land, in terms of the extent to which it is controlled by known laws of exchange.

Superficially, the gambling situation appears to be a real threat to the capitalist's economic model. It provides circumstances in which capital may apparently be accumulated without its prior possession. The man who wins the pools achieves overnight what can never be achieved through the sale of his labour throughout his life. He moves into a position where he can become an instant capitalist himself, and all he had to do for his trouble was to make arbitrary marks on a piece of paper.

Gambling has the appearance of being a threat to the economic *status quo*. This aspect is played up by both its opponents and its promoters. As we shall see when we come to consider the Christian moralist approach to gambling, great emphasis is laid on the fact that it 'undermines honest labour'. Some tractarians even suggest that it could lead to social unrest or revolution.

The corollary of this argument is the enthusiasm of gambling promoters over potential results of betting. Their literature hypes the big win as the only available release from the drudgery of alienated labour, and gambling is packaged as a private, quasi-revolutionary overthrow of capital, apparently assaulting it at its very economic roots.

Those who sought to politicize the working class, however cautious their own political positions, recognized gambling as a form of misdirected radicalism. Arthur Henderson, who was active in the development of the British Trade Union and Labour movements, once told a working-class audience, 'Gambling is a greater foe to labour than all the forces of capitalism.'[38]

In his study *The British Worker* Ferdynand Zweig reported the ideas of a number of workers about gambling. Interestingly, he discovered that the whole constellation gambling–religion–misdirected radicalism was specifically reproduced by the workers themselves. One man told him, 'I have nothing against the Church leaders who fulminate against the pools . . . provided that they can sell the same commodity – hope – either cheaper or better. But it seems to me they can't.' Gambling as an alternative to socialism was openly discussed:

Most workers do not believe they are lucky. They often say: 'If I was lucky I wouldn't be a worker. I was unlucky in one thing – I was born poor.' 'You must realize', a bus conductor, himself a gambler and a man who had studied his own state of mind, told me, 'that a working-class chap is an under-dog and feels like one. He is not satisfied with present conditions, so he often escapes into a world of dreams. This world he finds in religion, socialism, or gambling. Socialism is a dream both for him and for humanity as a whole, and gambling is a dream for himself personally. He can't hope to save enough to get out of his dreary existence. He can't work himself up; that is open only to a very few of the best men. The only way out of the mines, or cotton mills, or foundry work, or navvy work on the road, is to win in a big way. Only in that way can he gain his real freedom.[39]

This societal analysis of gambling as a form of misdirected radicalism parallels the psychoanalytic interpretation. In the individual, gambling as symptom-formation represents an unsatisfactory mode of coping with external and internal paternal authority. The gambling mechanism is engaged as an alternative to confronting that authority, as a means of evading the decision either to become it oneself (through the establishment of an ego-syntonic relationship between ego and super-ego) or to overthrow it (continue the struggle against the father). Engagement with the symptom allows the under-lying conflict to continue to exist and determine behaviour, without the real possibility of meaningful resolution.

Similarly, in terms of the class conflict, the worker's gambling as 'a dream for himself personally' apparently removes the need either to think in terms of becoming one of the 'very few of the best men', who successfully metamorphose them-selves into members of the ruling class which originally oppressed them (parallelling capitulation to the punitive super-ego), or to effect a radical solution, through socialist organiza-tion and action, to that oppression (the decision to carry on the struggle against the father). Politically and psychologically, gambling substitutes for both struggles and leaves men sus-pended within a conflict the resolution of which can only be achieved by accepting one alternative or the other.

But the concept of a gamble as a private revolution is a lie at every level. At best, gambling involves the reallocation of wealth within a given class, without affecting the total wealth available to that class. More often, the reallocation is the result of a pooling of limited economic resources, which are skimmed by both the state and the entrepreneurs, before being handed back to the winners. It emerges as just another form of economic exploitation. Far from providing a lever with which the capitalist machine can be disrupted or overthrown, gambling is another channel for its reinforcement. In Western industrial society, the working class is always the gross loser.

But this economic truth is submerged; the illusion, given

added impetus because it is reinforced by the opponents of gambling, is propagated. And the misconception itself has a political function for the ruling class. Gambling is a safety valve in the capitalists' system. By offering apparent potential wealth to a tiny minority, it seduces the mass of the people, and deadens inclinations which they might have towards organized, revolutionary activity. As long as a worker believes that he, individually, has a chance of freeing himself from the oppression of capital, however remote that chance, he will be less likely to feel class solidarity, or to engage in political activity. Gambling divides the working class against itself, substitutes for the development of revolutionary perspectives, and tends further to enrich those who are already rich through the exploitation of labour.

The apparent ambivalence in the nature of gambling – threat to capital on the one hand, reinforcer on the other – accounts for the ambiguous attitude of the state toward it in the West. Moral condemnation and pious concern about the 'social problem' combine with tolerance (gambling is either legalized, or laws against it are not enforced) and frequently a rapacious readiness to subject it to heavy taxation.

Sometimes, however, the state appears to be seduced by its own rhetoric. In England a Royal Commission pointed to 'the loss of industrial efficiency or possible disorder' as potential consequences of gambling.[40]

Bourgeois sociologists know better. They have seen that gambling exerts a hegemonizing function; far from being disruptive, they regard it as one of the cohesive factors by which the oppression of the capitalist order of things, in which they believe, may be continued. In order to make this point effectively, the sociologists have to deny that betting has anything to do with 'abnormalities' like addiction or neurosis.

In his study of East London betting shops Otto Newman, an academic British sociologist, started by summarily dismissing the psychoanalytic approach as 'entirely speculative'. He went on to argue that for most of the participants gambling was a wholly rational pursuit, entered into for calculated reasons related largely to social and cultural integration. He stated that 'irrefutably' in the community he studied 'the Gambler is the social norm, the Non-Gambler the deviant oddity'. This, he states, is probably true of most other similarly composed working-class communities . . . To try therefore to enumerate the personality characteristics of 'The Gambler', when this group forms approximately 75 per cent of the population under review, would not seem very illuminating. I have, accordingly, decided to designate as 'Gamblers' those individuals who confront the questioner with a positive ideological attitude to gambling, who will affirm that gambling is, even if not an absolute necessity, at least a valued and significant feature in their lives, who will declare that, were they to be deprived of gambling, an important and treasured component in their daily life would thereby disappear.[41]

Armed with this description of the 'normal' gambler, Newman goes on to paint an idyllic picture of the activity, as a harmless and integral part of our culture, even to the extent of insinuating that the betting shop is taking over as the natural centre for social interchange, in place of the public house. The analysts had, for him, got it all wrong because they were so wrapped up with 'the psychologically impaired compulsive', whereas he had discovered 'the "normal" regular and habitual gambler', who is a contented everyman.

Sociologists working in America have reached very similar conclusions. Robert Herman, in a study of on-course gamblers,[42] stressed that external factors, such as increased taxation on betting leading to poorer odds, or the statistical fate of favourites affected various groups of bettors in different but largely logical ways. He used this and similar evidence to emphasize the apparently calculated, rational behaviour of gamblers in general as opposed to the expected excesses of neurotic indulgence which he felt should be present if gamblers conformed to their psychoanalytic prototypes.

Irving Zola takes these arguments even further. He suggests that some forms of gambling are necessary reinforcements of a political *status quo* which he considers desirable. Writing about Hoff's Café, East Side, New England City, he says,

Though some betting may produce neither recreation nor monetary gain, this does not necessarily mean that it is a sterile, nonproductive, or even dysfunctional activity . . . For these men, gambling may be a way of harnessing or channelling their otherwise destructive frustrations. Instead of lashing out at society, they lash out at 'the system'. In this sense, gambling may be an activity which helps reinforce and preserve some of the major values of the larger social system.[43]

From their own positions, the sociologists are evidently correct. Gambling does indeed serve as a political safety-valve by diverting a potentially revolutionary impetus, but Newman's viewpoint is valid only if one denies the necessity of change. The error lies in the assertion that because gambling has a definable social function, which tends to preserve the *status quo*, the neurotic interpretation of it is either wrong or irrelevant. The parallel, as always, is with religion. Religion is another powerful political weapon in the hands of a ruling class: it hegemonizes the beliefs of the people and deflects their ambitions for social change. But it is able to do this effectively precisely because it exploits a universal neurosis of mankind.

To see how this works in the case of gambling, it is useful to provide a thumbnail historical sketch of the history of betting in Britain from the time of the emergence of an industrial working class. The late seventeenth and early eighteenth centuries were marked by a prodigious enthusiasm for all kinds of financial speculation. The excesses of this gambling mania, which seems to have affected all levels of society, culminated in the South Sea Bubble – the inflation of comparatively worthless stock – and the passing of the Bubble Act of 1721. Predictably, this did not quell gambling, but merely mitigated its disruptive effects on commerce. Turf, lottery and gaming activities developed rapidly as major forms of cultural activity.[44] Significantly, gambling began to coalesce in the highest and the lowest orders of society.

Throughout the eighteenth century it developed as the primary interest of the politically moribund aristocratic class. Gambling was a principal activity in the political clubs of the time, and a severe affliction of the landed aristocracy, the political high-flyers and their attendant retinues of beaux and lackeys alike. Horace Walpole, George Selwyn and Charles James Fox were among those most severely affected. Fox lost £140,000 in three years, and although he was an expert whist-player, and invariably won at the game, he chose hazard, a game of pure chance, instead, complaining that whist 'afforded him no excitement'.[45]

This singular obsession of the rich is exemplified in a story told about the prestigious club, White's. An unfortunate pedestrian suffered a stroke outside the club, and the porter hauled him into the foyer and set off to find a doctor. When he returned with the medical man, the members would not let the doctor approach their victim. They said they had laid wagers on the moment the man would expire, and the doctor's intervention would spoil the fairness of those bets.

But if gambling was a preoccupation of the upper social orders, it was also indulged to proportionate excess by the urban poor, who were dragged down by their lottery losses to scenes of Hogarthian squalour.

The gambling of neither class could be said to be motivated by a money dynamic. Fox, for example, would have stuck to his whist if even more cash had been his gaming objective. The poor realized that the King was the only real lottery winner; in any event, the records indicate[46] that the fortunate few who actually won the lottery dissipated their gains very quickly, and were quite unable to consolidate them.

The eighteenth-century lottery is a classic example of the economic and political functions of gambling. Lotteries were a favourite money-raising tactic of the Georges, although they had been used in Britain for specific projects since Elizabethan times.[47] They ensured the redistribution of wealth upwards. The only certain winner was the Crown as promoter. Extortionate profits could readily be extracted: the whole operation functioned as an additional form of taxation. The odds offered in relation to the size of the subscription were appalling. The *London Magazine*[48] calculated the chances in George II's £700,000 lottery with £10 tickets (brokers sold tenth or hundredth parts of tickets to the poor, and after the agency commission had been paid the deal was an even worse one):

> 34,999 to 1 against a £10,000 prize
> 11,665 to 1 against a £ 5,000 prize or above
> 6,363 to 1 against a £ 3,000 prize or above
> 3,683 to 1 against a £ 2,000 prize or above
> 1,794 to 1 against a £ 1,000 prize or above
> 834 to 1 against a £ 500 prize or above
> 249 to 1 against a £ 100 prize or above
> 99 to 1 against a £   50 prize or above
> 6 to 1 against a £   20 prize or any prize

Mathematics like this fully justify Adam Smith's description of a lottery as a 'tax on all the fools in creation', but still compare favourably with modern-day British football pools where, after deduction of profit, tax, and administrative expenses, less than 35 per cent of the pool is redistributed as prize money.

Despite the odds, the lotteries were greeted with feverish excitement. They were the occasion of all forms of divination, quasi-mysticism and prayerful dream-interpretation to invent the lucky numbers. Phantasy and irrational conviction combined, often producing tragic results. In the reign of George II a footman, serving in the household of a well-known lady,[49] saved for two years to buy two lottery tickets. When neither ticket drew a prize of any kind, he killed himself, leaving behind a letter in which he wrote about what his life would have been like if he had won. It included marriage to 'cross and coy' Grace Towers, who had spurned his life-time advances. He would have made her not just his wife, but his servant, too. At five o'clock every day he would have had 'tarts and jellies and a gallon bowl of punch'.

The only persons who grew rich out of gambling were the promoters, regal or otherwise. Early gaming entrepreneurs, like William Crockford, a Billingsgate Market man who discovered that it was far more lucrative to deal in chips than fish,[50] were among the first examples of the betting industry's own *nouveau riche*.

In 1796 Lord Kenyon wrote: 'It was extremely to be lamented that the vice of gambling had descended to the very lowest orders of the people. It was prevalent among the highest ranks of society who had set the example to their inferiors, and who, it seemed, were too great for the law.'[51] This was among the first rumblings of the nineteenth-century bourgeois position. For a complexity of reasons, which we shall describe in the next section of this introduction, the efflorescence of the entrepreneurial class in the nineteenth century was not associated itself with gambling among that class. The puritanical ethics which the capitalists adopted included a moralistic condemnation of gambling. In the 1820s the casinos were closed, the lotteries abandoned and the laws regulating betting introduced.

Nevertheless, these laws were never rigidly enforced. Realizing that gambling acted, in part, as a safety-valve, the bourgeoisie allowed its ambivalence on this issue to flourish. Abstaining from and denouncing the practice, it watched with satisfaction its debilitating effects on the moribund aristocracy,[52] and permitted the politically dampening growth of an illicit gambling subculture among the poor, knowing that the anticipation of illusory gains took their minds off real oppression. Only the occasional, atypical iron-foundry-owner was prepared to break the class taboo and muscle his way into the turf with a status string of thoroughbreds.[53]

This pattern continues up to the Second World War: mass engagement in illegal betting by the workers, repressive legislation combined with vociferous denunciation and tacit *laissez faire* from the ruling class, and a consuming over-indulgence on the part of the aristocratic appendage.

Casinos were banned altogether, but the dukes and dowagers had access to the watering-places of Europe. Legally, the only betting allowed was 'on-course', though the development of the telephone had led, via a legal loophole, to the possibility of off-course credit betting by phone – again, a facility which was available only to the rich. Working-class gaming was forced to rely on an illicit network of street bookies and runners.

After the war this started to change, partly because the erosion of the puritan values which had informed bourgeois orthodoxy was proceeding, particularly in those areas where the moralism had little apparent structural function. But also because religion itself was declining, and the ruling class needed to release and encourage another animistic practice which would have a similar effect on the mass of the people.

Eventually, and inevitably, the laws were changed. Harold Macmillan introduced his 'squalid lottery',[54] a state-run interest lottery, in the late 1950s. This gave gambling the official sanction and respectability it needed for a come-back, and the new bourgeoisie determined to participate in the economic exploitation of gambling. Lawful off-course betting shops arrived in 1960, and in 1963 came cash casinos. By 1970 legal betting through commercial channels had soared to a total turnover of £2,000 million a year.[55]

Britain experienced a change in its gambling mores, characterized by the intervention of the bourgeoisie for the first time. Throughout the 1960s this was intensified, in the form of increased taxation on betting, the introduction of levies, and the emergence of Lord Wigg, a product of Labour's meritocracy. As Chairman of the Betting Levy Board, he symbolized the end of the tyranny of the aristocrats over the Jockey Club, and hence the whole structure of horse-racing, the largest single betting medium.

The middle class embraced betting so whole-heartedly in this period that it allowed the emergence of a highly respectable entrepreneurial sector within the new enterprise. Perfect business gentlemen, like Cyril Stein of Ladbroke's with his accounting and banking background, took over from Rogue Honest Joe as the men behind the emergent safe industry of huge turnovers, high profits and low overheads. John Banks, a northern bookmaker, openly called his betting shops 'money factories', thus outraging his colleagues. But the legalized gambling entrepreneurs had come to stay: a few established chains of betting shops, more than 600 in some single companies, serving vast areas of the country on exactly the same principle as any other form of retail profit-making industry. The more it taxed them, the more the state appeared to be legitimizing their activities. As the industry became increasingly entrenched and respectable, the small-time bookies vanished altogether, and the biggest slice of the nations betting passed into the hands of the five largest companies: a process with the most reputable of bourgeois precedents.

The only voice in the wilderness crying halt to this carnival of connivance in betting was the Churches' Council on Gambling. As we shall show, the ecclesiastical authorities had their own good reasons for being both anxious and afraid.

Gamblers' accounts

Neither the outward moral indignation of the state, nor the rapturous enthusiasm of the promoters deceived the gamblers themselves, even before Freud. If we turn to the books written by gamblers, or about their practices, drawing on first-hand knowledge, we find a striking insight into the true nature of the gambler's motivation. Every gamester knew that the next best pleasure to winning at cards was losing at cards. Even though he put the two possibilities the wrong way round, he was nearer to understanding the real nature of gambling than the vociferous rabble of amateur philosophers and arm-chair theologians who condemned the practice, supposedly because it was based on a greedy desire for material wealth.

John Ashton could write in 1898, and expect consensus from non-gamblers, 'It is taken up as a quicker road to wealth than by pursuing honest industry, and everyone engaged in it, be it dabbling on the Stock Exchange, betting on horse-racing, or otherwise, hopes to win, for it is clear that if he knew he should lose, no fool would embark in it.'[56]

But the gamblers were far greater fools than Ashton gave them credit for, and most of them knew it full well.

An ancient Hindu epic dating from the second millennium before Christ describes the dice battle between two jealous and noble families, the Kauravas and the Pandavas. The Kauravas had the distinct advantage of Sakuni, who in modern gambling argot would be dubbed a 'dice mechanic', or cheat. He could win every throw on loaded die. Yudihishthira, who represented the Pandavas, was a bad dice-player, with no pretensions about his ability. He suspected that Sakuni was cheating at the start of the game. But he would not give up. His rationalization, similar to those which were later to be reiterated throughout the annals of gambling, was that his honour required him to carry on playing. In the words of one translation,

> Now when Yudihishthira had lost his Raj, the Chieftains present in the pavilion were of the opinion that he should cease to play, but he would not listen to their words, but persisted in the game. And he staked all the jewels belonging to his brothers, and he lost them; and he staked his younger brothers, one after the other, and he lost them; and he then staked Arjuna and Bhimra, and finally himself; and he lost every game.[57]

Finding himself a slave, Yudihishthira has only one thing left to stake: his wife. Sakuni offers him his freedom, against his wife, to be decided by the dice. He accepts and loses. She protests that as he was a slave when the cast was made, the bet was invalid; he no longer had any dominion over her, and thus had no right to wager her in a game. This dispute is again settled through Sakuni's dice, and the unfortunate Yudihishthira loses again. Yudihishthira's persistence, his refusal to learn by defeat, and his dogged pursuit of disaster make him the first known gambler to display the classic neurotic symptoms the significance of whose psychodynamics could not be understood until the discovery of psychoanalytic theory.

Since the sixteenth century there has been a spate of books by and about gamblers, accentuating the obsessional and compulsive elements of the practice, underlining how inevitable losses far outweighed the potential gains in their significance to the players. One of the earliest was *Liber de Ludo Aleae*, by Girolamo Cardano, who was mathematician, physician and gambler all in one.[58] Other classics include Charles Cotton's *The Compleat Gamester*, 1674,[59] and Lucas's lurid *Memoirs of the Lives of the Most Famous Gamesters . . .* , 1714.[60]

Among the most valuable, in terms of its explicit interest in loss, over and above winnings, is a curious confession left by Richard Minster, a seventeenth-century aristocratic rake, whose singular compulsion to gamble led him into such straits that he was eventually charged with a long series of felonies, brought to trial, found guilty and beheaded, his influential connections notwithstanding:

One night during Epiphany I suffered my most grevious loss of money in the whole of my damned life, and was forced to return to the world which I am now to be quit of by my own damnation.

During that se'nnight I had lost and recouped and lost again, and was much of an evenness in my reckoning. My harlot's jewels that she valued were gone, but in a flux of generosity I had bought her more and lain with her and ravished her in my joy and her lewdness. But ever the craze was upon me like a grumbling illness and perforce I went forth again on the Saturday minded to lose all I possessed. Lose! I say – for in my recollectiohs there lurked the feeling of a beast, a fornicator suffering a virgin to take his whim, at each toss of the dice that lost me a fortune; a mounting turmoil within me, retarded each time by a winning throw . . .

I played with Mountgarde and Hilbery and gained ninety guineas from them in an hour, taking their notes because they were penniless . . . My winnings sullened me, and in despair I raised my stake. Still I won. And so in the main it went on through the night. At one moment I had upward of fifty thousand guineas owed me, and still I went on, throwing scarce a losing die in all that time.

The room was in a hubbub of calls of Deuce! Trey! and the like. All of us had taken off our greatcoats and laid up our swords and the room was heady with the wine fumes and tallow. It was a wild scene of depravity and in its midst I stood surrounded for my fortune, some of the players touching me and rushing back to their own tables to see how their luck fared then. I felt as though marching at some great triumph against fortune. But in my heart I was despairing, for I was winning a battle I sought to lose.

But at last, toward morning (so I think; the notion of time was not with me) I gathered up my winnings – notes, gold, jewels, perukes, and all that the losers had been able to summon to their aid in their losses and cried to them to hear my last stake.

I lost on the throw and can scarce describe the feeling of relief that overcame me. It was like a solvent to the harsh world to which I must now return.[61]

There are many other examples of this curious branch of literature. These books, and others like them, provide concrete insights into gambling – and make nonsense of theories which regard loss as 'an unfortunate side effect'. Numerous stories and anecdotes illustrate the gambler's indifference to winning, his insatiable, self-destructive propulsion towards total loss, his frequent longing to be rid of something which he describes at best as 'an enchanting witchery', at worst as a disease. Yet all the gamblers admit that will-power, rationality and moral precepts are not enough to arrest the progress of the compulsion. There is a grim inevitability with which they repeat their destructive behaviour, even to the point where it endangers freedom or life itself.

One example from Steinmetz's extraordinary compendium of anecdotes, *The Gaming Table: Its Votaries and Victims*:[62] says it all:

The following incident is said to have occurred in London: two fellows were observed by a patrol sitting at a lamp-post in the New Road, and, on closely watching them, the latter discovered that one was tying up the other who offered no resistance, by the neck. The patrol interfered to prevent such a strange kind of murder, and was assailed by both, and very considerably beaten for his good offices; the watchmen, however, poured in and the parties were secured. On examination next morning, it appeared that one had lost all his money to the other and had at last proposed to stake his clothes. The winner demurred – observing that he could not strip his adversary naked in the event of losing. 'Oh,' replied the other, 'do not give yourself any uneasiness about that; if I lose I shall be unable to live, and you shall hang me, and take my clothes after I am dead, for I shall then, you know, have no occasion for them.' The proposed arrangement was assented to, and the fellow, having lost, was quietly submitting to the terms of the treaty when he was interrupted by the patrol whose impertinent interference he so angrily resented.

Scarcely indicative of a man seeking 'a quicker road to wealth than by pursuing honest industry' – but then, as we are going to argue, Christians and the apologists had good reason to cover up the real nature of the gambling neurosis.

Gambling and religion

We have produced evidence, both psychoanalytical and from the texts of gamblers themselves, which indicates that gambling is a complex – and widespread – neurosis. In fact, we do not know of any society in which it was wholly absent. However, we have already shown that conventional attacks on gambling, particularly those put forward by Christians, rely on false arguments. We will have to return to this point, but it is worth underlining the fact that the moralistic attack is two-pronged: it argues both that gambling is unhealthy materialism and, in the same breath, that it is potentially subversive to profit-based capitalism. The gamblers' own accounts, confirmed and explained later by psychoanalysis, and the willingness of the state to endorse betting stand in violent opposition to these theses.

In this section we are going to suggest that there is motive to this moralistic madness, a motive that concerns the very origins of gambling, and the reasons why it holds such exclusive sway over the minds of those who engage in it. The arguments put forward by religious men are deliberate rationalizations. In psychoanalytic language, they constitute a 'reaction-formation'. The moralists are concerned about gambling not because it is a wholly atheistic and alien activity, but because it is just too close for comfort. The player exclaiming, 'Don't push your luck!' is saying very much the same thing as the Christian when he proclaims, 'Do not tempt the Lord thy God!' Central to our thesis is the argument that gambling is a 'universal neurosis' – like religion itself.

Gambling emerged out of religion. In Professor Tylor's phrase it is 'secularized divination'.[63] The roots of gambling are in religion; it is an alternative way of explaining, and thus potentially controlling, the unknown. The paraphernalia of gambling derive from the paraphernalia of divination. We still tell fortunes with cards. Gambling was nurtured in the womb of religion, and it resembles it closely.

The astragalus, the ankle-bone of any cloven-footed animal, was the ancestor of the die. Many have been found on prehistoric sites of different cultures. They were used in religious and quasi-judicial ceremonies before being employed in games of pure chance. According to Greek mythology, the astragalus was the instrument which the gods used to determine the division of the world. The legend has it that after their successful battle against the Titans Zeus, Poseidon and Hades became lords of the universe. The method of determination as to who should rule what was an appeal to chance. This is a characteristic appearance of the gambling process at the core of mythology. It is used to explain that which is unknowable. It is only in an Einsteinian universe that 'our dear God does not cast dice'.

The Greeks even have a legend that accounts for the secularization of the gambling process, and its separation from the appeal to chance which lies at the centre of religious belief. The myth explains that Tyche, Goddess of Fortune, was strolling one day in the woods on Olympus when Zeus appeared and, as he was accustomed to do, ravished her by force. The only pleasure of the female child who resulted from this union was the invention of gambling games, and a malicious delight in the quarrelsome chaos which they sowed among men. Tyche gave her child houses which had lamps which burned for ever in their windows so that passers-by were constantly attracted to enter and dice at their peril with the Goddess of Chance.

(In the mythology of chance, Luck is usually female, though Destiny and Fate and, in the West, God himself are far more often male. This raises an interesting question in relation to the psychosexual symbolism of gamblers, and a comparative emphasis on either the male or the female surrogate may point to real differences in individual, infantile, Oedipal experience. It remains true, however, that Fate overrides the temporary favours of (Lady) Luck, suggesting the validity of Freud's view that gambling is primarily expressive of homosexual aggressive–libidinal impulses towards the father. It is reasonable to suppose that in individual cases the gambling ritual may be over-determined, and may additionally [or even exceptionally, primarily] give expression to comparable impulses towards the mother. An individual desire to elevate a female chance-symbol may be seen as paralleling the cultural growth of Mariology within the Catholic Church in the nineteenth century.)

In Egypt, too, gambling appears in both religious and, later, secular contexts. According to one Egyptian legend, the reason why there are 365, and not 360, days in the calendar is because Thoth, the God of Night, gambled with the moon and won one seventy-second part of her light. These winnings he presented to Nut, the Goddess of the Sky, who was in need of some consolation following her row with Ra, the God of Creation. The gift took the form of five extra days.

Just as Thoth had diced with the moon, we find paintings of games dating back to 3500 B.C. showing that the Egyptians themselves used the astragalus in board and counter activities, or games of chance. In the Judeo-Christian tradition, of course, casting lots was a favourite mechanism for determining the will of God, and the Old Testament is littered with references to the habit. Historians have pointed to similar practices and myths in all civilizations. Appeals to chance were used to explain the elements of mythology, and to determine the will of the gods for individual men before they became means of settling the ownership of arbitrarily risked sums of money. Wherever there was doubt about destiny out came the dice, the lots or the entrails. When mythology itself could not contrive a satisfactory explanation, it showed the gods themselves appealing to the ultimate authority of chance.

Gambling and religion remain close to each other in many primitive cultures. Burt and Ethel Aginsky, authors of several studies of the Pomo Indians, have reported that in this tribe gambling never left the immediate enclosure of religion.[64] Gambling is the full-time pursuit of a small, highly esteemed group of professionals who enjoy a status comparable to that of the priests. This, of course, is an atypical situation.

It is far more common to find that practices close to gambling are strong elements in primitive quasi-judicial procedures and religious practices whereas gambling proper – the 'secularized' version of divination – is either specifically condemned, or regarded with considerable suspicion.

But the appeal to chance lies behind diverse practices in many primitive cultures, in particular behind trial by ordeal, and related techniques. Some Australian tribes spin a mounted stick to determine the perpetrators of unsolved crimes, and the person to whom the stick points when it settles is treated as guilty, and punished by exile. In other cultures a coconut is substituted for the stick. Another variation, also reported among certain Australian tribes, relates directly to the astragalus. A bone is thrown in a circle, with the whole tribe gathered around its perimeter. The one to whom the bone points when it settles is treated as guilty and, after receiving the attentions of the sorcerer, dies within a few days.

This appeal to chance has not died out in either religious or judicial procedures in the West. The final selection of twelve jurors for trial by jury under the British legal system is made by drawing lots to determine which of the pool of potential jurors called to court will actually sit. Johan Huizinga, who studied the origins of games,[65] has argued that religion, judicial systems and play all have common origins. Certainly, chance-orientated appeals survive in many children's games determining both rewards – 'Pass the parcel' – and punishments – 'Musical chairs'. Significantly, in popular culture, appeals to chance are still considered the 'fairest' of all deterministic procedures. When we do not know how to solve any one of a myriad of small, everyday problems, like the gods dividing up the universe in myths, we toss for it, and let chance decide. In the 'democracies' of certain Free Church sects, lots still determine the will of God. In science, chance explains what we do not know; in life it determines when we cannot decide.

In all these instances chance emerges as both the ultimate authority and, paradoxically, the ultimate source of control. (The projected actions of all other agencies may be disrupted by chance itself.) These qualities compound its fascination for obsessional neurotics and, in part, account for their preoccupation with magic, and quasi-mystical, preventive rituals. These actions can be seen as attempts to control chance itself. In gambling, where the neurosis is so specifically bound up with attitudes to paternal authority, it is not surprising that we should find the fascination with chance specified and escalated. If one can control chance itself (win consistently at gambling) then all things are possible – including the discharge of one's direst unconscious impulses. The gambler is constantly relieved and reassured that such control is, in fact, unattainable.

The sexualization of the authority of chance undoubtedly

occurs through fear, or actual experience, of apparently random impotence. This loss of control, which so closely resembles the dreaded castration itself, will seem to have been imposed by an outside agency. As the individual male lacks voluntary control of his erectile tissue, chance, like the potentially castrating father, becomes a fascinating and terrifying vehicle for ultimate authority.

Gambling, which is a series of appeals to chance, emerges as a potent process. When a religion cannot wholly assimilate gambling into itself, it is certain to fear it, since it proposes another way of knowing the unknowable, of explaining the unexplainable, using the techniques of religious animism, but potentially short-circuiting the concomitant ideology of a specific religion. After all, some drama critics argue that it was by chance that Oedipus was propelled towards his tragic fate: murdering his father and marrying his mother. As the discoveries of dynamic psychology progress to the point where even certain accidents are no longer regarded as 'chance' events, the functioning of this agency in the affairs of men acquires a new complexion. Scientific psychology reduces the area of control which we ascribe to chance, but it cannot render it impotent. Both gambling and religion are actively and irrationally concerned with that possibility and its implications – precisely because chance is the ultimate authority which can override the will of the technologists and the gods alike.

The psychology of the 'universal neurosis'

The ethnological observations on gambling are well-known and have been extensively documented elsewhere. We wish to argue that just as gambling emerged from religion, and retains many of the characteristics of it, so the psychology of the religious man and the gambler continue to parallel each other very closely. This is particularly true of Western Judeo-Christian society, where, at one level, gambling and religion are very similar attempts at the resolution of the unsolved conflicts surrounding Oedipal development. As we shall argue, the link becomes closest in the post-Reformation, Puritan tradition through the mutually shared suppression of anality. Predictably, it is within this religious tradition that the reaction-formation against gambling is strongest.

The starting-point for this comparison is Freud's text, 'Obsessive Actions and Religious Practices', of 1907,[66] quoted in the first part of this introduction. Here Freud draws a parallel between religious ceremonials and obsessive actions: the rituals of the obsessional neurotic as he engages in his compulsive tasks have many of the same qualities as the liturgies of the Church, and the private practices of religious men and women. Similarly, Freud argued that believers did not know the real motives which impelled them towards religious practices, or represented them in their conscious minds with rationalizations and the neurotic does not know the real reasons why he carries out his ceremonials either. He wrote,

> The sense of guilt of obsessional neurotics, finds its counterpart in the protestations of pious people that they know that at heart they are miserable sinners; and the pious observances (such as prayers, invocations, etc.) with which such people preface every daily act, and in especial every unusual undertaking, seem to have the value of defensive or protective measures.[67]

These observations led him to his now famous conclusions about the nature of religion. 'In view of these similarities and analogies one might venture to regard obsessional neurosis as a pathological counterpart of the formation of a religion, and to describe that neurosis as an individual religiosity, and religion as a universal obsessional neurosis.'[68]

Freud returned to this theme in many of his later works, extending the argument considerably; in *Totem and Taboo*'[69] he maintained that 'what constitutes the root of every form of religion' is 'a longing for the father', and in 'The Future of an Illusion' he once again calls religion 'the universal obsessional neurosis of humanity'.[70] He followed this by saying, 'Like the obsessional neurosis of children, it arose out of the Oedipus complex, out of the relation to the father.'[71] In 'Civilization and Its Discontents' he stressed that, by extracting an enormous price, religion could, and sometimes did, prevent the formation of the clinical manifestations of private obsessional neurosis. But those who have sought to make much of this observation, and have used it as an apology for religion, have not been drawing their comfort from Freud. He went on,

> Religion . . . imposes equally on everyone its own path to the acquisition of happiness and protection from suffering. Its technique

consists in depressing the value of life and distorting the picture of the real world in a delusional manner – which presupposes an intimidation of the intelligence. At this price, by forcibly fixing them in a state of psychical infantilism and by drawing them into a mass-delusion, religion succeeds in sparing many people an individual neurosis.[72]

The comparison which Freud drew between religion and the obsessional neuroses was neither mechanical nor simplistic. In 'The Future of an Illusion' he warned, 'But these are only analogies, by the help of which we endeavour to understand a social phenomenon; the pathology of the individual does not supply us with a fully valid counterpart.' Moreover, in his earliest text of all on this subject, 'Obsessive Actions and Religious Practices', he stressed the differences between obsessional neurosis and religious activities. He argued that in obsessional neurosis the instincts which had been denied and displaced into private rituals were exclusively sexual, whereas in religion 'they spring from egoistic sources'. It was not until later, in *Totem and Taboo*, 1913, that he maintained that repressed sexuality had played its part in the formation of religions, and continued to influence their contemporary forms. But there were other differences, which he did not later adapt: he noted that the obsessional neurotic carries out his cere-monials in private, but the religious man frequently performs his rituals in public, often with some ostentation. Also, he stressed that the rituals of the obsessional neurotic are individually contrived, whereas those of the religious man are shared by large numbers of fellow believers. (But the religious man is likely to cling to the established liturgical practices which he has learned, and resist attempts to change them, just as the obsessional holds fast to his private ceremony.)

The most significant dissimilarity of all, in our context, is that the obsessional neurotic is frequently objective about his neurosis, and tends not to believe in his own rationalizations, whereas the religious man carefully develops the credulity of his ego. The bank clerk who washes his hands several hundred times a week does not really believe that these actions will forestall the infection he says he fears. But if he engages in daily prayer and obsessive bible-reading, he might well believe that these activities help to open the gates of heaven for him. Any rational doubts are rejected as temptations.

When we consider the question of gambling we are immediately confronted with a striking fact. Not only do gambling practices very closely parallel religious practices in their outward forms, but the attitude of the gambler towards his ritual differs from that of the everyday obsessional neurotic in precisely the same way as the attitude of the religious man differs from it.

The similarities between gambling and religion are numerous. We have already indicated that the paraphernalia of gambling emerged directly from the paraphernalia of divination. But the ceremonials which surround the use of those paraphernalia are still interrelated. What happens in a casino, in terms of ceremonial, closely resembles what goes on in a church. Both are ostentatiously opulent, remote from the norms of everyday life; inside both establishments a language, or style of speech, is used which is remote from that employed in ordinary social interchange. Men and women, in both places, engage in complex, irrational procedures, apparently alien to their usual style of behaviour. To participate in worship requires suspension of normal modes of behaviour, and a willingness to submit, absolutely, to a series of arbitrary activities; so does participation in roulette.

We can suggest precise comparisons of details. A crucifix worn round the neck resembles the luck-token of the gambler; it solicits the favour of the unseen power. The rosary resembles the pack of cards: it helps to draw the relevant emotions into a physical system, which can be manipulated, and a particular significance ascribed to each segment. The invocations of gamblers are prayers. The Bible, or the Prayer Book, used for daily guidance and containing absolute truth, if only it can be correctly deciphered, is the form-book, or the chosen system. In the words of one former gambler, 'I used many systems of picking out a horse – sometimes by taking a pin and closing my eyes, letting the pin-point land where it would. This, I thought, was divine guidance. Names also appealed to me and I would identify certain of them as "heaven sent".'[73]

Perhaps the best way of grasping these similarities is by looking at the relationship between Lourdes and Las Vegas. Both cities are filled with men and women performing endless series of mysterious rituals, clutching their lucky–sacred trinkets, waiting for the miracles from Lady Bernadette Luck which never come. Both require a long journey to reach – in the case of Las Vegas, a pilgrimage across the desert. Both are economic and cultural outposts, surviving only on their respective animistic promotions.

But our comparison of gambling and religion cannot stop at similarities in outward forms. The relationship between the Christian religion, specifically, and gambling goes much further. The gambler and the Christian have much in common in terms of their attitudes towards their chosen displacement activities.

Firstly, both gambling and religious practices can best be understood as unsatisfactory attempts to exert and impose control, externally and internally. They are responses to anxiety, which is experienced as a result of the appearance in the ego of intolerable impulses, which cannot be discharged. Impulses do not go away: they have to be coped with. The rigidity of belief in the religious man and the credulity of the gambler are manifestations of a determination to make the control mechanism work. (In this respect they differ from the obsessional neurotic who often possesses a certain critical insight and experiences his whole unsatisfactory defence mechanism as ego-alien activity.)

And so they share the belief that there is an external being, more powerful than themselves, whose favours can be sought, and who can be influenced by the most extraordinary physical and psychological activities enacted here on earth. Even the most hard-headed and cynical gamblers will admit, when pressed, to a complex system of superstitious belief. In both activities, then, there is a father surrogate, fate and God. In some circumstances, there can also be a mother surrogate, luck or the Madonna. The attitude of the believer to that surrogate, and the search for ways of influencing it, constitute one of the most important dimensions of both pursuits.

Similarly, in both religion and gambling, there is absolute conviction on the part of the participants. The gambler believes, consciously, that he will win, although logic, and his past performance, should combine to inform him that he will lose. His overt optimism is unaffected. Similarly, the Christian emphasizes 'faith', a crushing, irrational confidence in the existence of a deity, which cannot be shaken by scientific objections. Psychologists who have studied gambling, without psychoanalytic conclusions, have commented on the striking parallel which exists between the gambler and the religious man in this respect.[74]

Both Christianity and gambling are phantasy-goal-orientated activities. The Christian is seeking the unobtainable: eternal life in an elusive Elysium. The gambler believes that he is craving the financial cornucopia: the big win that never comes. Both neurotics are prepared to endure endless present suffering in the pursuit of these insubstantial goals.

And, finally, indulgence in either practice necessitates the suspension of usual attitudes to time and value. In the gambler, this is expressed in an oblivious indifference to the real purchasing power of the money with which he is playing. In the Christian, it involves the acceptance of beliefs about the origins of man, and his present estate, which bear no relation to his life experience, and of which he could not be convinced outside his religious beliefs.

The 'magic' and 'mystery' at the core of the gambling experience resemble the 'magic' and 'mystery' at the core of the religious experience. This is acknowledged even in the popular writing on gambling.

Tactics, magic, science – if none of these work how can you win? You can't. 'All horseplayers die broke,' said Damon Runyon, expressing a universal truth . . . Never, never ask how you can win. Ask, if you must, how you can lose less. Ask, above all, if it is better to have gambled and lost than never to have gambled at all.

The exception to all the above is me. I don't fool around with red telephones or wishbones, or form-books, or newspaper tips, or any of that fatally attractive beguiling rubbish. I just happen to have this tiepin. I was wearing it at Newbury the day I got that tremendous Tote Treble, and I know, I know, that one day, sooner or later, if I wear it faithfully . . .[75]

Longrigg's humourous account is close to the truth of the matter. Many religious people clinging to their crucifix, their secret private prayer, or their well-thumbed copy of the New Testament are doing exactly the same.

The interesting feature about these resemblances, as we have already suggested, is the way in which they accord with the *differences* which Freud pointed out between religion and obsessional neurosis. The gambler has to conduct his gambling with other people. His, too, is a social ritual. He tends to choose a particular form, or forms, of gambling, and stick to them. But the ceremonials involved are not of his own invention: the rules of the game, like the conventions of worship, are given. But the gambler, too, will become very anxious if the croupier spins the wheel in the wrong direction at roulette, or if the cards are not dealt in the correct way, even though such variations may have no effect on his chances. Like the Christian, his ego is supremely optimistic: it knows he will win, despite all the evidence and the efforts of the unconscious to lose. Few of the gambler's associates will consider placing a bet to be 'abnormal' any more than they would regard saying a prayer in this light. In all these respects, gambling differs from obsessional neurotic symptom-formation, and approximates the condition of religious practices.

We have described how in the gambler the ego adopts a submissive and masochistic position in relation to the super-ego. For the Christian, the situation is similar. 'What, after all,' asks Joachim Kahl, the former Protestant theologian, 'is the Cross of Jesus Christ? It is nothing but the sum total of a sado-masochistic glorification of pain.'[76]

The unique proximity of the gambling and religious neuroses has already been suggested in this introduction in Reik's observations on the reasons for Dostoyevsky's gambling. Two-way traffic between them is to be expected. As Lindner points out, an oppressive religious background in childhood is one of the commonest characteristics of the gambler. More interesting, perhaps, is the evidence provided by self-help therapeutic groups such as Gamblers Anonymous.

Members of Gamblers Anonymous have found their gambling constitutes a major personal problem, and have joined a group, consisting solely of other gamblers, with the intention of giving it up. Their literature specifically denies the efficacy of self-knowledge: 'None of us have found a knowledge of why we gambled to be especially useful in freeing us from the obsession to gamble.'[77]

However, the Twelve-Step Recovery Programme, which each new member is taken through and admonished to read daily (many G.A. members refer to the Twelve-Step leaflet as 'my bible') is full of encouragements to substitute a form of religious practice for the old gambling activities.

Steps Two and Three, for example, say, 'Came to believe

that a Power greater than ourselves could restore us to a normal way of thinking and living . . . Made a decision to turn our will and our lives over to the care of this Power of our own understanding.' Step Eleven re-emphasizes the theme: 'Sought through prayer and meditation to improve our conscious contact with God as we understand Him, praying only for knowledge of His will for us and the power to carry it out.'

We have already seen in 'Gambling Sickness' how the religious element in Gamblers Anonymous supplied one member with a more socially acceptable form of displacement activity for his Oedipal conflicts which remained intact and unresolved. So it is with most members of Gamblers Anonymous; God is readily substituted for the gaming table. 'I have found that the most successful G.A. members I know are the ones who actually make a decision to turn everything over to a power greater than themselves,' writes Larry R. of San Francisco. Bob J. of Boston says that G.A. has enabled him to 're-enter my church and ask for and receive help and guidance from God'. Charles I. of San Francisco writes of his G.A. experience: 'I professed a new faith and understanding of God, a thing I had never done before.' And so it goes on.

The structure of a G.A. meeting itself – in which member after member confesses and re-confesses the sins of his former gambling life, and receives applause and praise when he finishes – mobilizes guilt, publicly, just as the gambling experience did. But also, the introduction of the abstracted father surrogate, the Power Greater than Ourselves, means that the guilt is never confronted, it is merely channelled into the ritualized format of the meeting, with its endless series of prayerful acts (reading out of invocations and the Twelve-Step Programme) and humiliation, through abject confession which parallels the masochism of the gambling experience.

The activities of this group indicate that the gambling displacement has such similar origins to the religious displacement that in many individuals they can be exchanged without difficulty. However, this process requires the renunciation of the possibility of self-knowledge.

Chance was just as much a 'Power Greater than Ourselves' as any other agency which reformed gamblers chose to describe as determinative in their decision-making process. The subservient relationship of the ego to the super-ego which characterizes the gambler's behaviour at the race-track and the casino, and forms the basis of his insatiable need for punishment, is transferred to the confessional format of the G.A. meeting. Guilt continues to be activated by the insistence on sins past. E. Moran, honorary psychiatrist to the group in Britain, has even reported on the case of the gambler who joined the organization and used it in exactly the same way as he had used his former gambling. He spent so much money and time on telephone calls and fares that he continued to punish himself and his wife financially, just as he had been doing when betting.[78]

We have traced the strong resemblances between the outward forms of gambling and those of religion, and between the psychological dynamics of the gambler and the religious man. Both entail a passionate, unshakeable search for love and approval from an illusory and indifferent outside agency; both seek signs of that approval in prizes or miracles, winnings or answered prayers, and both are backed up by an unquenchable ego-optimism, despite what is learned about reality. However, it would be wrong to suggest that gambling and religion were the same thing. Gambling could foster a Dostoyevsky, but not a St Thomas Aquinas; a mafia, but not a papacy. Indeed, it is always likely to be a less satisfactory displacement than religion because of its unfortunate financial consequences, and the fact that it is still socially stigmatized. As the G.A. members point out, acceptance of the religious alternative can bring 'peace of mind', simply because the displacement of Oedipal conflicts is a more viable one, but it is still a displacement, and it involves the denial of the underlying forces which motivated the compulsion in the first instance. Repressed conflicts remain unresolved, and continue to determine behaviour.

Christianity, capitalism and the gambler

Given this close interrelationship between religion and gambling, and specifically between Christianity and gambling, the history of the attitude of the Churches to the pursuit explains a great deal about its psychological mechanisms. As we have indicated, this history is largely comprised of a reaction-formation against gambling, a denunciation that almost reaches hysteria in the case of the nineteenth- and early-twentieth-century puritanical moralists. But the interesting thing about the development of this literature is that it is almost exclusively a post-Reformation phenomenon.

Before the Reformation there were isolated attacks on gambling, but the Church had no official position on it. Only after Luther, and after the emergence of a Puritan Christian tradition specifically wedded to the ideology of capitalism, did the tirade against betting really begin, reaching a crescendo in the most highly industrialized countries.

Up until the late fifteenth century, with few exceptions, the Church endorsed the secular position on gambling, exemplified by pragmatic British Medieval laws introduced to prevent the dispersal of feudal estates by gaming war-lords, and to encourage more bellicose pursuits, such as archery, among serfs and vassals.[79]

In contrast to the Koran, which specifically condemned gambling,[80] there is no direct biblical justification for rejecting it and so the Catholic Church never saw any reason to condemn it as 'inherently' immoral. This was to remain a point of difference with the Protestant tradition into the twentieth century.

In fact, Catholic and pre-Reformation Church of England divines frequently emphasized the structure and symbolism of gambling as being a metaphorical equivalent of the Christian hierarchy. Cards, in particular, presented a ready-made simile for the Great Chain of Being; the gambler's attitude to those cards, with all its optimism, blind faith, irrational certitude, struggle and acceptance of arbitrary decisions, paralleled what the Church considered to be a desirable attitude towards God, and his ordering of the universe.

It is not surprising, therefore, to discover Bishop Latimer's Christmas 'card sermons' of 1529.[81] Christmas, by tradition, was a festive time when everyone gambled at cards. Latimer took the opportunity to explore and elaborate the metaphor of the Church and the pack as far as it was possible to pursue it.

As long as the Church was secure in its monopoly of faith, it could afford to admit this popular parody of itself: so absolute was its intellectual dominion that there was no possibility of gambling presenting a viable alternative. Indeed, we find that despite the significant changes that were to be brought about by the Puritan tradition this parallel continued to survive in folklore. In 1744, when Richard Lane, a private in the Forty-seventh Foot, was brought before the Mayor of Glasgow, accused of playing cards in church, he made an elaborate plea, which began by claiming that when he saw the Ace, he thought of God, when he saw the Deuce, he thought of the Son and the Holy Ghost. When he saw the 'Tray', he thought of the Trinity. And so on, throughout the pack, concluding that there were 365 spots in the pack, the number of days in the year, and fifty-two cards, corresponding with the number of weeks. Not surprisingly, this reminded him of the Bible and Prayer Book, the almanack of the church for the year. The mayor was so impressed with this explanation that he pardoned the private forthwith[82] and the incident became a popular legend that still survives in a contemporary folk song, about a soldier fighting in Vietnam.

The private, however, had been doing no more than appealing to a tradition firmly established by the early leaders of the Church. Buckenham, prior of the Dominicans at Cambridge, had once advised Christians to 'confound Lutheranism by throwing quatre and cinque: the quatre being the four doctors of the church and the cinque being five passages from the New Testament selected by the preacher'.[83] At this point, the practice of gambling was firmly within the precincts of the truth; it was an ally against the Reformation heresy.

Lutheranism itself, and the subsequent development of the Puritan tradition in opposition to absolute Church hegemony over ideas, reversed this alliance. For post-Reformation Protestant Christianity, gambling rapidly became a cardinal sin, involving denial of faith in God, the worship of false deities, like chance, and, paradoxically in the light of the alliance which emerged between Puritanism and capital, the pursuit of worldly goods in a way which was deemed incompatible with the ideals of good Christian living.

And so we find Thomas Gataker, a Puritan theologian, producing a treatise *Of the Nature and Use of Lots* in 1619. Lots, it should be remembered, had been considered a very good way of determining the will of God. But Gataker is incredulous. Although he advises their occasional use for 'the confirmation of doubts', he goes on to point out that they are often 'plain witchery', or worse, giving the Devil's side of the problem rather than God's. He argues that they are always so when handled by unbelievers. Looking at the dice, he is not reminded of God's Church, or formulae for combating heresy; on the contrary, he sees 'an whole alphabet of evils that usually accompany these games, even as many as there be aces or points on the dice'.[84] A man who throws dice, he concludes, is certainly making an appeal to the Devil, and not to the true God.

Similarly, Jeremy Taylor, in his *Ductor Dubitantium*, was of the opinion that gambling belonged to the 'arts of geomancy', and that 'God hath permitted the conduct of such games of chance to the Devil'.

To understand this theological volte-face, we have to refer to the doctrine of justification by faith, which was introduced into Protestantism at the time of the Reformation, and subsequently became one of the major points of conflict with the given theological superstructure of Catholicism, to which believers were simply required to assent, following mediation by the priests.

'Justification by faith', the crux of Lutheranism, was the central discovery of the post-Reformation, Puritan, Protestant tradition; it is the key to much of its subsequent development, and it permeates every level of the Protestant's social, political and religious life. It was a doctrine that required individual struggle on the part of every believer to find God for himself. Obedience to ceremonies, sacraments and priests was no longer enough to ensure salvation. A man had to search for his deity on his own; he had to 'let Jesus into his heart'. Salvation was achieved, at least in part, by a private battle against the forces of evil, by a private attempt to internalize God.

There were liberating aspects to this development. A man was no longer required to accept so absolutely the faith as mediated by the priestly caste, but there were also new dangers.

False gods and devils could emerge all along the route. Any system of thinking or acting which contained within it an alternative explanation of the unknown other than the ordained relationship with the true God was suddenly fraught with new dangers.

Luther came to see devils everywhere and not just in the

abandoned precincts of Rome. Any way of grappling with the unknowable, any potential animistic path which explained the inexplicable and sought favours of an all-powerful exterior being became heretical. It could not be contained and assimilated by an external superstructure of faith.

Gambling was just such a diabolic phenomenon. After all, in his version of the Gospel the writer now known as St John had written:

Then the soldiers, when they had crucified Jesus, took his garments, and made four parts, to every soldier a part; and also his coat: now the coat was without seam, woven from the top throughout.

They said therefore among themselves, Let us not rend it, but cast lots for it, whose it shall be: that the scripture might be fulfilled, which saith, They parted the raiment among them, and for my vesture they did cast lots. These things therefore the soldiers did.

On Calvary, itself, there was a suggestion that the scripture might be fulfilled in two ways. Gambling stands there next to the Cross, the central Christian symbol, as the alternative practised by the unbelievers. They are dicing; Jesus is dying. The reader can chose which of these masochistic activities is the more significant to him. They are similar, exclusive alternatives. Another evangelist tells the story of the centurion who repents and admits that Jesus, whom he had helped to crucify, was the son of the true God. But those who prefer the mysteries of chance, argues the Christian, will not be able to find God. They are the kind of men who gamble at the foot of the Cross. As J. A. Spender, a moralist and tractarian, wrote, 'The lights of the casino shut out the stars.'[85] One mode of divination is exclusive of others.

But what was to make gambling a particularly dangerous competitor for Puritan Protestantism was the masochistic element in its dynamic. The struggle to find God (as we saw in 'Gambling Sickness') is gruellingly masochistic. The introduction of 'justification by faith' made it even more hazardous, and with Calvinistic notions about predestination, religious faith itself became little better than a bad bet. The prize at the end of the road was no longer guaranteed. Gambling inevitably appealed to a precisely similar psychology. Guilt surrounding parricide is at the core of the symbolism of both the Cross and the pack of cards.

The hostility of the Churches in the post-Reformation period can be seen not as opposition engendered over a wholly alien activity, but a genuine reaction-formation against a practice that was, in so many respects, very similar.

But the reaction against gambling cannot be explained in purely theological terms. A paradoxical process was taking place within Protestantism by which it wedded itself, inextricably, with the ideology of capitalism. This alliance gave enormous impetus to the efflorescence of industrial capitalism in the nineteenth century. Particularly in Britain, the structural fusion of the interests of capital and Puritanism was absolute. Puritanism provided the entire ethic of hard work for small rewards, of suffering in this world for a prize in the next, of subservient, laborious dedication, and humble acceptance of one's lot, which acted like oil in the oppression perpetrated by the capitalist machine.

This association compromised the very essentials of Christianity. It ran completely contrary to scriptural doctrines about poverty and love. But the Christians were particularly anxious to absolve capitalism from criticism. Gambling was a convenient scapegoat onto which they could hive off the responsibility for all the pernicious and really intolerable effects of capital's exploitation of labour. And so the moralists came to attack gambling on every front. They argued that it was a heresy, in that it denied the existence of a universe ordered by God. They insisted that it was 'materialist', and therefore incompatible with Christian living, thus hoping to evade the real issue of Puritanism's pact with capital. And they added that it was a devastating, pernicious force, murderously marauding labour, and potentially leading to revolution. This was a lie, but again it deflected interest away from the real effects of the industrialists' sweat-shops on the down-trodden and subjected proletariat.

More books were produced containing these curious arguments than the vast number attacking drink.[86] We have chosen Major Seton Churchill's *Betting and Gambling*,[87] of 1894, as a characteristic example. Unlike so many of the dry, pedantic guardians of public morality, Churchill writes with a rolling rhetoric, and his single short volume takes care to encompass every one of the main arguments put forward by the many other Christian writers who tried to dissuade men from gambling:

O, young men, who are starting in life with perfect liberty and freedom, preserve that sacred heritage of yours. You are free to choose between all that is noble, good, and pure on the one hand, and all that is vile, selfish, and degrading on the other. Beware of the slippery incline which may lead you or others on to a gambling hell. Many others before you have entered that path, full of the most perfect confidence in themselves, but they have been allured on to their own destruction, and they have found that the bright hopes held out to them by the Goddess of Chance were never fulfilled, and that she wreaked her vengeance on their confidence and devotion in a way they little anticipated at the outset.[88]

The biblical language, and the description of chance as a deity, is significant. The gambler believes, irrationally and despite all the evidence, that chance will be favourable to him, if he only dedicates himself to her more fervently, and the Christian believes likewise. The Lord *his* God is 'a jealous God' who will only offer the prize of paradise to those who afford him the most servile devotion in this world, whatever suffering it causes them. Both are equally fanatical in their absolute conviction of the veracity of their beliefs, without any rational evidence to support them.

Having posed gambling as a heresy, Churchill switches to his other major argument: gambling is a perniciously pervasive force for evil in society, which could upset the whole social structure. Gambling is 'a dark cloud of moral pollution hovering over the country'. It is a 'disintegrating force in society, the nation that yields to its influence must degenerate, and approach more nearly its old savage condition'.[89]

To back up these arguments he quotes one Henry Thorne: 'There is in the gambling spirit a certain feverish reliance upon chance, which is a bad passion because it puts fate in the place of conduct, and an imaginary and non-existent personality in the place of the living God.'[90] Then he cites Prebendary Harry Jones who believes that 'gambling disintegrates the grit of true humanity. It weakens belief in honest work. It tends to destroy that genuine individual self-reliance which is the social hope of a people. It directs energy from productive operation and, above all, puts us out of touch with a living God, who in his economy, leaves nothing to "chance".'[91]

To these moralists gambling appears to comprise not just a means of exchange, which they say is detrimental to the existing capitalist order of things, but to constitute an attack on the whole cosmology that envisages God as the lynch-pin of a capitalist-ordered economic system. It presents another God, who has another kind of economy, and one which is apparently not based on the exploitation of labour.

Churchill admits this direct comparison in his colourful descriptions of Monte Carlo. 'Atheism, or the absence of any God, could more truly be called characteristic of the place. And where there is no God, some substitute is soon found; hence that palace or casino in which is enshrined the Goddess of Chance who daily attracts her devotees.' He then goes on, in an elaborately detailed description, to compare the casino with a cathedral,[92] noting, in contrast to the 'stinginess' of Christians, 'the Devil's servants, reckless of expenditure, provide all that is needed to carry on the work of their master'.[93]

For Churchill, chance takes the place of God; the casino substitutes for the Church, the bait of winnings for the lure of paradise, and gambling ritual for ecclesiastical ceremonial. The moralists, however, were left with one problem: the gambling prize was at least theoretically situated in this world. That of the Christian was not even purported to be anywhere else but in the next. Ironically, the supporters of capital found themselves denigrating gambling winnings. Writing about the victory of 'Romney Marsh', labourer, in a Hamburg lottery (he picked up £4,000) all Churchill could manage was, 'What an enormous amount of demoralization that large sum must have induced.'

'If working men accustom themselves to sudden gains and losses,' he explained later, 'they cannot be expected to work steadily at their occupation when the profits are small, and the work is hard.'

Soon he turns on the rhetoric again, in a direct appeal to the working class. 'O, working men of England! arouse yourselves to face this cursed evil . . . You working men of England are now masters of the grandest empire ever created, and your votes at any election can settle what is to be the future of this inheritance.' He warns against voting for candidates who are not interested in the morality of their constituents.

Ultimately, we shall all be engulphed, but it is the masses and not the classes who will be first affected. Are you going to allow men who do not work to grow rich at the expense of your families and your-selves? Are you going to permit the parasites of society to absorb the wealth of the labouring classes? Are you going to permit pro-fessional gamblers who do nothing to enrich their country, to run up huge balances at their bankers, which you know to be the price of blood, and that the blood of your own countrymen, of your own kith and kin?[94]

These 'parasites' of society, who do not work but grow rich on the price of the blood of the labouring classes, have a familiar ring about them. But surely they cannot be the relatively innocent gamblers whom Churchill claims to be describing. As we have seen, their lot is usually ruin, not 'huge bank balances'. Churchill seems quite consciously to be deflecting the real criticisms which can be made of a bourgeois class on to the gamblers, attacking them viciously because the activities he ascribes to them are precisely those about which the entre-preneurial Christian capitalist is likely to have the most exten-sive guilt feelings.

Churchill drives this point home by quickly trying to exon-erate the true capitalists from any of the blame. 'The law of exchange', he reminds his readers, features prominently in God's Word. It, and all its effects, are therefore quite accept-able. 'England would not be the leading country of the world had her sons never embarked in any enterprise involving risk. Enterprise is an essential to success and few can succeed in life who shrink from the possibility of running risks.'[95]

The argument for the moralists is complete: gambling cannot be tolerated because it provides a similar alternative to Christianity. In the process of rejecting it, it is saddled with the blame for all the vices which really do result from capitalist exploitation of labour. It is a process that psychoanalysts will recognize as all too familiar in the development of many specific personality types.

The arguments which Churchill put forward were not excep-tional. They represented the orthodox attitude of the Protestant tradition. Other tractarians were even more extreme. Reverend Glass, Vicar of Leyton, gave a series of lectures to City business-men in 1924.[96] He told them,

The man who takes the gamble to get rich quickly is a danger not only to commerce, but to his country. His moral integrity is impaired and it affects the society in which he moves. He is a contradiction of good citizenship for he lacks the spirit of self-sacrifice and self-control. His methods in the long run will lead to an indolence which has a bad effect on efficient industry. One of our leading financiers, Sir Robert Kindersley, of today, puts it in strong words: 'reduction in individual effort to save and to work'.[97]

Here, the Christian exposes his pact with capitalism, just as earlier the good Vicar had gone to the most tortuous lengths to 'prove' that commodity brokers could not be classified as gamblers.

Drawing his arguments together, Glass said, 'On the day of Calvary, the Roman soldiers gambled beneath the Cross for they knew no better. We are living on the side of Calvary where the light of the Cross of Christ has been shining through the ages. Yet there are multitudes of men and women who ought to know better who are gambling beneath it still . . .'[98]

Again, it is a question of choice between two essentially similar forms of animistic practice. When moralists argue that gambling is to be opposed because it is a materialist pursuit of wealth, they are using false arguments. Avarice hardly figures in the gambler's motivational repertoire. Indeed, if acquisitive avarice were gambling's dynamic, it would have proved as acceptable to the Puritan tradition as the Stock Exchange, the cocoa market and capitalism itself. After all, it was not commodity broking in which the soldiers were engaging at the foot of the Cross. Capitalism satisfies no one's animistic needs, and is therefore compatible with Christianity.

Writing, also in 1924, R. H. Charles, Archdeacon of Westminster, said,

This appeal to chance is . . . the perversion of a natural and right love of adventure . . . till it becomes the debased thrall of a world that is arbitrary and fortuitous, irrational and unknown. But Christianity does not content itself with condemning the appeal to chance; it does more, it seeks to rescue man's spirit of adventure from this thraldom and set it free to achieve the chivalrous, noble and ideal tasks to which it was predestined.

And what is this true, noble adventure which Charles is proposing in contrast to the irrational chaos of the gambler? Nothing other than the precisely comparable search of the Christian for 'eternal life'.[99]

Later moralists have acquired more sophisticated polemical

techniques deploying sociologically-orientated data about gambling. But they use it to reach the same conclusions. Benson Perkins[100] declares that gambling is

against such a conception of life that the teaching of Jesus and the New Testament bears witness. True, our knowledge is limited, but as Jesus made it clear, 'Your Heavenly Father Knoweth.' The whole teaching concerning the character of the God and Father of Our Lord Jesus Christ whose very spirit is love, who cares for his children, knowing their every need, is the direct antithesis of the gambler's foolish, superstitious, childish and unscientific belief in luck.

On any objective criterion, belief in God is just as 'foolish, superstitious, childish and unscientific'. 'Resort to gambling', Perkins concludes, 'is virtual denial of faith in God and in an ordered universe, putting in its place an appeal to blind chance . . .' which is certainly a fair description of what the gambler does, at one level. However, what is interesting in this description is the similarity between the system which Benson Perkins is proposing and the one he is rejecting.

The arguments of the moralists persist today. Christians attack gambling because they say it is a threat to capitalism. As we have tried to show in our description of the class role of gambling, it is more often a reinforcement of the system. The argument, as put forward by the moralists, is full of duplicity. On the one hand, it is produced as a means of exonerating themselves from the social evils resulting from their own structural alliance with capitalism: as in Churchill, gambling can be blamed for oppression of the masses. On the other hand, it has recently acquired a protective function. Christians know that for the first time capital is prepared to shed, or at least dilute, its liaison with the Christian–Puritan tradition. In some respects, the elevation of gambling by the state in post-war Britain has been a conscious substitution of another animistic practice for that one that, as an institution, is visibly on the decline. Evidently, it suits the Christians to assert and reassert the erroneous argument that gambling threatens capital and leads to social unrest. This is more likely to receive sympathetic official treatment than the old line that gambling denied faith in God. This accounts for the reduction in moralism of the recent reports of the Churches' Council on Gambling.[101] These have concentrated on statistical, rather than moralistic, evidence. The fact that the Churches' Council was, until recently, the only body in Britain collecting gambling statistics is significant.

So now the moralists lay greater stress in their work on gambling's disruptive effects. Lycurgus Starkey, writing in a well-known Christian magazine, commented: 'The prevalence of gambling points to a breakdown of the Puritan ethic of work which held that in one's daily calling honesty, industry, thrift and service to God and man should be stressed.'[102]

There is one aspect of this which we have so far left to one side, and that is the continuing attitude of Catholicism to gambling. Gambling never posed the same problems to the indomitable, unquestioning theology of Rome as it did to the hazardous route of late Protestantism. The similarities between gambling and Roman Catholicism are as evident as those which exist between the Puritan tradition and gambling. But Rome could admit of the practice by assimilation. Where 'justification by faith' was not involved, chance did not emerge as an alternative god. Pursuit of chance was just a parallel of the religious experience, acceptable as long as the sacraments and ceremonies of the Church continued to be observed.

This continues to be a major point of difference with the Protestant Churches. In Britain, for example, the Roman hierarchy has seen no need to contribute to the work of the Churches' Council on Gambling. In 1950, after a Royal Commission had been set up to investigate gambling in Britain,[103] Roman Catholic officials sent a memorandum stating: 'We hold then that it is not wrong to play for stakes, even for large stakes, provided the players can easily afford it.'[104] This position infuriated the Puritans, particularly the strictest Non-Conformists. Benson Perkins commented that the Catholics had 'gratuitously offered the opinion that it was difficult to establish the inherent immorality of gambling', and soon after the Methodist Church published an official declaration stating, 'Resort to gambling is a virtual denial of faith in God and an ordered universe, putting in its place an appeal to blind chance, prompted neither by love nor rectitude.'[105]

This was a public explosion of a major point of difference that had been simmering, and continues to simmer, with strong words spoken on both sides. Another arena for the debate was the use of gambling within the Church as a fund-raising gambit. Scarcely surprisingly, Roman Catholics had managed to assimilate it without any theological qualms, which again infuriated the Puritans.

In 1924 Charles wrote angrily:

In the Roman Church lotteries are a recognized means of procuring funds for religious purposes. In the southern provinces of Ireland this evil is, so far as I can discover, wholly unrestrained. I will give but one example. Thus in a raffle organized on behalf of a religious institution before the establishment of the Free State the prizes included a cameo of Leo XIII specially presented by the Pope himself.

Charles goes on to denounce gambling as a 'satanic ally'. In our discussion of the anality of gambling in the next section we return to the extensive implications of this comment.[106]

Others have agreed with Charles, if resorting to more sober language. Thus Gordon Moody, the present Secretary of the Churches' Council on Gambling,[107] puts forward similar arguments in *Notes on the Use of Gambling for Fund Raising*. He makes special mention of the prevalence of gambling in the Roman Church, and suggests that it drives out true charity.[108]

But if the Puritan tradition had ultimately failed to integrate the lucrative source of funds, it was not through want of trying. Ezell, in his detailed and scholarly study of the development of the lottery in the United States,[109] comments:

With the exception of the Quakers, every major denomination and most of the minor groups drank from this fount. Among the latter groups were the Pacific Congregational; Universalist Society; Free Will, New Connexion, Six Principles, First Day and Catholic Baptists; English Episcopal; German Presbyterian; German Reformed Calvinist; Hebrew; Church For All Denominations; German Religious Society of Roman Catholics; High German Reformed Presbyterian; French Evangelical Church Society; and Dutch Presbyterian Protestants.

There was something fundamental and structural in the inability of Protestantism to assimilate gambling, and its consequent reaction-formation. That fundamental factor concerned the attitude of the Puritan tradition to repressed anality, and forms the subject-matter of our next section.

So far, we have established that the animistic roots of gambling, detailed by ethnologists and anthropologists, indicate an indelible link with religious practices. This link accounts for the strong reaction-formation of the Puritan tradition against gambling. Unable to assimilate in part because of their theological positions, Puritans went as far as to suggest that it was a devilish mode of exchange. The association with the Devil, introduced by Gataker and Taylor, has continued to be employed in this century. This exaggerated fear of gambling results from its many similarities with religion. Because it appealed to similar psychological types, it was in a real sense a competitor. As the state, in recent years, has come to abandon its alliance with the Puritan ethic, and sought to establish a secular ideology, the Christian moralists have responded by over-emphasizing the erroneous argument that gambling is a threat to capital, thus hoping to rekindle the dying alliance between industrialists and Christians against a common enemy. The Catholics, for whom gambling was never a problem because of alternative theological conceptions which allowed for assimilation, have disdained involvement in this campaign. For them it is possible for a man to be a gambler and a Christian, as long as he goes through the necessary formalities.

The intensity of the debate and the volume of literature produced by the Puritan moralists are indicative of the extent of their fears. They seem to sense that increasingly gambling is taking over from religion as the animistic orthodoxy for the mass of the people.

Anal strategy

As we have already pointed out, the strategic role of anality in the gambling neurosis, although raised in much of the existing psychoanalytic literature, has been insufficiently discussed. This is a serious omission.

The concept of the anal-erotic character type was introduced by Freud in 1908 and subsequently substantially elaborated, both by Freud himself and by several of his colleagues and associates.[110] Freud observed that there was a certain character type that was orderly, parsimonious and obstinate. He related this constellation of characteristics to anal retentiveness in infancy. 'As infants, they seem to have belonged to the class who refuse to empty their bowels when they are put on the pot because they derive a subsidiary pleasure from defecating.'[111]

From these apparently straightforward observations derived

one of the most influential of the specific discoveries of psychoanalysis. Freud soon realized that the anal-erotic character in later life substituted money for faeces. Ferenczi, following up this lead, traced the precise 'Ontogenesis of the Interest in Money', which we have included in this volume, and Elvio Fachinelli extended this research to a study of anal money-time.

Fachinelli specifically sought to update Freud on money, noting the virtual absence in earlier work of the concept of the gift, developed by Marcel Mauss.[112] Fachinelli also indicates the links between the work of Freud and that of Marx on money, sketching out a comprehensive schema for analysis.

But the influence of anality, as Freud indicated, extends even beyond influencing attitudes to money, to time and to value. Freud, at first puzzled by the significance of stubborn obstinacy in the anal constellation, eventually traced it to the role of punishment in the infantile toilet-training process. He noted that a 'self-willed parting with stool'[113] would lead to punishment on the buttocks. This was intended 'to break [the subjects'] obstinacy and make them submissive'.[114]

To support this thesis, Freud observed, 'an invitation to a caress of the anal zone is still used today, as it was in ancient times, to express defiance or defiant scorn, and thus in reality signifies an act of tenderness that has been overtaken by repression. An exposure of the buttocks represents a softening down of this spoken invitation into a gesture . . .'[115]

But Freud also extended these discoveries about anality to encompass the role of the Devil in religion: 'We know that the gold which the Devil gives his paramours turns into excrement after his departure, and the Devil is certainly nothing else than the personification of the repressed unconscious instinctual life.'[116]

These observations began to propose a historical and social role for anality, relevant on a far wider basis than that which concerned the neurosis of the individual patient on the consulting-room couch. We will shortly return to the determinative role of anality in the universal neuroses. First, however, we must sketch the significance of the anal element in gambling as it appears clinically.

In so far as gambling is playing *with* money, rather than *for* money, it is a straightforward displacement of the universal childhood desire to play with faeces. In other words, it represents a general regression to the anal stage of development. Ferenczi's essay traces very clearly the way in which money, and ultimately abstract systems, displace excreta by a process of progressive repression, and there is no need to restate that argument here.

However, it is worth noting how the anal element constantly erupts through the repressive defences in gambling in such a way as to indicate the cistern of repressed instinctual forces lying beneath. Faeces are associated with success at gambling: when a man treads in animal excrement on the street in France, a popular superstition informs him that he is likely to be successful in a forthcoming lottery. One of the most persistent of the Monte Carlo legends concerns a man who, on his way to the casino, received pigeon-droppings on his hat. He won a fortune. Subsequently, he would wander round the streets, waiting for a similar incident to recur. News of his success spread, and a craze developed for the reception of a comparable heavenly faecal blessing before commencing play. Ferenczi has reported, too, that a patient of his from Erdely told him that when someone had a piece of extraordinary luck, such as winning in a lottery, the local expression was, 'He is as lucky as though he had eaten filth as a child.'

Similarly, perhaps the least inhibited of all commercial gambling games is American table dice. It is the only game in casinos which is conducted noisily, and unlike in games of roulette or cards emotions are undisguised, exclamations and expletives are common. Significantly, the anal references are strongest here. The name of the game is 'craps'; terminology includes 'coming out the hard way', 'they're rolling', 'come-out bet' and a 'don't pass line'. A 'roller' can throw one of two combinations, a 'pass' or a 'crap'. Even in games like poker, where phallic and masturbatory references appear to be much stronger than anal preoccupations, the money which is played with in any given round of the game is always referred to as 'the pot' – and it is of central interest to the players. Floor managers in casinos are called 'pit bosses'. Comparison with Ferenczi's account of the progressive repression of the faecal element into money is revealing when applied to gamblers' argot. We often find that first-degree displacement has already taken place: thus dice become rollers and then marbles (cf., the significance Ferenczi gives to marbles on the road from faeces to gold) and money itself becomes 'rocks', a cautious step backwards in the shit–mud–sand–pebbles–marbles–gold–cash continuum which Ferenczi proposes.

But gambling is much more than a displacement for a generalized regression to the anal stage of development. The singular preoccupation with the handling of money which gambling invariably necessitates indicates a relationship with traumatic or particularly pleasurable anal sensations in infancy, with unresolved conflicts surrounding the infantile bowel-training procedure.

As we have seen, Freud proposed a relationship between the desire of the infant to retain his faeces for the stimulation of pleasurable sensations and subsequent development of orderly, parsimonious and obstinate character tendencies. But an integral part of the retentive mechanism was the later, gratifying, sudden expulsion of faeces, and a particular satisfaction in that expulsion was associated by later psychoanalysts with conceit, suspicion, ambition and loveless generosity in later life.

Ernest Jones has indicated how these apparently irreconcilable character-traits, which result from the various stages of infantile anal pleasure, become resolved in later neurotic displacements.[117] He quotes many convincing examples, including the relatively common case of the man who for long periods of time is unable to write letters to anyone, but suddenly turns to his letter-writing with a feverish enthusiasm, clearing up all his backlog with one fell swoop, and often writing letters in this period which are far more informative, thorough and well-constructed than is required by social convention. This pattern is often paralleled by attitudes to tidiness, for example, where a man, or woman, might leave his or her papers and possessions in an appalling jumble, and then suddenly and impulsively spend a considerable period of time over-organizing them, refusing to be deflected by other more pressing priorities. Jones saw such behaviour as relatively benign attempts to reconcile the conflicts between the retentive and expulsive moments in displaced anal activities.

Gambling is a very efficient medium for such reconciliation. The meanness, avarice and orderliness of the retentive moment can be satisfied by systems-play, and the avaricious, obstinate optimism of the ego. The 'loveless generosity' in the abandoned moment of loss, with all the necessary suspicion and ambition, particularly in games in which bluff plays its part, emphasizes the expulsive moment. As money is the medium, the relationship to faeces is particularly direct.

But, as Fachinelli has indicated, early anal experience also affects attitudes to value and to time. The child becomes regulated by his bowel movements; as Freud put it half a century before, faeces are his first gift. He knows that their expulsion at the right moment will bring pleasure to his mother. But this regulation is only achieved at a price – the denial of his own pleasurable time-system, including the retention of faeces until such a moment as their expulsion will yield maximum satisfaction. A resistance to the new, adult value-time scale is likely to remain. But gambling is an attempt to subvert this imposed parentally-instigated time-value system. Gamblers turn cash into chips or betting slips. Cash, thus metamorphosed, is separated from its reality value. A player who complains about a £2 casino or race-course entrance fee may well be prepared to lose up to £100 once inside. In cards and casino play particularly, normal attitudes to time are completely suspended: there are no clocks in casinos and, as every card-player knows, it is almost impossible arbitrarily to impose time limits on a game. Most activities – eating, sleeping, defecation, work and leisure – are regulated at least according to an approximate timetable which is only marginally adaptable according to the individual's immediate desires. Gambling refuses to be contained within such a pattern. In these implicit attitudes to value and to time we can see an uneasy attempt to reassert the old infantile structure, to sabotage the imposed time- and value-scale.

Finally, the masochistic element in gambling evidently has an anal as well as an Oedipal significance. Self-willed parting with stool (loss at gambling) leads to punishment. We know of the case of a man who, after suffering high gambling losses, felt impelled to visit a flagellation brothel. In this instance, the displacement was not enough in itself. Every gambler may expect punishment for his obstinate refusal to learn by experience, his insistence on the pleasurable expulsion of his money, but the gambling substitution may well not be sufficient on its own to cope with the conflicts aroused by the underlying anal neurosis.

Unaccountably, this vital connection between gambling and the progressive repression of anal conflicts seems not to have been traced in any of the existing psychoanalytic literature. Hans von Hattingberg hinted at it and Lindner pointed towards it in a single sentence, but hitherto it has not been developed. We consider that it is at least as significant in the understanding of gambling as Freud's important discovery concerning regression to phallic preoccupations and masturbatory conflicts.

This outline of anality in gambling is central to our thesis because it relates to a body of literature which has grown up around the analysis of the role of anality in history, specifically in the development of that other great, universal neurosis, the Western Christian religious impulse.

Here, there is extensive documentation, and it is both relevant and informative because it illuminates the whole Catholic–Protestant contradiction on the admissibility, or otherwise, of the gambling syndrome. Norman O. Brown starts from Freud's observation about the relationship between gold, the Devil and repressed instinctual impulses.[118] His purpose is the reinstallation of Freud's hypothesis of the death instinct, which has often been either ignored or diluted by short-sighted post-Freudians. He argues that man has repressed the fact of his death, in contrast to animals, who allow death to be a part of life and make use of the death instinct in the act of dying itself. 'Man aggressively builds immortal cultures and makes history in order to fight death.' From this basis Brown went on to discuss the scatology and anality of the Lutheran Reformation, and the subsequent suppression of its specifically anal moment by the capitalist-linked Puritan tradition. The key to his theory is the *apparently* fortuitous fact that Luther's *Thurmerlebnis*, his moment of blinding discovery when he realized the doctrine of 'justification by faith', was made while sitting on a latrine. Brown does not emphasize the additional biographical fact that Luther suffered from persistent constipation throughout his life.

Perhaps this is because he rejects 'vulgar psychoanalytical dogmatists – those for whom psychoanalysis is a closed system rather than a problem', who over-emphasize, according to his theory, the specificity of the anal character. Although he considers that the investigation of private trauma over infantile toilet-training may be useful in the treatment of individual

77

neurotics, he argues that we must reject such a simplistic approach in dealing with the socio-historical phenomenon of anality. He warns that if we do not, we shall be in danger of the kind of gross reasoning that argues that Protestantism itself came about by a change in toilet-training procedure, and that the only way to overthrow capitalism, in which the anal character is the social orthodoxy, is by a new revolution in toilet-training patterns.

Brown turns to studying Luther's forgotten texts, the passages in 'Table Talk' filled with anal preoccupations and diabolism, and he reveals a middle term connecting anality with Protestantism on the one hand and with capitalism on the other. This middle term, as Freud had already hinted, is the Devil. For Luther, in what Brown describes as his 'deepest sentence on capitalism', 'Money is the word of the Devil, through which he creates all things, the way God created through the true word.'[119]

Consequently, Brown argues, the subsequent development of Protestantism, its espousal of capitalism, was the very anti-thesis of the Lutheran position.

. . . the psychological commitment of Protestantism to capitalism is mediated by the notion of the Devil, not God, and can be understood only in the light of Luther's new *theologia crucis*. First of all it is a consequence of Luther's notion of the objective autonomy of the demonic that bondage to capitalism, like bondage to tyrants, can no more be avoided than bondage to original sin: the Devil is lord of this world. 'The world cannot go on without usury, without avarice, without pride, without whoring, without adultery, without murder, without stealing, without blaspheming of God and all manner of sins; otherwise the world would cease to be the world, and the world would be without the world and the Devil without the Devil. Usury must be, but woe to the usurers.' To those who argued that his position on usury was unrealistic, in view of its prevalence, Luther replied, 'It is nothing new or strange that the world should be hopeless, accursed, damned; this it had always been and would ever remain.' Hence capitalism is the inevitable bondage to Satan consequent on original sin: 'In truth the traffic in interest is a sign and a token that the world is sold into the Devil's slavery by grievous sins.'[120]

It is but one step then for Brown to argue that, in the light of original Protestant theology, the deification of capitalism is at best a confusion between God and the Devil, at worst a deification of the Devil himself. Interpreting the Devil as death, and equating capitalism with that death, he states that the Puritan–capital alliance is complete surrender to the death instinct.

Finally Brown explores the vitriolic anality of the early Lutheran attack on Rome and he argues convincingly that for Luther the real error of the Papacy was its insistence on a transformation of anal instincts into art, objects and gold, rather than an admission of anality which characterized Luther's own work. Such a transformation relies on deception, lies and tricks. The Papacy, for Luther who never lived to see the efflorescence of capitalism, was the Devil. For Brown, 'The precipitating factor in a psychological upheaval such as the Protestant Reformation is not any change in toilet-training patterns, but an irruption of fresh material from deeper strata of the unconscious . . . The dynamic of history is the slow return of the repressed.'[121]

This observation is of crucial importance in our understanding of gambling. Brown's theory, at times hypothetical and at others quivering with paradoxes, illuminates one of the great hidden strata in the religious experience of Western man. Luther's own historical moment was one of true perception and real insight. Rejecting the gilded displacements of Rome, he allowed man's anality to surface into consciousness. But the course of Protestantism after Luther was to be the vigorous re-repression of that anality. The scatology, and 'Devil's ordure' writing of the 'Table Talk' and other essential Lutheran texts have been steadfastly repudiated by Protestant theologians. Although Protestants have never accepted the gold–art-object displacement of anal instincts, the process of their re-repression inevitably required another form of displacement. This was adequately provided by the alliance with capitalism.

Unlikely as Brown's theory may sound on first acquaintance, it is supported by a mass of substantiating evidence. When Max Weber came to characterize the 'capitalist type' Erich Fromm examined his categorizations psychoanalytically and concluded that the essential capitalist, with his parsimony, Puritanism and strenuous work ethic, was, indeed, the epitome of the Freudian anal character type.

Puritanical capitalism, when administered as an ideology, is a retentive displacement of anality. Its ethics, as they relate to work, money, time and value, closely parallel what we know about individual displacement of the reality of anal experience. It relies on a sterile denial of the body, and yet it retains its traditional revulsion for that other form of denial implicit in the opulent sublimative processes of Catholicism. The capitalist, historically, is a philistine. His anal experience is channelled into his manipulation of money and labour. It does not re-surface as art. In its emphasis on stasis, stability, strenuous effort for faith and productivity on the one hand, and sudden conversion and a continuous guilt dynamic on the other, in the refusal of its theologians to re-open the closed chapters of Luther's 'Table Talk' or to consider the question of diabolism, Protestantism underlines its literal constipation. Its alliance with capital is an uneasy and unsatisfactory one, simply because, as a medium for displacement of the historical anal consciousness, it requires contravention of what appear to be fundamentals of Christian theology. These, of course, include poverty rather than possessive retention and accumulation of wealth, and charity rather than anally regressive oppression.

This thesis sheds considerable light on the Protestant attitude towards gambling. If we see the Protestant as rationalizing his alliance with the Devil (capital) we can see that he will be searching for another means of exchange, a method of handling money other than that which he has espoused that he can label as the Devil's. Again, such a logic is well-known to psycho-analysts. Gambling is a convenient substitute activity. It is a closed, autonomous system that can be hysterically denounced, as in Churchill's writings, and fused with all the real evils of capitalism. The existence of gambling clears the Puritan's conscience; as long as it is there, there is something else to which he can point as the Devil's medium. As Jeremy Taylor wrote, 'God hath permitted the conduct of such games of chance to the Devil'; this is the Protestant's imprimatur for his liaison with capital. 'The law of exchange', after all, is in God's Word. He can forge forward into the golden fields of usury, profit and exploitation, rationalizing that diabolism exists only in that means of exchange which brings no 'good' to either party.

But for the Puritan, the attack on gambling had an added advantage. Because Rome had internalized betting, his attack was also an attack on the whole sublimative process of the

scarlet woman. The Puritan, espousing capitalism, did not feel
the need to seek the beam in his own eye before attacking the
Catholic over his displacements for repressed anality.

We may conclude by saying that one of the functions of a
religion is to cope with repressed anality on a strategic historical
and cultural level. This is also a function of gambling, and again
it is another respect in which gambling approaches the condition of a religion. In the West, the differences between ways of
coping with that repressed material constitute the most significant differences between Christian denominations. They also
always involve contradictions with the theological cores of those
religions. Catholicism has chosen one characteristic mode of
confronting such repressed material: its sublimation into art,
culture and object-filled civilization. Protestantism chose an
equally characteristic developmental mode in its anal displace-
ment-formation. That was an alliance with capitalism. This
alliance was in contradiction to the truly liberating investigations of Luther, who had, for a single moment in history,
attempted to confront the reality of anality in his scatological
writings and investigations. Gambling had been assimilated in
the complex tapestry of the Roman sublimative process. For
Protestants, a virulent reaction-formation against gambling
was almost inevitable. By labelling it as the true satanic means
of exchange, they could unload and escape their own guilt
about the extent and consequences of their liaison with
capitalism. The Protestant moralist needs to be able to shriek
against gambling, or else the guilt surrounding his own anal
displacement may well become intolerable.

Plugging in the punter

In approaching the phenomenon of the gambler the psychoanalyst argues that gambling, like all neurotic behaviour
patterns, is a symptom of a central neurosis, a manifestation of
anxiety which has its origins in the emotions and events of early
childhood. It follows that Freudians are convinced that it is
worse than useless to try to remove symptomatic patterns of
behaviour without uncovering the complex motivational
forces which lie, indelibly, behind them. In particular, psychoanalysts stress the necessity of helping patients to confront the
repressed events and conflicts of their infancy and childhood –

and in conjunction with insight, within the context of a trans-ference relationship, to abreact the affects associated with them.

If the symptoms are 'cured' without such comprehension of internalized conflicts, the neurosis will certainly reassert itself, or the underlying anxiety will re-formulate and re-emerge in a different but potentially just as disturbing way.

The gambler may turn to God, and find himself tormented by a ravaging, religious guilt.

But psychoanalysis itself is a lengthy and expensive form of treatment, applicable only to certain kinds of neurotic. The development of other forms of therapy, relying on its basic principles and leading the patient towards insight, is a pressing psychiatric priority.

Despite the emergence of some encouraging tendencies, and the enormous popular interest in insight therapies, far too few resources are channelled toward the realization of this possibility. The reasons for this are complex and lie outside of the scope of this introduction – but it is essential for our pur-poses to point to one of the historical causes. Although there are now a large number of clinical psychologists and psychiatrists prepared to evade the fact, theoretical psychology continues to be split into two irreconcilable approaches (both of which are themselves subject to a myriad of subdivisions and internal groupings).

The origins of this division can best be understood historically and, although there are grounds for objecting to such a simpli-fied contrast, it may be expressed in terms of the polarity dividing the work of J. B. Watson from that of Sigmund Freud.

Watson, reacting against the 'mentalist', 'functionalist' and psychoanalytic schools of his day, determined to construct a psychological system which took no account of concepts such as consciousness. Psychology, he claimed, if it was to become a 'science', should be built only on observable data which could be quantified and measured. Thus, in marked contradistinction to Freud, many of whose theories had become consolidated during a period of intensive and prolonged self-analysis, Watson insisted that the only proper area of study was overt behaviour, to be examined in terms of the correlations existing between visual, auditory, tactile and kinaesthetic stimuli and the responses which an organism made to them. The internal dynamics of the psyche were regarded as an unfathomable irrelevance.

Watson first put forward his views in the *Psychological Review* of 1913, with an article entitled 'Psychology as the Behaviourist Views It'. Much of what he said derived from the researches of his contemporaries: Thorndike's discovery of the Law of Effect in terms of stimuli and response reactions among rats, Yerkes's comparable studies among apes, and Pavlov's examination of the nature of conditioned responses and reflex action among dogs. But Watson was the first man to draw together general conclusions from this material and to systematize a methodology for human psychology based on it. He stressed, controlled, experimental observation of the interrelationship between stimuli and response – many of the conclusions being drawn from the study of laboratory animals.

The attraction of Watson's theory was that it appeared to be able to claim for itself the status of an experimental science. Freud himself had hoped that his psychology would prove explicable in terms comparable to those of physics, and had only with the greatest reluctance abandoned the quest for such a psychological model. Perplexing aspects of his libido theory, where he frequently uses the metaphor of a discreet quantum of a hypothetical force, bear witness to the continuing hankering for such a solution. Watson, who never exhibited great subtlety in methodology, determined that this problem could simply be resolved by refusing even to consider any aspect of human or animal mental functioning except that which could be empirically observed and measured.

His own career was brief: by 1920 he had abandoned psychology and set out on a career in advertising. He was later to compare favourably the rising sales graph of J. Walter Thompson, of which he eventually became president, to laboratory graphs depicting behaviour among rats. Regrettably, despite the extraordinary naïveté of his positions and the inadequacy of a psychological system based on the denial of the relevance of a large part of the very area which it purported to be studying, Watson's ideas swept America in the 1920s and 1930s, rapidly establishing themselves as the psychological orthodoxy. Foremost among the reasons for this was the illusion that by concentrating only on those manifestations of behaviour which could be quantified, psychologists could claim to be 'scientists'. It should be noted that this conception of 'science' is itself open to dispute. Science had never before claimed that the way to comprehend the dynamics of complex structures could be found by formulating one's research as if those structures did not exist at all.

After Watson, behaviourism became more sophisticated: in the work of Guthrie, Holt, Hull, Hunter, Kuo, Osgood, Skinner, Weiss and others, distinct varieties of learning theory were put forward, but all shared basically the same premise. Human behaviour could best be understood by the observation of pigeons in a cage, or rats in a box. What is significant is the interrelationship between stimuli and response: learning advances by a process of conditioning. Any other considerations must be ignored in that they do not coincide with what is required for a preconceived notion of 'scientific' methodology.

After the 1930s behaviourism as a distinct school lost ground. It had failed in its aim to produce a consensus theory which was universally accepted by all its practitioners. Interestingly, even having so drastically limited their field of investigation its protagonists could not reach agreement, and were unable to establish the laws of human behaviour in the simplistic form for which the founders of the movement had craved.

Nevertheless, despite its barrenness the behavioural approach became widely dispersed, and particularly influenced the emergent faculties of psychology in British and American universities. It is still true to say that the dominant emphasis in academic psychology derives from the misguided behavioural conception of the nature of 'scientific' psychology.

One can see the effects of this process in the work of men like H. J. Eysenck, Professor of Psychology in the University of London. In his writing he makes much play with the assumed fact that there is an agreed body of scientific behavioural literature. This myth has been exploded by other writers.[122] However, Eysenck continues to deploy it as a weapon in his irresponsible and ill-informed outbursts against psychoanalysis.[123] He is undeterred in these assertions by the fact that his own theoretical positions, despite their reliance on what he considers to be rigid 'scientific' experimental evidence, are of a highly distinctive nature and are often disputed by precisely those authorities among whom he claims there is a consensus of agreement.

The barrenness of the legacy of behaviourally orientated psychology can be understood from the contradictions implicit in its premises and in its historical evolution. However, what is most disturbing about these denials of the psychodynamics of the human mind is the justification which they give for clinical application of forms of treatment categorized as behavioural therapy. In his latest book, *Beyond Freedom and Dignity*, B. F. Skinner wrote, '. . . we do not need to try to discover what personalities, states of mind, feelings, traits of character, plans, purposes, intentions, or the other perquisites of autonomous man really are in order to get on with a scientific analysis of behaviour'.[124] The therapeutic corollary of this is that no insight or knowledge of the precise ontogenesis of symptoms is necessary before attempting to eliminate them. Abnormal behaviour becomes the result of a failure to condition appropriately, and one can proceed immediately to its adaptation by intensified application of 'correct' conditioning processes.

The implications of these conclusions are disturbing at every level: in their most alarming forms they have led men like Skinner to devise complete 'technologies of control', which, he argues, should be applied for the purposes of government and societal organization. Abnormal behaviour which can be appropriately reconditioned ranges from political dissidence to homosexuality, or gambling. Opposition to theoretical approaches of this kind lies outside the context of a study of gambling, and we can do little more than register our unqualified rejection of them. However, on a more immediate level, the study of the psychology of gambling does reveal the inadequacies of those methods of 'treatment', broadly derived from behavioural psychology, which deny the efficacy of insight and rely on the application of force.

In his introduction to V. Meyer's and Edward Chesser's *Behaviour Therapy in Clinical Psychiatry*[125] Max Hamilton states, 'Behaviour therapy is at once among the newest forms of treatment in psychiatry – and one of the oldest: sticks and carrots have always been used to modify human behaviour.' It is the 'sticks' which gives rise to most cause for concern (particularly as aversion therapies are practised in clinical situations by persons who frequently would neither describe themselves as behaviourists nor always appear to comprehend the shakiness of their theoretical premises.)

Introduction

Forceful eradication of the symptoms, in fact, lies behind most aversion techniques[126] which are one of the stocks-in-trade of behavioural therapy. For example, Feldman and MacCulloch have 'treated' homosexuals by punishing them into heterosexuality.[127] For the behavioural therapist neurosis consists only of manifest symptoms: the adaptation or the elimination of those symptoms is his only goal. If those symptoms change in the required direction during 'treatment', even if neither patient nor therapist approached insight at any stage, the patient may still be deemed to be 'cured'.

We learn our correct responses, and when we make the wrong ones we get punishments instead of rewards. So, according to the behaviourists, we do not fall into the same trap again. Learning itself is no more than the process by which individuals become conditioned.

In an article critical of behaviourism Robert Allan asks:

Why then does the psychological establishment, long run out of ways of defending behaviourism, still cling to it like a limpet? Individual psychologists still like to think they are scientists, just like physicists, dealing in causes and measurements, but as a main current, how does the ghost survive? The answer is ideological and political. If everything can be reduced to a question of 'human nature' and 'human nature' can be studied scientifically, then it should be possible to abolish the contradictions in society by building a 'human technology' on this 'human science'. Consequently, in the ideal world of the psychologist, conditioning can be planned, neatly organized, and social forces, simply the sum of individual human natures, can be controlled. Behaviourism is the pseudo-scientific warrant for ideological – and even physical – repression. Contented housewives, satisfied workers.[128]

But, sometimes, the behavioural therapists expose their own weaknesses. The following striking passage was written by leading professors of behavioural science at the University of California:

Experimental literature shows numerous examples of reactions that were not specifically expected or desired. Some of these are pain, frustration, increased aggressiveness, arousal, general and specific anxieties, somatic and physiological malfunctions, and the development of various unexpected and often pathological operant behaviors . . . Some of these reactions are temporary (pain), others may be long lasting and even fatal (gastric ulcers).

Current theory and research does not yield complete under-standing and control of this problem. We consider that the ethical justification for research on aversive stimulation derives from its importance in human experience. Aversive control is a traditional and common form of human social persuasion. Prevalent social practice among Western European and American middle classes appears to favor indirect forms of aversive stimulation, such as verbal aggression or the deprivation of verbal affection rather than methods that involve actual pain. But even here, use of actually painful stimulation is common in child rearing. Psychologists, as scientists, can hardly be justified in neglecting such powerful and persuasive methods of behavior control . . .[129]

There is nothing new in arguments which favour coercion in 'treatment' of mental disorders. Such thinking led to the mistreatment of patients until well into this century, and has never been wholly discontinued.[130] What is disturbing, of course, is the elevation of these processes to the status of a quasi-science, and the attempt to disguise them behind a curtain of medical verbosity.

Gambling, perhaps more than any other neurosis, reveals the barrenness of the behaviourists' theoretical positions. Superficially, it is an area in which one would have expected the behaviourists to have made exhaustive studies. After all, it provides a continuous, uninterrupted stream of rewards and punishments leading to the establishment of operant behaviour patterns. But behaviourists have had very little to say about it indeed.

The reason is that it is impossible to comprehend the gambling neurosis without taking motivation into account. Simple conditioning theories just will not work. When a man becomes a gambler, and persists in gambling despite repeated losses, he flies in the face of behavioural learning theory. He is like a rat who keeps returning to the pot for food, even after it has been conditioned long enough to learn that all it will get from that particular source is an electric shock. And, irritatingly for those who wish to equate human behaviour precisely with that of rodents, no such rats exist.

When pressed, a behaviourist might try to patch up some sort of defence of his theory as applied to gambling. For example, he could try to argue that the reward was in anticipation, not in winning. The discerning of the reward in a behaviour pattern is always a complex procedure. But the whole theory comes perilously close to collapse when it has to be argued that an internal reward is preferred to such a tangible external stimulus as money. It is hard to imagine a serious defence of such a position without some reference to the unconscious mind. (But see below, Skinner's 'explanation' of gambling, note 135.)

Ironically, it is the behaviourists themselves who have carried out the tests which confirm the analytical position that the gambler is motivated by a desire to lose, but they have been unable to handle their own findings. The first experiments were carried out in 1948 by Preston and Baratta.[131] They established the concept of 'subjective probability' as distinct from objective probability. The investigators found that subjects overestimated their chances of success when the odds were heavily against them, and underestimated their chances of success when the odds against them were low.[132]

In 1953 Edwards extended these investigations to situations specifically studying gambling.[133] He wrote,

Neither in the experiments of Preston and Baratta nor in real life, do people follow the objective model. Why not? Several possibilities exist: it may be wrong to assume that people try to maximize monetary returns (or anything else, for that matter) when they gamble. Or it may be that people try to maximize returns but don't know how. They may misinterpret the probabilities or amounts of money involved, or both. Or they may not know how to combine probabilities and amounts of money to determine the best bet.

Edwards does not suggest another alternative: one which would erode the premises of behaviourist theory, the possibility that, unconsciously, players were actually seeking loss, and their play was organized in such a way as to make this outcome more probable. Drawing on other experiments by Mosteller and Nogee[134] he tries to rationalize his findings by arguing that experiments have shown that both rats and humans tend to alternate preferences in proportion to their probability of being correct, whereas the potentially most gainful strategy would be always to choose the outcome most likely to occur. He says that Jarrett has shown that this irrational behaviour occurs most frequently when subjects believe that there is a problem to be solved. They are more likely to behave strategically in the best way when they do not believe there is a solution to be found which will enable them to win 100 per cent of the time. He does not point out, of course, that many gamblers suffer from such a belief or consider why this should be so.

Perplexed and surprised, he concluded that subjects do not make choices to 'maximize expected winnings or minimize expected loss'. This was to become a troubling problem for behavioural psychologists. What was the 'utility' of gambling? How could it be seen to be compatible with learning theory?[135] In 1970 Brigitte Hochauer published the findings of her experiments on the spot in a Salzburg casino.[136]

According to the expectation maximization principle, the best strategy for the gambler should be to minimize loss. The normative model is contradicted by observable behavior. Only 4 out of 15 Ss [subjects in an experiment] have chosen the bet with the smallest Negative Expected Value [N.E.V.] . . . A possible explanation for this behavior may be that it would be too boring to bet for the smallest amount with the lowest risk during the whole evening . . . In his paper about probability Edwards writes, 'The dominant fact about N.E.V. bets is that Ss do not like to lose – they rather consistently prefer the alternative which had the lower probabilities of losing.' I cannot confirm this result. A great number of gamblers preferred long shots and avoided almost fair bets. This indicates a general preference for risk-taking.

Scarcely an illuminating conclusion about the psychology of gambling.

If these observers allowed themselves to consider unconscious motivation, they might have arrived at conclusions about gambling compatible with the evidence they produce. The psychoanalyst is not surprised to hear that the majority of players gamble in such a way that loss is a more likely outcome than winning. Nor is he surprised when the behaviourist confirms that players usually diverge widely from the optimum winning strategy. But for the behaviourists themselves, these findings are confusing and destructive, as they underline the error which lies at the centre of their psychological prejudices. The detailed statistics and quasi-scientific language are unable to cover up the perplexity which overtakes them in the light of their own results.

Unfortunately, the experiments have not been confined to the laboratory or the statistical survey. Behaviourists, despite the theoretical contradictions faced by their clinical researchers, have been active in the so-called 'cure' of gamblers. This has been effected by use of intensive aversive techniques. Considerable documentation on this subject exists,[137] but the case conducted by A. B. Goorney, a Royal Air Force neuropsychiatrist, is characteristic.[138]

A thirty-seven-year-old man was referred to Goorney, following his wife's complaints about massive debts as a result of repeated gambling bouts. He had gambled, on and off, for thirteen years. Goorney sets out the 'stimuli' for the patient's behaviour: 'The gambling had been started off by newspaper publicity of a forthcoming classical race or by receiving ready cash as expense repayments; there was also another factor, for the patient later admitted that at the time his relationship with his wife was particularly poor.'

Beyond outlining these 'stimuli', Goorney is not concerned with motivation at all. Briefly, he informs us that the patient's father was a heavy drinker, that his mother was a chronic, shy, retiring invalid, that the subject himself, as a child, had been 'timid, puny and shy', and that the gambling had started within a year of his marriage to a woman described as 'wearing the pants'. After this material has been mentioned, it is never again referred to, and is not treated as being significant in either the formation or 'cure' of the gambling neurosis. We are, however, told that the *reason* for the patient's last gambling bout was reading information about a big race in a newspaper.

The method of 'treatment' is then described in detail. This consisted in isolating the components of the habit: the making of daily selections, telephoning or visiting the bookmaker, having phantasies about projected winnings and listening to results on radio or television.

Aversion therapy to all the individual components of the habit was by random faradic shocks of 1–2 seconds' duration and unpleasant intensity (35 volts) to the upper arms (right if writing, otherwise varied), from an apparatus based on the design described by McGuire and Vallence . . . In all, nine days of treatment were given over two weeks (forty-five sessions, 675 shocks).

On the fourth day of treatment, the patient volunteered that he was having to force himself to open the paper and make selections. He also revealed that he was having difficulty in evoking and maintaining thoughts of selections and anticipated profits during the aversion sessions directed at the imagery. He still thought about selections between sessions and anticipated with pleasure the checking of results. By the seventh day thoughts of the selection were no longer occurring between sessions, and he had no desire to watch televised racing or to listen to the results.

Objective and subjective concomitants of anxiety were noted on the second day of treatment. The patient expressed the opinion that it was only the realization that he must obtain a cure that was keeping him going. Objective evidence of emotional stress was suppressed by the third day, but recurred briefly on the sixth day, with barely controlled anger towards the therapist, and again on the ninth day whilst listening to the radio results. He did not, however, refuse or request to terminate any session.

Goorney specifically goes out of his way to attack the psychoanalytic concept of 'insight'.

It might be proposed that, as the patient displayed insight during initial interviews, this factor in itself could explain the resolution of the gambling habit. Insight had been present, however, for some considerable time at the level expressed by the patient, but had not reduced the frequency of his gambling. Indeed, the way in which the insight was expressed might lead to the conjecture that it added to the strength of his gambling drive as the most suitable weapon he possessed to attack his wife.

Of course, such a superficial and inadequate definition of 'insight', which is evidently lacking in this instance from therapist and patient alike, tells us nothing, even conjecturally, about the value of true insight, acquired after only a long course of free association and analysis, or about its value in confronting and overcoming neurosis.

Goorney discusses analytic theories:

Analysts have interpreted compulsive gambling as an outlet for repressed ano-sadistic [*sic*] impulses (Simmel), a form of masochism (von Hattingberg and Bergler), satisfaction of the demands of a punitive super-ego (Menninger), an unresolved Oedipus conflict with fate the father projection (Freud). In terms of Learning Theory, on the other hand, compulsive gambling could be considered a maladaptive behaviour response acquired by learning. There are indications in the history of this case of psychopathological factors pertinent to analytical interpretations. There is also evidence of opportunity for the 'learning' of gambling responses from childhood associations. Where time is limited and a patient requests relief from a behavior pattern which is causing unfortunate consequences, behavior therapy techniques may provide the treatment of choice.

The behaviourist realizes, as indeed he must, that his comprehension of the problem is inadequate, and yet resolves to apply his punitive techniques and ignore the patient's underlying neurosis. Such an approach to human personality must be resisted. The use of force in the absence of insight on the part of the patient, or knowledge on the part of the therapist about the dynamics of the phenomenon he is treating, constitutes a reckless assault on the subject.

In the case of gambling, we can suggest, and it is no more than a hypothesis, that there is a further disturbing aspect to this method of treatment. Psychoanalysis has demonstrated that problem gambling is invariably masochistic in its dynamics. Most of the 'therapeutic' techniques used in aversive treatments involve the use of pain in a punitive situation. We have already quoted the California behaviourists who liken their therapies to the use of corporal punishment by parents. Such therapies require the frequent, ritualized repetition of that pain in an institutionalized fashion.

There appears to be a strong possibility that the process of aversive treatment itself could provide a substitute for the masochistic elements in gambling. One has only to recall the examples of the patients described earlier who used the organization of Gamblers Anonymous, and the Church, as gambling substitutes to realize that this is a distinct possibility.

Treatments which utilize punitive techniques on masochistic neuroses, and deny the necessity of examining the psychodynamics involved, appear to present patients with very real psychological dangers. Therapists engaged in the administration of aversive treatments have frequently reported the arousal, or strengthening, of unexpected masochistic tendencies in their patients.

Aversion therapy consists in beating patients into 'normal' patterns of behaviour. Gambling illustrates the flimsiness of its quasi-scientific theoretical base. Aversive techniques do not radically differ from the traditional violence which has been used down the centuries in the 'treatment' of mental disorders.

Pre-Freudian theories, post-Freudian omissions

The behavioural theory tells us nothing about why men gamble; behavioural therapy is, at best, unsatisfactory as a mode of treatment. However, it would be wrong to give the impression that Freudian theory emerged from nowhere, solved, among many other problems, the nature of gambling, and was then suppressed into obscurity by the development of behavioural psychology.

Freud stated several times that he was merely ordering into a scientific framework the truths which the poets and writers had discovered before him. Dostoyevsky's novel *The Gambler* is a striking example of this, and we have seen how gamblers themselves, in their memoirs, virtually invariably admitted that they were governed and dominated by powerful masochistic impulses which they did not fully understand. Many of the pre-Freudian psychologists had attempted to grapple with the nature of gambling, and had come close to understanding it even before the first publication of relevant Freudian texts.

Professor Lazarus, writing in 1883, was the first man to fly in the face of the prevailing ethical orthodoxy and state that financial greed was the lowest of all the motivational factors affecting the gambler.[139] Significantly, he sought the evidence for his book, *Über die Reize des Spiels*, at the gaming table and in written accounts by gamblers of their activities. He noted that 'pleasure in all chance play consists fundamentally in suspended activity'.

What Bergler was later to call the 'pleasurable–painful anticipation'[140] was, indeed, to prove crucial in the understanding of the neurosis. Lazarus suggested that the superstitious, animistic elements in gambling were connected with a desire for certainty and a need to test fate, to discover whether it was disposed to be favourable to its supplicant. He came close to indicating the parricidal and Oedipal conflicts which lie just under the surface in gambling although, faced with loose ends in his arguments, he tended to overstress simplistic and superficial motivational factors, such as the desire to escape from boredom and the need for vicarious excitement.

W. I. Thomas, writing in 1901, elaborated Lazarus's thesis, arguing that the gaming instinct, as he called it, was 'a powerful reflex fixed far back in animal experience. The instinct is,

93

in itself, right and indispensable.'[141] Curiously, he implies that the gambler might possess a superior, perceptive intellect. But Thomas was the first writer to base his theory on extensive clinical evidence, systematically gathered through interviews and correspondence with scores of gamblers. An embryonic Jungian, he appears to be suggesting that gambling is a residual manifestation of the hunting instinct, frustrated by industrial society. His theory is given some support by the existence of phrases like 'the green felt jungle'[142] as descriptive of the gamblers' world.

The various prevalent approaches to gambling psychology were drawn together by France in a detailed compendium,[143] part of which is included in this volume. France produced what is certainly the most perceptive and accurate of the pre-Freudian texts. He was aware of many of the major elements in the process which were to prove pivotal in later studies, although he was unable to make sense of them because he had no conscious knowledge of the Oedipal situation. 'The significant fact, however', he wrote, 'which the study of the gamblers' consciousness, as well as that of men acting in uncertainty in general, impress upon us is that the feeling of certitude frequently exists even in a state of great uncertainty.' Speaking of gamblers' hunches and belief in success against all known odds and experience, he wrote, 'It is more definite than what we in general term self-confidence. It is the feeling: I have a special tip, a cue in touch with the very ground principle, who wills.' Had he possessed knowledge of the unconscious mind and the nature of guilt and anxiety, one suspects that France would readily have accepted the Freudian theory of 'infantile omnipotence', (the tendency of the child to believe that thoughts have effectual power) and realized its relevance to the gambling situation. He also, everywhere, stressed the common origins of gambling and religion in an all-powerful, residual animism and, though tending, like Thomas, to look for explanations which were too simple to account for all the evidence he had produced, he pushed comprehension of the phenomenon almost as far as was possible before Freud.

But probably the first psychologist to attempt therapeutic activities was Dr Erik Kroger.[144] In the early part of the nineteenth century Kroger observed that gambling was a clinical condition comparable to alcoholism. He set up a study spa in

Zürich and began collecting alcoholics and compulsive gamblers for observation and treatment. He noted their superstitious and self-destructive tendencies. However, his activities were eventually curtailed by the Swiss authorities. Clearly, he was an early supporter of the 'addiction' theory.

The significant feature about all the pre-psychoanalytic texts is that they appear to be groping toward solutions to problematic features in gambling which have substantially been solved by the body of Freudian analytic literature. The features of gambling which they point to, the paradoxes which they document, no longer appear inexplicable, nor do they need to be reburied in generalized simplistic solutions.

However, there are aspects of gambling which Freudian theory leaves unresolved. The most striking weakness is one which applies to the entirety of Freudian literature, as well as to the specific neurosis of gambling: the virtual absence of discussion of women gamblers.

Freud's thesis on gambling is founded on a concrete physical and anatomical analysis. But the interpretation which he applies to Dostoyevsky is structurally inapplicable to women, quite apart from the problematic of the Oedipus complex. Freud's thesis must therefore be extended and adapted to encompass female gambling, or an alternative theory constructed which will apply to women. After considerable research we have been unable to discover any critique of the Freudian position on this, nor could we find anyone prepared to undertake such a critique.

Perhaps because they have been concerned with more central issues, none of the recent feminist analyses of Freud seem to have dealt with this aspect, which is of importance in terms of sexual relations, money, economics and leisure.

This is a large gap in the theory of the gambler's psychology, particularly significant because of the post-war increase, in Britain, in the number of women participating in all forms of gambling, and the spread of games like bingo, specifically promoted to stimulate and cater to the housewife gambler. Women, too, are making increasing use of Britain's 15,000 betting shops, initially a male preserve.

Empirical observations indicate that there are many significant differences between male and female gambling. Several writers have pointed out that women prefer involvement with the person they are winning from or losing to: they tend to chat with the bookie about their bets[145] and they are likely to prefer cards to roulette, where the enemy is just an impersonal wheel.[146] Common assumptions, such as the belief that women prefer to trust to luck whereas men choose quasi-rational or system-determined selections, may spring from real differences in the psychosexual dynamics of female gambling, but we still do not have enough information to grasp their significance.

There is one other area in which the Freudian theory of the nature of gambling is inadequate, and that is the phenomenon of gambling without gamblers. We have suggested above that the usual psychological distinction between the punter and the habitual compulsive is not very useful, but there still remain men who engage in gambling activities who are not, themselves, subject to the kind of psychological dynamics which we have characterized. The cheat, the card-sharper, the organized gaming promoter, the bookmaker, possibly even the tiny minority of true 'professional' percentage-takers, who act on genuine inside racing information, are all clearly motivated by the commercial impetus. They ask no questions of fate; they are not motivated by masochistic neurosis; because of the virtual impossibility of loss for them, they are often required to take less risk in their activities than the small businessman. Their psychology in no way resembles that of the gamblers with whom they deal.

More problematic is the psychology of the pools or lottery gambler. There are grounds for believing that the autonomous dynamic of gambling is not necessarily wholly or exclusively engaged in pools or large-scale lottery play. The desire for material gain can be the incentive for gambling where the stakes are minimal (even repeated regular losses falling well below the punitive financial level) and potential rewards are enormous. Evidently, the imagined utility of a prize that could never be obtained by any other means far exceeds the negative utility of numerous small losses, even where the odds against winning are very heavily biased against the player.

We need not expect to find masochistic, animistic, Oedipal forces invariably at work in persons who confine their play to such promotions. Some writers have even indicated that willingness for small-stake-and-high-reward investments is incompatible with the true gambling dynamic. Newman has noted that confirmed pools-players tend to be uninterested in other forms of gambling, whereas regular gamblers are often bored by the thought of pools or lottery play.[147] Cohen has argued that while persons engaged in true gambling activities become more expectant of winning after a period of loss, persons holding Premium Bonds, British state-run interest lotteries, get progressively less hopeful of winning the longer their ticket is not drawn, suggesting a completely different psychological dynamic.[148]

But this separation of low-stake gambling from the true gambling neurosis is frequently overstressed. As the odds in pools play are reduced, and the stakes increased in size or frequency, the true gambling dynamic quickly becomes apparent. For many participants it is probably present the whole time, in a more benign form. This can be seen in bingo play, or in the workings of the numbers rackets in Harlem, which are accompanied by the most elaborate mysticism, professional divinations, prayers, phantasies and extreme improbability of winning, which we have come to expect of gambling proper.

However, in British pools play, where 30p–40p is characteristically staked in a week, at odds of over 1,000,000 to 1, the quasi-rationality of 'form' sometimes takes over from magical divination of the result. Although there is no evidence that 'pools experts' assist competitors any more than clairvoyants, their popularity might suggest that more emphasis is being placed on the prize than on the animistic process.[149]

However, several commentators have underlined the inability of many large pools winners to consolidate on their success. There is a tendency towards dissipation of substantial winnings and irrational expenditure. This is usually attributed to the overwhelming effects of the receipt of such a large sum of money – however, it may be indicative of much deeper-rooted psychological mechanisms, perhaps the unconscious preference for loss which characterizes gambling proper.

Gambling as pornography

Earlier in this introduction we explored the anal elements in gambling and traced their interrelationships with the Protestant ethic and capitalist practice. Freud, as we have seen, emphasized the phallic preoccupations involved, specifically stressing that gambling was a form of displaced masturbation.

In this section we wish to argue in support of Freud's theory by indicating links between the processes of gambling and masturbatory stimuli, specifically pornography as used by men. The gambling neurosis is capable of embracing a complexity of submerged conflicts, and it appears that anal and phallic elements constantly coexist within it.[150]

The first similarity which we wish to trace is that which exists between gambling and pornography – sado-masochistic pornography in particular, which gambling most closely resembles.

Pornography is limited in its context; it rejects as irrelevant all information except that which is immediately pertinent to its specific objectives. It is repetitive, endlessly contriving around a limited number of possible sexual variations. Detail becomes supremely important, over and above generality: whether the participants conform to types usually considered attractive becomes less important than the positions in which they are placed. The detailed description of, or, in pictorial pornography, the visual concentration upon the fetish objects or anatomical parts provides the source of the habituating appeal.

Within these general outlines, the pornography of masochism has specific, relevant characteristics. At any rate in Britain, it is usually concerned with beating phantasies, which have consistently, since the early part of the nineteenth century, occupied a dominant position in the total pornographic output. Its emphasis is on anal aggression, in situations in which the sexuality of the participants is frequently ambiguous, and the genitals take second place to the anal regions.

Freud, in his essay 'A Child is Being Beaten',[151] studied the significance of these phantasies. He argued that for those who are obsessed by such preoccupations, the person being beaten in the phantasy, whose sex is often indeterminate, is conjured up as a way of reassuring the masturbator that the father, who is doing the beating, loves the masturbator, who is reassured because he or she is not the person being beaten. If another child is being punished, it means that another child is alienated from the territory of parental tenderness, which provides reassurance to the phantasist that he or she is still the loved one.

It is one way of ritualizing the ambiguity, of freezing the question 'Does my father love me?', just as gambling is. The answers which the beating phantasist receives are just as unsatisfactory as those obtained by the gambler, however. The sexual activity which accompanies the phantasy rekindles the guilt over masturbation. No sooner has the individual been reassured by conjuring up another child alienated from the father, than the incestuously orientated, masturbatory guilt has to be confronted. The question must be asked again; the phantasy becomes an endlessly repeated obsessional thought.

The emotions involved, and displaced, are of overwhelming strength, concerning the most basic of the child's fears and phantasies. The pornographer, who caters for this complex of feelings, is confronted by several difficulties. First, he has to assuage the guilt which surrounds indulgence by producing rationalizations for the masturbator – suggesting that his interest is a 'scientific' one, or concerned with correct procedures for child-rearing. Second, he has to overcome the limitations of the process itself: the emotions involved may be powerful and consumingly compulsive; the activities themselves are endlessly repetitive. So we find in this literature that the instruments of punishment, the situation, the positioning of the participants and, above all, the 'painful–pleasurable' moments between the decision to punish and the instigation of punishment are described in the most painstaking detail. The format is often quasi-scientific, and a pretence is made that the production is a manual, or guidebook, an accurate, scientific inventory: this acts as both rationalization and vehicle for the provision of an infinite series of minimal variations.

Genital sexuality is often absent: anality takes its place (though the specificity of anal preoccupations is often diffused into a general obsession with the entirety of the anal–genital region), and the mechanical instruments of punishment become substitutes for the penis itself.

Gambling literature closely parallels pornography in general, and sado-masochistic pornography in particular. The closed, limited terms of reference of the gambling situation exclude everything else: essentially the literature is repetitive, and meaningless outside its own context. (Interestingly, it also parallels astrological horoscopes in these respects, underlining, again, links with divinatory animism.)

It takes many forms, in graphic descriptions of gambling escapades, or tabulation of 'how to win' systems; in the former we find repeated emphasis on displaced anal detail, 'the painful–pleasurable' anticipation of punishment, and the insistence on microscopic description. In the latter, we find endless, spurious variations upon a theme. The rationalization is that they are a serious attempt to provide information which will assist in the selection of a likely winning chance; but with all their repetitive reiteration, and their actual ineffectiveness, they function by assisting the reader to engage in phantasy gambling: they are a form of pornography.

This is a characteristic passage from the memoirs of a 1920s gambler:

> The rings of spectators, standing in rows behind the players, the game inspectors on stools or high chairs, the ever-changing *changeur*, or money-changer, and the adroit, keen-eyed croupier, paying, collecting, or calculating great stakes, all contribute to the production of a scene pregnant with suggestion and without parallel except in the inner sanctuaries at Deauville and Cannes.
> Baccarat becomes a dramatic spectacle.
> Each slanting row of great pink squares, counters at 100,000 francs apiece, means that millions await those punters with the luck to win. De Mesa has probably won and lost more than anyone else on record. After the pink counters come large ovals, a sickly bile yellow, every one worth 50,000 francs. And then down the scale: oblong ivory counters at 20,000 francs, green counters at 10,000, pearl at 5,000; then those of chocolate hue, a modest 1,000 each. Sometimes, even small, cherry-coloured ovals worth only 500 francs make their timid appearance on the table.[152]

More recently Patrick O'Neill-Dunne, a roulette enthusiast who wrote a book about the longest roulette game in the world at Macao casino, which he organized, wrote:

> I am fond of roulette. The wheel is a work of art, beautiful to look at; the chips sensual to feel; the whole ceremony aristocratic. I love the low hum of the wheel, the clatter of the ivory ball as it hesitates, wriggles, bounces, and drops with authoritative finality into a numbered slot. My wife and I adore the constant drama of the players, spectators, and operators around the green tables. We enjoy the solid luxury of the casinos, the comfortable chairs, the refreshments: exquisitely prepared caviar sandwiches and Dom Pérignon champagne at one's elbow; the quiet, unhurried attention

of the croupiers and waiters, who if one is known to be a good sport and a generous tipper, win or lose, will reward your kindness with that affection, service, and flattery which makes life so pleasant.[153]

The book goes on to list and examine 20,080 consecutive spins of the wheel at Macao: O'Neill-Dunne and his team of assistants even went so far as to record the casino sounds throughout the month's play. The rationalized purpose of the book was simply to show that no system could work, though every variation was tried. O'Neill-Dunne's *Roulette for the Millions*, in its preoccupations and mode of presentation, is the *Hundred and Twenty Days of Sodom* of gambling.

Sometimes, particularly in fictional accounts of gambling, the masturbatory element erupts through its defences: gambling becomes the habit for which it substitutes. In *The Strip*, Aben Kandel wrote:

The fantasy with Lady Luck, in which he was the captive figure sitting inside a rainbow-colored bubble, had to be played out slowly, painfully, to its last drawn-out detail, the dream dictating the pace – the way it crashed to the ground, shocking him with release, but with the same spittle that licked his wounds, he was already creating a new bubble and eagerly taking his place inside it, rising again, lighter than air, the memory of the last craps loss already somewhere down below, a dark speck on earth while he soared and soared. Sucking greedily on euphoria, ten silver dollars on the first third of the board, number 9 red comes up, the pay-off is two to one. He arranges the thirty dollars in one confident pile and awaits the second spin of the wheel. The number is two black and now he has ninety dollars, chips as well as silver, and all of it is skillfully, prophetically moved down to the last six numbers, a ninety-dollar sentinel guarding 31, 32, 33 and 34, 35, 36, and the ball obediently plops into 36 and the pay-off is five to one, four hundred and fifty dollars plus the ninety he bet and a generous tip to the croupier and away to another table, the chips growing heavier in his pockets, the trips to the cashier's window more frequent, the crisp C notes stacked away in an inside breast pocket, and again the ball, the wheel, the numbers, the winnings, churning, spinning, blending madly, color, numeral, metal, orgiastic rise incited by luck, until the bubble bursts and he again picks himself up off the ground. And again, pausing only to note mournfully that the supply of spittle, fantasy, and mockery are endless.[154]

A model for the gambling neurosis

We are now in a position to formulate a tentative model for the interpretation of the gambling neurosis among males in Western, Judeo–Christian, capitalist society. In contrast to those writers who have stressed gambling's relationship to the addictions (or the 'impulse neuroses') we consider that it may best be understood as an unsuccessful obsessional defence.

Inevitably, the ontogenesis of interest in gambling in the individual derives from infantile Oedipal conflicts. In the gambler we may expect to find a repressed tendency to homosexuality, or bisexuality, arising from the fact that at some time during the development of the ambivalent relationship with the father the male gambler-to-be sought to make himself the object of his father's love. In part, he identified with his 'castrated' mother, seeking to become her rather than striving for dominant possession of her. Gambling emerges as a questioning of fate, the father surrogate: it takes the form of a question, 'Does my father love me?' But either answer (win or loss) is intolerable. If the gambler wins (receives a positive answer to his question) he also comes to accept that his infantile belief in the supreme power of thoughts was justified. This strengthens the guilt felt for his repressed unconscious incestuous and parricidal impulses. Winning takes on the meaning, 'Yes, my father loved me, but I only sought to destroy him with my murderous thoughts.' The antidote to winning is losing: this is actively, though unconsciously, sought as a relief from the symbolic implications of winning. On the one hand, it alleviates guilt, by providing punishment for the ambitions against the father and, on the other, it symbolizes castration itself: the necessary precondition to becoming a love-object for the father. But, as Freud pointed out, neither in infancy nor in terms of subsequent displacements was that castration a satisfactory solution to the problem. And so the gambler again seeks to win – and the whole cycle is set in motion once more.

Of course in the adult gambler this conflict will be largely internalized and will be expressed in terms of the relationship between the super-ego and the ego, which becomes sado-masochistic. Father-love re-emerges as the ego makes itself the willing, passive recipient of the mistreatment inflicted upon it by the super-ego. The ego accepts the castrating punishment of gambling losses, which themselves appear to reinforce the validity of the authoritarian, moralistic strictures issued by the super-ego.

In these respects, with its capacity to cater for every nuance of ambivalence in relation to parental introjects, gambling closely parallels neurotic symptom-formation. But it gains its particular complexion from its relationship to two forms of infantile sexuality: genital masturbation and anal erotism. In relation to the former, it is not only a substitute for masturbation (which gives it its 'addictive' qualities) but it is also again a form of questioning of the fate-father, 'Do you approve of my masturbation?' Unconsciously, the gambler knows that the penalty for this practice is castration, and again this is meted out to him in terms of the displacement in the form of loss. Gamblers who lose everything no longer have the where-withal to bet, any more than the castrated child can continue masturbating.

But behind these masturbatory similarities (which often lie close to the surface, so that genital sensations may be associated with winning or losing) lie the deeper, formative anal preoccupations. It is these which give gambling its essentially obsessive structures. These structures are expressed in the relationship to money, to value and to time, which can be seen as attempts to reassert the infantile pleasurable anal system as a violation of that which was imposed during the bowel-training procedure.

But gambling is not always experienced as an ego-alien activity (unlike the obsessional neurotic symptoms which it resembles). Some writers have seen in this grounds for relating gambling to the addictions, the 'impulse neuroses', or the perversions. We prefer to draw a parallel with religion, which in so many respects gambling closely resembles. The emphasis which it places on shared ritualistic practice, divination, and ways of controlling the ultimate authority of fate [the father], are all essentially obsessional devices – as is the ultimate ambivalence towards that authority. While we accept that there are differences between gambling and obsessional neurosis, we have pointed out that to a very remarkable extent these differences are identical with those which Freud saw as existing between religion and obsessional neurosis. On account of the similarities existing between religion and gambling, and on account of their mutual divergences from the patterns of obsessional neurotic symptom-formation (which they both resemble in so many respects), we consider it appropriate to describe gambling as one of man's 'universal neuroses'. The evidence drawn from sociology, anthropology and comparative religious studies would appear to add additional weight to this conclusion.

Notes

1. Anonymous, 'Gambling Sickness', in *Gamblers Anonymous* (Los Angeles: G.A. Publishing Co., 1964), pp. 232–48.
2. Sigmund Freud, 'Dostoevsky and Parricide', (1928) *The Standard Edition of the Complete Psychological Works of Sigmund Freud*, ed. and trans. James Strachey, 23 vols. (London: Hogarth Press, 1953—), Vol. 21, pp. 177–94.
3. E. Benson Perkins, *Gambling in English Life*, rev. edn (London: Epworth Press, 1958).
4. Erving Goffman, *Where the Action Is* (London: Allen Lane The Penguin Press, 1969), pp. 111–12.
5. John Cohen, 'The Nature of Gambling', in *Psychological Probability* (London: Allen & Unwin, 1972), pp. 65–92.
6. James Hunter and Arthur Brunner, 'Emotional Outlets of Gamblers', *Journal of Abnormal and Social Psychology*, Vol. 23, No. 1 (1928), pp. 38–9.
7. E. Moran, 'Varieties of Pathological Gambling', *British Journal of Psychiatry*, Vol. 116 (1970), pp. 593–7.
8. Edmund Bergler, *The Psychology of Gambling* (London: Bernard Hanison, 1958; New York: Hill & Wang, 1958. All references are to paperback edition: New York: International Universities Press, 1970.) Extracts in this volume pp. 115–201.
9. David Cooper, extract from an unpublished manuscript, kindly made available by the author.
10. Sigmund Freud, 'The Future of an Illusion' (1927), *Standard Edition*, Vol. 21, pp. 1–56.
11. Sigmund Freud, 'Obsessive Actions and Religious Practices' (1907), *Standard Edition*, Vol. 9, pp. 126–7.
12. Hans von Hattingberg, 'Analerotik, Angstlust und Eigensinn', *Internationale Zeitschrift für Psychoanalyse*, Vol. 2 (1914), pp. 244–58.
13. Ernst Simmel, 'Zur Psychoanalyse des Spielers' ('On the Psychoanalysis of the Gambler'), lecture delivered at the sixth International Psychoanalytic Convention, September 1920; published, in précis (abstract) form, in *Internationale Zeitschrift für Psychoanalyse*, Vol. 6 (1920), p. 397.
14. Sigmund Freud, 'Some Character-Types Met with in Psychoanalytic Work' (1916), *Standard Edition*, Vol. 14, pp. 309–33.
15. Freud, 'Dostoevsky and Parricide'. See note 2, and note 21.
16. Charles Rycroft, *A Critical Dictionary of Psychoanalysis* (Harmondsworth: Penguin Books, 1972), p. 12.

17. Tadashi Uematsu, 'Parricides in Japan', *Annals of the Hitotsubashi Academy*, Vol. 2, No. 2 (Tokyo, 1952), pp. 205–17. Uematsu also notes that in parent-killing in Japan both men and women overwhelmingly go for the father. *Japan Times Weekly*, 13 May 1972.

18. Sigmund Freud, 'Civilization and Its Discontents' (1930), *Standard Edition*, Vol. 21.

19. ibid., p. 130.

20. 'Play with yourself' is the formulation used by prostitutes when instructing clients to masturbate – significantly most frequently employed when the prostitute is punishing a client according to his instructions. The masturbatory use of the hands in a gambling situation can readily be seen in the manual language of racing's 'tic-tac' signalling code, and the complex finger-talk of commodity speculators in the broking exchanges.

21. Theodor Reik, 'The Study of Dostoyevsky', in *From Thirty Years with Freud* (London: Hogarth Press, 1940), pp. 142–57. Although many psychoanalysts have subsequently taken Freud's paper as a definitive explanation of the ontogenesis of interest in gambling Freud himself held no such high estimation of it. Replying to Reik's criticisms of the text in a letter, he once wrote, 'I think you have applied too high a standard to this trivial essay. It was written as a favour for someone and written reluctantly. I always write reluctantly nowadays.'

22. René Laforgue, 'On the Eroticization of Anxiety', *International Journal of Psycho-Analysis*, Vol. 11 (1930), pp. 312–21.

23. Ernest Jones, 'The Problem of Paul Morphy', *International Journal of Psycho-Analysis*, Vol. 12 (1931), pp. 1–23, first read as a lecture before the British Psycho-Analytic Society, 19 November 1930. It was subsequently included in Ernest Jones, *Papers on Psycho-Analysis*, 5th edn (London: Ballière, Tindall & Cox, 1948).

24. See especially the writings of Reuben Fine, both a trained psychoanalyst and chess-player.

25. Charlotte Olmsted, *Heads I Win – Tails You Lose* (New York: Macmillan, 1962), has written: 'The face cards represent the old European family system of father, mother, and eldest son or heir; our pack is very good at playing out the family role conflicts and is often so used. It does reflect a particular type of family structure – one where father-son conflicts are seen as more important than mother–daughter conflicts, since there is only one female in the pack, wife to one and mother to the other. The unattached female is not seen as important enough to have a card to herself, although the mother–wife is central to the family structure. You would expect such a society to have a great many Oedipus conflicts – they would probably be based so solidly on family structure as to be all but universal. There would also probably be a strong drive on the part of unmarried females to secure a husband and thus a place in the family structure for themselves, probably not matched by a like desire on the part of the male, who could continue to use his mother for emotional support if he chose. These are, of course, all features that are very prominent in the European area where this pack arose.' Charlotte Olmsted's theories on cards are

reprinted, 'Analyzing a Pack of Cards', in Robert D. Herman, ed., *Gambling* (New York: Harper & Row, 1967), pp. 136–52. See also G. B. Milner, 'The Red and the Black', *New Society*, Vol. 398 (1970), pp. 816–19.

26. Edmund Bergler, 'On the Psychology of the Gambler', *Imago*, Vol. 22 (1936), pp. 409–41, and 'The Gambler: A Misunderstood Neurotic', *Journal of Criminal Psychopathology*, Vol. 4 (1943), pp. 379–93. Bergler also discussed the gambler in *The Basic Neurosis: Oral Regression and Psychic Masochism* (New York: Grune & Stratton, 1949) and eventually drew together all his ideas on this theme in *The Psychology of Gambling*. Bergler was a thorough, clinical researcher. He was often contemptuous of other analysts who wrote learned papers about complex neuroses, such as gambling, after examining a single patient who manifested the symptoms. He also tried to get his ideas across to a wider public by writing books and articles accessible to the layman as well as the professional analyst. However, he became possessive about encroachments on what he regarded as his chosen field. He believed that he was the first man to elucidate the theory that the gambler was motivated to lose – although, of course, Freud was not alone in anticipating him in this respect.

27. Karl Menninger, 'Criminal Behavior as a Form of Masked Self-Destructiveness', *Bulletin of the Menninger Clinic*, Vol. 2 (1938), developed Freud's concept of the severe super-ego, whose demands on the ego were satisfied by large, punitive losses at gambling. Ernst Kris, 'Ego Development and the Comic', *International Journal of Psycho-Analysis*, Vol. 19 (1938), pp. 77–90, developed the masturbation–play–gambling theory of Freud's, but he believed that under certain conditions the ego could not control the process on which it had embarked, and, craving for the reassurance of winning, switched from playfulness to a life-and-death involvement. He again underlined the association between ruin at gambling, orgasm and death.

28. Otto Fenichel, *The Psychoanalytic Theory of Neurosis* (London: Kegan Paul, French, Trubner, 1946), pp. 372–3.

29. Ralph Greenson, 'On Gambling', *American Imago*, Vol. 4, No. 2 (1947).

30. For further discussion of the problems posed by women's gambling see this introduction, pp. 95–6.

31. George Devereux, 'The Psychodynamics of Mohave Gambling', *American Imago*, Vol. 7, No. 1 (1950), pp. 55–65.

32. Cf. Ferenczi's observation on his patient from Erdely in the section of this introduction 'Anal Strategy', p.74.

33. Robert Lindner, 'The Psychodynamics of Gambling', *Annals of the American Academy of Political and Social Science*, Vol. 269 (1950), pp. 93–107.

34. E. Moran, 'Pathological Gambling', *British Journal of Hospital Medicine*, Vol. 4, No. 1 (1970), pp. 59–70.

35. Bergler, *The Psychology of Gambling*, p. 81.

36. Iago Galdston, 'The Psychodynamics of the Triad – Alcoholism, Gambling and Superstition', lecture delivered at the New York Academy of Medicine, March 1951; published in *Mental Hygiene*,

October 1951. Summarized in Bergler, *The Psychology of Gambling,* pp. 81–2.

37. Herbert I. Harris, 'Gambling Addiction in an Adolescent Male', *Psychoanalytic Quarterly,* Vol. 33, No. 4 (1964), pp. 513–25.

38. Quoted in Perkins, op. cit., pp. 63–4.

39. Ferdynand Zweig, 'Gambling and the Belief in Luck', *The British Worker,* (Harmondsworth: Penguin Books, 1952), pp. 140–8.

40. The Royal Commission on Lotteries and Betting, 1933, *Report,* Cmnd. 4341.

41. Otto Newman, *Gambling: Hazard and Reward* (London: Athlone Press, 1972), pp. 9, 222.

42. Robert Herman, 'Gambling as Work: a Sociological Study of the Race Track', in Herman, op. cit., pp. 87–104.

43. Irving Kenneth Zola, 'Observations on Gambling in a Lower-Class Setting', *Social Problems,* Vol. 10, No. 4 (1963) pp. 353–61, and reprinted in Herman, *Gambling,* pp. 19–32.

44. See John Ashton, *The History of Gambling in England* (London: Duckworth, 1898).

45. George O. Trevelyan, *The Early History of Charles James Fox* (London: Longman, 1880; Silver Library Edition, Longman, 1899) p. 454. This book contains extensive information about eighteenth-century aristocratic gambling. See especially pp. 450–61. Andrew Steinmetz, *The Gaming Table: Its Votaries and Victims,* 2 vols. (London: Tinsley, 1870), also comments on Fox's reputation as a gambler. 'Though it was calculated that he might have netted four or five thousand a year by games of skill, [Fox] complained that they afforded no excitements.' See also Rev. J. Glass, *Gambling and Religion* (London: Longman, 1924), part 3, where it is estimated that in one session of gambling lasting twenty-two hours, Fox lost an average of £500 an hour.

46. In 1808 a committee of the House of Commons was appointed to investigate lotteries; in an appendix to the report submitted to the House by the committee are feverish and gruesome accounts of lottery addiction and dissipation of winnings.

47. For the history of British lotteries see John Ashton, *A History of English Lotteries* (London: Leadenhall Press, 1893). The best account of the lottery's development in America is John Ezell, *Fortune's Merry Wheel: The Lottery in America* (Cambridge, Mass.: Harvard University Press, 1960).

48. Quoted in Ashton, *A History of English Lotteries.*

49. ibid., pp. 310ff.

50. A. L. Humphreys, *Crockford's; or The Goddess of Chance in St James's Street: 1828–1844* (London: Hutchinson, 1953).

51. Quoted in Steinmetz, op. cit., Vol. 1, p. 123.

52. For an account of this see Henry Blyth, *The Pocket Venus: A Victorian Scandal* (London: Weidenfeld & Nicolson, 1966).

53. Mr James Merry, a Glasgow ironmaster, won the Derby in 1861 with Thormanby, and a reputed £40,000 in bets besides.

54. Harold Wilson's phrase, as Leader of the Opposition in the British

Parliament, for Premium Bonds, a lottery held for the interest on investment, which was distributed according to a weekly computer draw. As participants could withdraw their stakes at any time, win or lose, and redeem the bonds for full face value, the speculation in interest represented a minimal gamble for a potentially large prize. Now £50,000 prizes have been introduced, and it has been calculated that the odds on drawing this prize with a single bond in any one year are 800,000,000 to 1 against.

55. The best available source for statistics about the overall volume of betting in Britain is the material put out by the Churches' Council on Gambling (C.C.G.). See especially 'The Facts about the "Money Factories" ', (London: C.C.G. Report, 1972), p. 14.

56. Ashton, *The History of Gambling in England*, states, 'The money motive increases as chance predominates over skill.' This is the opposite of the discoveries of all twentieth-century psychologists who have studied the phenomenon.

57. Steinmetz, op. cit., Vol. 1, pp. 34–42.

58. See Oystein Ore, *Cardano, the Gambling Scholar* (Princeton, N.J.: Princeton University Press, 1953; & Dover Publications Inc., 1965.

59. Cyril Hughes Hartmann, ed., *Games and Gamesters of the Restoration* (London: Routledge, 1930). This volume contains both Cotton's and Lucas's texts.

60. See note 59. But this edition has expurgated two of Lucas's most obscene and revealing anecdotes.

61. Quoted in Alan Wykes, *Gambling* (London: Aldus Books, 1964), pp. 18–19.

62. Steinmetz, op. cit., Vol. 2, p. 97.

63. E. B. Tylor, *Primitive Culture* (New York: Harper & Row, 1958).

64. Burt W. and Ethel G. Aginsky, 'The Pomo: A Profile of Gambling among Indians', *Annals of the American Academy of Political and Social Science*, Vol. 269 (1950), pp. 108–13.

65. Johan Huizinga, *Homo Ludens* (London: Routledge, 1949).

66. Sigmund Freud, 'Obsessive Actions and Religious Practices', (1907) *Standard Edition*, Vol. 9, pp. 115–27.

67. ibid., pp. 123–4.

68. ibid., pp. 126–7.

69. Sigmund Freud, 'Totem and Taboo' (1913), *Standard Edition*, Vol. 13, p. 148.

70. Sigmund Freud, 'The Future of an Illusion' (1927), *Standard Edition*, Vol. 21, p. 43.

71. ibid., p. 43.

72. Sigmund Freud, 'Civilization and Its Discontents' (1930), *Standard Edition*, Vol. 21, pp. 84–5.

73. Margie H., 'Margie's Story', in *Gamblers Anonymous*, pp. 186–94. Margie's way of choosing horses resembles a common practice among Christians of allowing the Bible to drop open at a random point, and accepting the first verse they see as God's word for them, for the day. Muslims also use the Koran in this way.

74. See Cohen, *Psychological Probability*, p. 68. Cohen maintains that this

'belief which admits of no doubt' is found in religion and gambling, and also, 'in a coarser form' in 'political ideologies'. This latter addition is not one which we accept; the motivation for belief in a right-wing political ideology, for example, is often cynical, calculated, self-interested materialism. See also R. H. Thouless, 'The Tendency to Certainty in Religious Belief', *British Journal of Psychology*, Vol. 26 (1935), pp. 16–31.

75. Roger Longrigg, *The Artless Gambler* (London: Pelham Books, 1964), p. 9.

76. Joachim Kahl, *The Misery of Christianity* (Harmondsworth: Penguin Books, 1971), p. 30. Kahl shows no signs of a Freudian formation, yet he also writes, 'Submission to human domination was glorified as an act of submission to God. Man's psychological apparatus for punishing himself – his bad conscience – was used to regulate all his impulses and he came to think that what was violently imposed from outside was the consequence of his own free will. Existing suffering was overcome by the power of religion and ontologized, never criticized.'

77. Anonymous, *Gamblers Anonymous*, pp. 34–5.

78. E. Moran described this case to me in the course of a discussion on gambling; it has not, so far as I know, been documented. P.F.

79. Wykes, op. cit., p. 46.

80. See the Koran, sura v: 'Satan seeketh to sow dissension and hatred among you by means of wine and lots, and to divert you from remembering God and prayer . . . Therefore abstain from them.'

81. Quoted in Ashton, *The History of Gambling in England*, pp. 28–9: '. . . whereas you are wont to celebrate Christmas by playing at Cards, I intend, by God's grace, to deal unto you Christ's cards wherein you shall perceive Christ's rule.' Latimer found the games of primero and trump particularly appropriate to his purpose.

82. ibid., pp. 34–6.

83. ibid., p. 28.

84. T. Gataker, *Of the Nature and Use of Lots* (London, 1619), p. 194.

85. Quoted in Perkins, op. cit., p. 104.

86. Apart from those quoted elsewhere in this introduction, the following publications will give a representative sample of the moralist position: W. Douglas Mackenzie, *The Ethics of Gambling* (1895); B. Seebohm Rowntree, ed., *Betting and Gambling* (1905); J. M. Hogge, *The Facts of Gambling* (1907); Cecil H. Rose, *Gambling and Christian Ideals* (1930); R. C. Mortimer, *Gambling* (1933); John Bretherton, *Why Gambling Is Wrong* (1936); Maldwyn Edwards, *Why Gamble?* (1946); Geoffrey Martin, *Gambling and the Citizen* (1949); Free Church Federal Council symposium, *Gambling, Right or Wrong?* (1952); Rev. J. Clark Gibson, *Gambling and Citizenship* (1955). There are literally hundreds of these slim volumes in existence; many of them plagiarise earlier texts.

87. Major Seton Churchill, *Betting and Gambling* (London: James Nisbett, 1894).

88. ibid., pp. 19–20.

89. ibid., pp. 26–7.

90. ibid., p. 25.
91. ibid., pp. 25–6.
92. ibid., p. 162.
93. ibid., p. 163.
94. ibid., pp. 78–9.
95. ibid., p. 129.
96. Glass, op. cit.
97. ibid., p. 37.
98. ibid., p. 98.
99. R. H. Charles, *Gambling and Betting* (Edinburgh: T. & T. Clark, 1924), p. 78. Charles also claims: '. . . the Christian religion denies that there is such a thing as Chance', p. 74.
100. Perkins, op. cit., pp. 103–4.
101. The phenomenon of the Churches' Council on Gambling underlines many of the points made in this introduction: all the British Churches contribute to the work of C.C.G., financially and practically, except the Roman Catholic Church. Rev. Gordon E. Moody, the long-standing secretary to C.C.G., and a Non-Conformist minister, described himself in a recent magazine interview as 'too mean' to threaten himself through gambling (*Observer Magazine*, 10 Sept. 1972). His own writing goes to characteristically tortuous lengths to explain how profiteering and capitalist speculation are not comparable to gambling activities.
102. Lycurgus Starkey, 'Christians and the Gambling Mania', *The Christian Century*, Vol. 80 (1963), pp. 267–70. Reprinted in Herman, op. cit., pp. 225–33.
103. A Royal Commission on Gambling was set up on 4 June 1932 to inquire into 'the existing law and the practice thereunder'. In 1933, it issued an interim report, and in 1934, a bill was introduced in the House of Lords on the Royal Commission's recommendations. It declared lotteries illegal, except those held, under carefully formulated restrictions, by 'art unions', but it licensed dog-tracks and football pools. In 1950 another Royal Commission was established which published a full report in 1951.
104. Royal Commission, *Minutes of Evidence* (1951), p. 341.
105. Quoted in Perkins, op. cit., p. 109. Perkins commented: 'This declaration also rejects, implicitly, the Catholic position by referring to attempts to make gambling and Christianity compatible as being drawn from "sub-Christian and non-Christian levels of thought".'
106. Charles, op. cit., p. 65.
107. Rev. Gordon E. Moody, *Notes on the Use of Gambling for Fund Raising* (C.C.G., n.d.).
108. The concept of 'fund'-raising as an activity engaged in by Churches is itself interesting: 'Funds' are money, the source by which things are made possible, but, as Ferenczi and Freud argue, money is also faeces. 'Fundament' is used to describe anal regions and functions, yet 'Fundamental', meaning basic or essential, is never used to describe phenomena relating to waste matter. 'Fundamentalist', however, has specific religious overtones: it refers to that kind of

Protestant whose religious thinking insists on an obsessively literal interpretation of biblical writings. These words, and their usage, give a very vivid parallel of the ambiguous attitudes to money, capitalism, anality and religious belief which underlie the whole of puritan writing and religious practice.

109. Ezell, op. cit., p. 140.
110. Sigmund Freud's two basic texts on anal erotism are 'Character and Anal Erotism' (1908), *Standard Edition*, Vol. 9, pp. 16–75, and 'On Transformations of Instinct as Exemplified in Anal Erotism' (1917), *Standard Edition*, Vol. 17, pp. 12–33. But see also Karl Abraham, 'Contributions to the Theory of the Anal Character', *Selected Papers* (London: Hogarth Press, 1927), pp. 370–92; and Ernest Jones, 'Anal Erotic Character Traits', *Papers on Psycho-Analysis*, pp. 413–37.
111. Freud, 'Character and Anal Erotism', p. 170.
112. Marcel Mauss, *The Gift: Forms and Functions of Exchange in Archaic Societies*, trans. Ian Cunnison (London: Cohen & West, 1954).
113. Freud, 'Character and Anal Erotism', p. 170.
114. ibid.
115. ibid.
116. ibid., p. 174.
117. Jones, 'Anal Erotic Character Traits'.
118. Norman O. Brown, *Life Against Death: The Psychoanalytic Meaning of History* (London: Routledge & Kegan Paul, 1959; Middletown, Conn., Wesleyan University Press, 1959. All references are to paperback edition: London: Sphere Books, 1968.)
119. ibid., p. 197.
120. ibid., p. 198.
121. ibid., p. 205.
122. Among the most useful attacks on behaviourism, particularly on the 'concensus' theory of behavioural knowledge, is L. Breger and J. L. McGaugh, 'Critique and Reformulation of Learning Theory Approaches to Psychotherapy and Neurosis', *Psychological Bulletin*, Vol. 3 (1965), pp. 338–58.
123. H. J. Eysenck attacks psychoanalysis in ill-considered articles on Freud in 'men's' magazines and in irresponsible books on psychology. See his *Fact and Fiction in Psychology* (Harmondsworth: Penguin Books, 1965), pp. 95–131.
124. B. F. Skinner, *Beyond Freedom and Dignity* (London: Jonathan Cape, 1972; Harmondsworth: Penguin Books, 1973), p. 15.
125. V. Meyer and E. Chesser, *Behaviour Therapy in Clinical Psychiatry*, (Harmondsworth: Penguin Books, 1970), p. 9.
126. See, for example, the techniques described in H. J. Eysenck and S . Rachman, *Causes and Cures of Neurosis* (Oxford: Pergamon Press, 1965).
127. M. P. Feldman and M. J. MacCullough, *Homosexual Behaviour: Therapy and Assessment* (Oxford: Pergamon Press, 1971).
128. Robert Allan, 'Bahaviourism', *Seven Days*, No. 18 (1972), p. 21.
129. Cited ibid., p. 19.

Introduction

130. A number of cases of brutality to patients in mental institutions by nursing and medical staff have been reported in Britain in recent years. Perhaps the most sensational, the Whittingham Hospital affair, was made the subject of a full-scale government inquiry. See *Report of the Committee of Inquiry into Whittingham Hospital* (H.M.S.O., 1972), Cmnd. 4861.

131. M. G. Preston and P. Baratta, 'An Experimental Study of the Auction Value of a Certain Outcome', *American Journal of Psychology*, Vol. 61 (1948), pp. 183–193.

132. We are not, of course, trying to discredit the value of clinical psychologists' discoveries about the existence and nature of subjective probability as such. In recent years one psychologist, John Cohen, has made a detailed study of the subject and, unlike his colleagues quoted in this section, has not ignored the historical origins of gambling, nor sought wholly to reject the Freudian interpretation, although he remains critical of it. Cohen is Professor of Psychology at Manchester University. His principal publications on the subject are: *Risk and Gambling: The Study of Subjective Probability* (New York: Philosophical Library, 1956); *Chance, Skill, and Luck: The Psychology of Guessing and Gambling* (Harmondsworth: Penguin Books, 1960); *Behaviour in Uncertainty* (London: Allen & Unwin, 1964); and *Psychological Probability* (London: Allen & Unwin, 1972).

133. W. E. Edwards, 'Probability Preferences in Gambling', *American Journal of Psychology*, Vol. 66 (1953), pp. 349–64.

134. F. Mosteller and P. Nogee, 'An Experimental Measurement of Utility', *Journal of Political Economy*, Vol. 59, No. 5, p. 371. See also P. Slovic and S. Lichtenstein, 'Importance of Preferences in Gambling Decisions', *Journal of Experimental Psychology*, Vol. 78, No. 4, part 1.

135. B. F. Skinner, *Science and Human Behavior* (New York: Macmillan, 1953) briefly and unsatisfactorily attempts a reconciliation. He returns to the subject in his latest book, *Beyond Freedom and Dignity* (London: Jonathan Cape, 1972; Harmondsworth: Penguin Books, 1973); again, he has to explain gambling solely in terms of a search for a repeat of an initial win, a thesis which is quite inadequate to meet the facts: 'A gambling enterprise pays people for giving it money – that is, it pays them when they make bets. But it pays on a kind of schedule which sustains betting even though, in the long run, the amount paid is less than the amount wagered. At first the mean ratio may be favourable to the bettor; he "wins". But the ratio can be stretched in such a way that he continues to play even when he begins to lose. The stretching may be accidental (an early run of good luck which grows steadily worse may create a dedicated gambler), or the ratio may be deliberately stretched by someone who controls the odds. In the long run the "utility" is negative: the gambler loses all.'
The most notable of many absurdities in this argument is the notion that commercial gambling operators are able to tailor-stretch the odds to provide early wins for a new bettor. But one can see why Skinner introduces it; apart from the 'accidental' early win, he has no other way

of explaining repeated indulgence in an activity which produces repeated losses, and consummates in overall loss.

136. Brigitte Hochauer, 'Decision-making in Roulette', *Acta Psychologica*, Vol. 34, Nos. 2 and 3 (1970), pp. 367–74.

137. See also J. C. Barker and M. Miller, 'Aversion Therapy for Compulsive Gambling'. *British Medical Journal*, No. 2 (1966), p. 115; and C. P. Seager, M. R. Pokorny and D. Black, 'Aversion Therapy for Compulsive Gambling', *The Lancet*, No. 1 (1966), p. 546.

138. A. B. Goorney, 'Treatment of a Compulsive Horse-Race Gambler by Aversion Therapy', *British Journal of Psychiatry*, No. 114 (1968), pp. 329–33.

139. Moritz Lazarus, *Über die Reize des Spiels* (Berlin, 1883).

140. Bergler, *The Psychology of Gambling*.

141. W. I. Thomas, 'The Gambling Instinct,' *American Journal of Sociology*, Vol. 6, No. 2 (1901), pp. 750–63.

142. E. Reid and O. Demaris, *The Green Felt Jungle* (London: Heinemann, 1965), a book about gambling and organized crime.

143. Clemens J. France, 'The Gambling Impulse', this volume, pp. 115–56.

144. Wykes, op. cit., pp. 15–16.

145. Newman, op. cit., p. 129.

146. Judah Binstock, *Casino Administration: The House and the Player* (London: Bodley Head, 1969), pp. 135–8.

147. Newman, op. cit., p. 222.

148. Cohen, 'The Nature of Gambling', p. 78.

149. See Hubert Phillips, *Pools and the Punter* (London: Watts & Co., 1955). In his evidence to the Royal Commission on Betting, Lotteries, and Gaming, 1951, Phillips demolished the concept of 'skill' and 'expert advice' affecting the outcome of pools predictions in any way. See also St Clair Drake and Horace Cayton, 'Policy: Poor Man's Roulette', in Herman, op. cit., pp. 3–10, for an account of mystical divinatory practices among New York's numbers-racket-players.

150. This fusion of two pre-genital elements need not surprise us. Freud himself recognized a close relationship between anal erotism and the development of the castration complex. He pointed out that in the unconscious the concept of the faeces, the penis, and the baby were frequently indissolubly inter-connected: for the child, all three are 'little ones' regarded as parts of the body which may become detached. 'Since the column of faeces stimulates the erotogenic mucous membrane of the bowel,' he wrote, 'it plays the part of an active organ in regard to it; it behaves just as the penis does to the vaginal mucous membrane, and acts as it were as its forerunner during the cloacal epoch. The handing over of faeces for the sake of (out of love for) someone else becomes a prototype of castration; it is the first occasion upon which an individual parts with a piece of his own body in order to gain the favour of some other person whom he loves. So that a person's love of his own penis, which is in other respects narcissistic, is not without an element of anal erotism.'
Freud points out that disturbances in attitudes to money and to gifts, and intestinal disorders, at one level manifestly anal, are thus fre-

quently bound up with the fear of castration: they may represent either unsuccessful defences against castration (anal retentiveness paralleling the desire not to be parted from the penis) or eruptions of the repressed, passive attitude towards the father (anal expulsiveness indicating the unconscious activity of the wish to become a 'castrated' love-object for the father). Interestingly, these ideas were first put forward in relation to the Wolf-Man, the subject of one of Freud's case histories, of whom he wrote: 'It was hard to say whether he ought to be called a miser or a spendthrift. He behaved now in this way and now in that, but never in a way that seemed to show any consistent intention.'

Freud's study of the Wolf-Man is primarily concerned with the latter's infantile neurosis – and the development of obsessional symptoms between the ages of four and a half and ten. Many of the characteristics we have indicated as typical of the gambler appear to be applicable in this case: marked anal fixation; obsessional symptoms; neurotic piety; and a passive attitude towards the father, bound up with repressed feminine impulses. Gambling was not one of the symptoms which the Wolf-Man presented to Freud during his analysis – although chronic disturbances in his attitudes to money and gifts were. However, from Muriel Gardiner's book, *The Wolf-Man and Sigmund Freud*, we learn that subsequently the Wolf-Man became caught up in gambling and reckless financial speculation of all kinds. It was only after repeatedly experiencing severely punitive losses that he finally abandoned the habit: his case demonstrates clearly the interrelationship between gambling, anal erotism, the fear of castration (particularly as punishment for masturbation) and repressed feminine impulses towards the father.

See Sigmund Freud, 'From the History of an Infantile Neurosis'. This case study is reprinted within *The Wolf-Man and Sigmund Freud*, edited by Muriel Gardiner, (Harmondsworth: Penguin Books, 1973). The Wolf-Man's own memoirs, also contained within this volume, include the accounts of his gambling activities which took place after his analysis with Freud. Many of the ideas demonstrating the unity in the unconscious of the concepts of the baby, the rod of faeces, and the penis are contained in Freud's paper, 'On Transformations of Instinct as Exemplified in Anal Erotism'. (See note 110.)

151. Sigmund Freud, 'A Child is Being Beaten' (1919), *Standard Edition*, Vol. 17, pp. 175–204. See also Freud, 'The Economic Problem of Masochism' (1924), *Standard Edition*, Vol. 19, pp. 155–70; and Steven Marcus, *The Other Victorians* (London: Weidenfeld & Nicolson, 1964), pp. 252–65.

152. S. Beach Chester, *Round the Green Cloth* (London: Stanley Paul & Co., 1928), pp. 31–2.

153. Patrick O'Neill-Dunne, *Roulette for the Millions* (London: Sidgwick & Jackson, 1971), p. 3.

154. Aben Kandel, *The Strip* (New York: New American Library, 1961), pp. 112–13.

Clemens J. France

The Gambling Impulse*

The present study is an attempt to investigate the origin and nature of the instincts and motives involved in chance plays and gambling. The writer has followed the biological or genetic method approach, calling upon the facts of biology, anthropology and history as aids in the solution of the problems encountered. The historical side has been especially emphasized as the writer has had in mind the ethical and sociological value of a contribution to the subject of gambling, as well as the psychological. From this point of view the historical aspects appealed to the writer as being of especial significance.

* * *

Section 1

Historical

Gambling seems to be indigenous among all races. There is evidence of its antiquity both in Egyptian paintings and in

*Clemens J. France's text, 'The Gambling Impulse', is of particular interest as it indicates how pre-Freudian psychologists, when confronted with the gambling neurosis, began to think uncharacteristically in terms of solutions involving complex unconscious mechanisms. France's long and heavily annotated text surveys gambling in its historical perspective – and he finds himself compelled by his material to recognize the gambler's motivation to lose, and to relate that motivation to religious experience. This is remarkable before the advent of a body of psychoanalytic theory, and it indicates the particular ability of the gambling neurosis to challenge and cause a departure from superficial psychological positions, just as the gambling neurosis continues to undermine the behaviourist interpretation today.

Some of the references are highly abbreviated; there is a possibility that a number of them may not be absolutely accurate. In addition, France has sometimes reproduced as quotations passages which are in fact paraphrases of the original. – Eds.

Originally published in the *American Journal of Psychology*, Vol. 13, No. 3 (July 1902), pp. 364–76, 382–407. Reprinted by permission of the University of Illinois Press.

materials of undoubted genuineness found in the tombs of this same people, among whom the practice was even attributed to the gods.[1] Evidence of the extent and danger of the habit is given from the fact that a man convicted of gambling in Egypt was condemned to work in the quarries.[2] Certain gambling games of the Chinese and Japanese are said to have been invented by the Emperor Yao, 2100 B.C.[3] Gambling among the ancient Hindus, Wheeler tells us, became a madness. There are certain Hindu legends of Rajahs, playing for days in succession, until the loser is reduced to the condition of an exile or a slave.[4] Among the ancient Persians gambling was a common diversion. Plutarch in his life of Artaxerxes relates that Queen Parysates, the mother of the younger Cyrus, at one time 'used all her skill in gambling to satiate her revenge and accomplish her bloodthirsty projects against the murderers of her favourite son'.[5] The prohibitions in the Koran are unable to suppress the practice among the modern Persians.[6] History furnishes examples of people risking their lives on a single throw of the dice. St Ambrose informs us that this was common with the ancient peoples, especially the Scythians. He also tells of how the Huns were ready to play at all times, even when at war; that they always carried their dice with them, guarding them as they would their arms.[7] There is not much evidence that the ancient Jews ever gambled, except by drawing lots.

This practice was very common, and we know that the 'promised land' was thus divided. Disney tells as that, in later days, the Jews did gamble and that gamesters were excluded from the magistracy, and were incapable of being chosen into the greater or lesser Sanhedrin; and that they could not be admitted as witnesses.[8]

'In China,' says Huc, 'gaming is prohibited and yet is carried on everywhere with almost unequalled passion . . . China is, in fact, one vast gaming-house . . . The games are very numerous. They play day and night, till they have lost all they have, and then they usually hang themselves.'[9] Williams says,

Gambling in China is universal. Hucksters at the roadside are provided with cup and saucer, and the clicking of dice is heard at every corner. A boy with but two cash prefers to risk their loss on the throw of a die, to simply buying a cake without trying the chance of getting it for nothing. Gambling houses are kept open by scores by paying bribes to the officers.[10]

In ancient Greece, also, gambling prevailed to a large extent. Philip of Macedon favoured the practice, recognizing its corrupting influence on the Greeks. Aristotle ranked gamblers with thieves and plunderers (*Nicomachean Ethics*, Book iv), and the Athenian orator, Callistratus, speaks of the desperate gambling in vogue (Xenophon, *History of Greece*, Book vi, ch. iii).[11]

Evidence of extensive gambling at Rome is derived from the excavations of Pompeii and other places. 'Sig. Rodolfo Lanciani says that, so intense was the love of the Roman for games of hazard that whenever he had excavated the pavement of a portico, basilica, bath or any flat surface, accessible to the public, he always found gaming-tables engraved or scratched on the marble or stone slabs.'[12] Ashton writes: 'Notwithstanding the laws against it, there was hardly in Rome a more common or more ruinous pastime.'[13]

Steinmetz devotes a chapter to the gambling amongst ancient Roman emperors.[14] Augustus was passionately addicted to the practice, and even gloried in his character of a gamester. Caligula stooped even to falsehood and perjury at the gaming-table. 'The Emperor Claudius played like an imbecile and Nero like a madman.' Nero would stake 400,000 sestertii (£20,000) on a single throw of the dice, and Claudius had the interior of his carriage arranged so that he could gamble on his journeys. Domitian was also an inveterate gambler. Juvenal, the contemporary of this emperor, writes: 'When was the madness of games of chance more furious? Nowadays not content with carrying his purse to the gaming-table, the gamester conveys his iron chest to the playroom. It is there you witness the most terrible contests. Is it not madness to lose 100,000 sestertii and refuse a garment to a slave perishing with cold?'[15] The rage at Rome seems to have kept on increasing until 'finally at the epoch when Constantine abandoned Rome never to return, every inhabitant of that city, down to the populace, was addicted to gambling'.[16]

That the ancient Germans were devoted to this form of play Tacitus testifies. They would not only stake all their wealth, but also their liberty.[17] In modern times, it was in Germany where there existed the most celebrated gambling resorts of all Europe – Baden-Baden, Ems, Homburg, Aix-la-Chapelle, Wiesbaden. It was to these resorts that the wealth

and nobility assembled during the 'cure season'. 'Princes and
their subjects, fathers and sons, and even, horrible to say,
mothers and daughters, would hang side by side, for half the
night, with trembling hands and anxious eyes watching their
chance card.'[18]

The early French annals record that the 'haughty and idle
lords were desperate gamblers', and that the exercise of this
impulse formed their chief occupation. In the reign of Charles
VI, who himself gambled heavily, we read of the Hôtel de
Nesle – famous for its terrible gaming catastrophes. 'Gambling
went on in camp, and even in the presence of the enemy.
Generals after having lost their own fortunes compromised the
safety of their country.' Play among the lower classes was not
excessive at this time;[19] but under Henry IV, everyone seemed
to catch the frenzy, all professions and trades being carried
away by it. Magistrates sold for a price the permission to
gamble. An Italian, a professional gambler, Pimentello, made
£100,000 in the course of a year; and there was scarcely a
day but someone was ruined. The result of this state of things,
says Steinmetz, was incalculable social affliction. All this
gambling took place in the face of the most stringent laws
against it.[20] In the reign of Louis XIII the passion was pretty
well suppressed, but in that of Louis XIV the practice prevailed
in high circles, and, as the King and Queen Regent both played,
everyone who had an expectation at court learned to play
cards. Steinmetz says:

> Before this, there was something done for the improving of con-
> versation; every one was ambitious to qualify himself for it by
> reading. But on the introducing of gaming men likewise left off
> tennis, billiards and other games of skill, and consequently became
> weaker and more sickly, more ignorant, less polished, more dissi-
> pated . . . The women, who till then had commanded respect,
> accustomed men to treat them with familiarity by spending the
> whole night with them at play . . . At the death of Louis XIV three
> fourths of the nation thought of nothing but gambling.[21]

Dusaulx writes: 'I have found cards and dice in many places
where people were in want of bread. I have seen merchants
and artisans staking gold by the handful. A small farmer has
just gambled away his harvest, valued at 3,000 francs.'[22] In
the reign of Louis XVI the passion prevailed unabated, and
was undoubtedly increased by the French revolution. At this

time gambling was a source of not a little revenue to the government.

The English have always been notable for their propensity to gamble; a writer familiar with the visitors at Monte Carlo says that the majority are English.[23] Hence we are not surprised to find that the use of dice in England is of great antiquity, dating from the advent of the Saxons, Danes and Romans.[24] Ordericus Vitalis (1075–1143) tells us 'that clergymen and bishops are fond of dice-playing', and John of Salisbury (1110–82) calls it the damnable art. An edict of 1190 shows that gambling was common among the lower classes; also in the thirteenth and fourteenth centuries we have evidence of its prevalence.[25] Cotton in his *Compleat Gamester* gives a vivid description of the practice in the time of Elizabeth. And Lucas in his *Lives of Notorious Gamblers* gives proof that high play was common in the reigns of Charles II, James II, William III and Queen Anne.[26] Legislation against card-playing was made in the reign of Henry VIII, prohibiting the common people from playing except at Christmas.[27] A book entitled *The Nicker Nicked, or the Cheats of Gaming Discovered* (1619) furnishes a good account of the gambling-house of that period. The author says: 'Most gamesters begin at small game; and, by degrees, if their money or estates hold out, they rise to great sums; some have played first of all their money, then their rings, coach and horses, even their wearing clothes and perukes; and then such a farm; and, at last, perhaps, a lordship.'[28]

In the reign of Queen Anne the evil seems to have increased, especially among the women. Ward in a satire, *Adam and Eve Stript of their Furbelows* (1705), has an article on the gambling lady of that period entitled 'Bad Luck to Him who has Her; or the Gaming Lady'. Steele devoted No. 120 of the *Guardian* (29 July 1713) to female gambling, in which he points out the ruinous effects attendant on the indulgence of it amongst ladies. 'Nothing,' he says, 'so quickly wears out a fine face as the Vigils and cutting Passions of the card table. Hollow eyes, haggard looks, and pale complexions, these are the natural indications of a female gamester.' He speaks of the danger to the moral nature and purity of a woman who has lost heavily. 'She has then only her person to dispose of.' Pope, also, in his *Rape of the Lock* (Canto III), gives a picture of the gambling lady and of the corrupting influence that the practice exerts upon her.[29] In the reign of George II the state of affairs continued as in previous reigns. A letter in the *Grub Street Journal* says, 'The canker of gambling is surely eating into the very heart of the nation.'

Gambling-houses kept by women which had long existed and for a period were closed were re-opened at the end of the eighteenth century.[30] Gambling at this period was the chief amusement of women, as well as of men. Says Steinmetz: 'At social gatherings it was vain to attempt conversation. The intellectual was inhibited by the impulsive. The time presents a picture of dissolute manners, as well as furious party spirit. The most fashionable ladies were immersed in play. The Sabbath was disregarded and moral duties neglected.'[31] Seymour Harcourt in his *Gaming Calendar* (1820) gives a vivid picture of the universality of the habit among all classes in the latter part of the eighteenth century. Gambling clubs, which later played so great a role, began now to rise into prominence. Two of these, White's and Brooks's, deserve especial mention.

It was at White's Club that play was carried on to an extent, which made ravages in large fortunes, the traces of which have not disappeared at the present day. It was at White's that General Scott won £200,000. It was at Brooks's that Charles James Fox, Selwyn, Lord Carlisle, Lord Robert Spencer and other great Whigs won and lost hundreds of thousands. The number of great men who played heavily, the number of fortunes wrecked at this time, is almost incredible.[32]

The Duke of Wellington in his early career lost a large sum of money at play, and was on the point of selling his commission to relieve himself from his debts of honour.[33] Duels and suicides caused by gambling were common, as is shown by the Annual Register.

In the early part of the nineteenth century the passion had not abated. Ashton says: 'The West End of London literally swarmed with gambling-houses.' One writer speaks thus of these gambling hells:

To these places thieves resort and such other loose characters as are lost to every feeling of honesty and shame. A table of this nature in full operation is a terrific sight; all the bad passions appertaining to the vicious propensities of mankind are portrayed in the countenances of the players . . . Many in their desperation strip themselves on the spot of their clothes, either to stake against money or to pledge to the keeper of the table for a trifle to renew their play, and many instances occur of men going home half naked, having lost their all.[34]

Crockford's Club was the most noted of all the gambling-houses in London. It is estimated that Crockford netted £300,000 in the first two seasons alone. Ashton writes: 'One may safely say without exaggeration that Crockford won the whole of the ready money of the then existing generation.'[35]

The great gambling institution of England is that of horse-racing, or the turf, as it is commonly called. Everyone has read of the famous English Derby. Today, by means of a system of bookmaking, published in the daily papers, everyone is enabled to gamble, and the extent of the practice is enormous. In the English *Political Science Quarterly* of November 1900 attention is called to the extent and evil of this practice and an urgent plea made for reform.[36]

Brief reference only can be made to the few leading countries remaining. We know that the Russians, Italians, Spaniards and Japanese are all addicted to gambling. Alfonso X of Castile endeavoured to prevent the practice, by founding in 1332 the Chivalric Order of the Band, in which it was forbidden. A further ordinance was issued by John I, King of Castile, in 1387, forbidding the subjects to play backgammon or dice. In 1506, because of the misery in Italy arising from the in-dulgence of gambling, the Council of Ten forbade all forms of this play and all sale of dice and cards. This did not eradicate the evil. Toward the end of the last century gambling raged furiously at Venice. In 1774 the Graded Council ordered the close of a large public gambling-house known as the Ridotto. Today the state lottery in Italy is still in existence.[37]

The United States has not been excelled by the countries of Europe and Asia in their proneness to this form of play. Stein-metz says: 'It is not surprising, that a people so intensely speculative, excitable and eager as the Americans, should be desperately addicted to gambling. Indeed, the spirit of gam-bling has incessantly pervaded all their operations, political, commercial and social.' We cannot go into the history here, but all know well the struggles our large cities have had and are still having to suppress this practice. Nor is it confined to large cities. The excessive gambling among the miners and lumbermen in the West is well known; the notoriety of Saratoga as a great gambling resort a few years back is still fresh in our memories. A collection of stories by Mr Lillard will give the reader an inside view of some aspects of the gambling carried on in the United States.[38] Mr Lillard informs the writer that he has gambled and seen gambling in every state in the union, and that the stories which he gives are very fair examples of many of his own experiences.

The history of lotteries and an account of the role they have played in society is a subject too extensive to be more than touched upon.[39] The lottery existed in ancient Rome and has flourished continuously until comparatively recent times. State lotteries have existed from the fifteenth century, and have been, in many countries, one of the chief sources of revenue. As an illustration of this, the following facts, of the part lotteries played in our own country, are instructive. MacMaster tells us that in 1790 cash had become so scarce that it was impossible to obtain money to pay the cost of local governments or to carry on works of public improvement, and that in consequence recourse was had to lotteries.

In a short time there was a wheel in every town large enough to boast of a courthouse or a jail. Wherever a clumsy bridge was to be thrown across a stream, a public building enlarged, a schoolhouse built, a street paved, a road repaired, a manufacturing company to be aided, a church assisted, or a college treasury replenished, a lottery bill was passed by the legislature, a wheel procured, a notice put in the papers, and often in a few weeks the money was raised.

It was with the money collected from the sale of lottery tickets that Massachusetts encouraged cotton-spinning, and paid the salaries of many of her officers, that the city hall was enlarged in New York, that the courthouse was built at Elizabeth, that the library was increased at Harvard, that many of the most pretentious buildings were put up at the Federal City. The custom, indeed, continued for several years, and the State wheel became as regular an item in the papers as the ships' news or prices current.[40]

The following is a list of some of the lotteries and their purposes, collected at random by MacMaster from the newspapers for the year 1788-9: West River Bridge Lottery, Brattleborough, Vt; Furnace Lottery, Fair Haven Iron Works, Vt; Windsor County Grammar School Lottery, Vt; Massachusetts Semi-Annual State Lottery; Leicester Academy Lottery, Mass.; Hartford Bank Lottery, to build a bank along Connecticut River at Hartford; Bell Lottery, to procure a bell for the German Reform Church, Maryland; Petersburgh Church Lottery, Va.; Alexander Lottery, to pave certain streets; Fredericksburg Academy Lottery, Va.; Lottery to enable the Hebrews to pay the debt on their synagogue, Penn.; Lottery to build a city hall at Philadelphia; New York City Lottery to enlarge the city hall for the use of Congress.

The result of this was very injurious to industry and business, as a general rage for speculation arose among all classes. Mac-Master says: 'Farmers and artisans, tradesmen and merchants were neglecting their businesses to watch the drawings of innumerable wheels.'[41] In 1817 lotteries still existed. 'The lotteries were almost as bad as the dram-shops and tippling-houses. The depression and excitement, that so invariably followed the drawing, diverted the laborer from his work, weakened his moral tone, consumed his earnings, and soon brought him to pauperism.'[42]

To realize the extent of gambling in Europe at the present time a few facts about the expenditure of the greatest of modern gambling resorts, Monte Carlo, are instructive.[43] The expenditure of the Casino runs into gigantic figures; for police and courts the administration pays per annum £20,000; for roads £8,000; for lighting and water £19,000; for clergy and schools £9,000; for maintenance of the Casino, including salaries, management, gardens, lighting, heating, etc., £800,000; for charity £6,000; for carnivals and prizes £11,000; for printing £2,000; for agents, pensioners, etc., £9,000; for the viaticum £12,000; for the reptile press £25,000;; for theater and orchestra £40,000; an expenditure of upwards of £1,000,000. And yet the shareholders received in 1897 dividends to the amount of £570,000. During 1891 the total revenue from the tables was a little over 23,000,000 francs. The dividends paid average about 38 per cent.

In closing this brief historical sketch the writer gives the following list of persons of note who have been especially addicted to gambling.[44] Guido, the great painter, Voiture, Montague and Descartes in early life, Cardan, Lords Halifax, Anglesey and Shaftesbury, Lord Carlisle, Selwyn, Charles James Fox, Wilberforce, Pitt, Sir Philip Francis, Horace Walpole, Marie Antoinette, Nell Gwyn. Webster and Clay, according to Lillard, were both great poker-players.

Anthropological

The passion for gambling is nowhere so strong as among savage and barbarous races. The American Indians are the most desperate and reckless gamblers in the world. Some of them will not only lose all their possessions, but also will stake their wives and children and even their own liberty. The practice is thus a cause of much distress and poverty in their families.[45] Property changes hands with the greatest rapidity, a single throw at dice or a heat in a horse-race often doubling the player's fortune or sending him forth an impoverished adventurer.[46] Among the Nahua nations the great national game is one played with a ball – the end being to throw the ball through a small opening, a feat seldom done except by chance. The successful player, Bancroft tells us, was made as much of as the winner at the Olympic games. All classes gambled heavily on the issue. Among the Hurons the chief game is that of the dish (*jeu du plat*).

Large parties assemble to play this, during which the people not only lose their rest, but in some measure their reason. The players appear like people possessed, and the spectators are not more calm. They all make a thousand contortions, talk to the bones, load the spirits of the adverse party with imprecations, and the whole village echoes with howling.[47]

The game is in great repute as a medicine, the gambling parties often being ordered by the physician. The people all convene in a hut, the sick being brought in on mats.[48] Among the Iroquois whole townships, and even whole tribes, play against each other. The assemblage would last sometimes eight days, meeting every day, every inhabitant of each township tossing the dice once.[49]

The Senecas had a popular belief that a certain gambling game would be enjoyed by them in the future life of the Great Spirit – which was an extravagant way of expressing their admiration for it. Among the Zuñis 'kicked stick' (*Ti-kwa-we*) is the great national game, and is indulged in from boys of five to men of forty. Everyone, man, woman and child, takes sides and gambles on the issue.[50] In many tribes women are as much addicted to this practice as men, and among some there are games peculiar to the women alone.[51]

Gambling is the chief recreation of the Malays of Sumatra, all classes indulging extensively in play. They risk high stakes on their success; in some instances a father will stake his wife or children; or a son, his mother and sisters.[52] The Battas are also passionate gamblers. 'They do not hesitate to risk all they possess, and often stake their own person, and if unable to pay are sold as slaves.'[53] The Javanese,[54] Balinese,[55] Sulus,[56] Bugis,[57] are all addicted to the practice. The ancient Mutsams were inveterate gamblers, the gambling crowd being called together by the sound of the drum.[58] So also the Patagonians are much devoted to gambling, the women as well as the men risking their valuables.[59] Among the Usbegs, a nomadic people of Central Asia, the favourite game is the *Ashik* (*ahsek* – ankle-bones of sheep) 'played in the manner of European dice, and with a degree of passionate excitement of which one can form no idea'.[60] So we find mention of gambling all over the world – among the Melanesians, Malayans, Alaskans, Koreans, Hawaiians, African Negroes, in Brazil and in all the Latin Republics; amongst the natives of South America, amongst the natives of the Isle of Man, and even amongst the Icelanders.

The extremes to which the gambler in his passion is led are almost incredible. 'It is well known that they have eaten up cards, crushed the dice, broken the tables, damaged the furniture, only to end in fights with each other.'[61] We have record of a man who, enraged at play, jammed a billiard-ball into his mouth, where it stuck fast until removed by a surgeon,[62] of one who, having put a candle into his mouth, chewed and swallowed it;[63] of a mad player at Naples, who bit the table with such violence that his teeth went deep into the wood, and who thus remained, nailed as it were, until he expired.[64] Steinmetz[65] gives cases where loss at play resulted in stupefaction – some players neither knowing what they did nor what they said, of a case of a man who cut off all the fleshy part of one of his ears to obtain money to play; two cases of men who, having tossed for each other's money, tossed to see which one would hang the other, the loser actually submitting to be hanged.[66] Jean Barbeyrac cites a case of a man who, having gambled all his life, made in his will an injunction that his skin and membranes be used to cover a table, a dice-box and draught-board, and that dice be made out of his bones.[67] Archdeacon Bruges mentions a similar case. There are a number of examples of men who have staked their wives.[68] Parchasus Justus, who wrote a book to cure himself of the habit, tells of people who staked their teeth and eyebrows. Hyde found some Chinamen who staked the fingers of their hands; Schouten, of Chinamen who staked the hairs of their heads.[69] A gambler has told the writer he has seen a man shot in a game of poker, and thrown into a corner, while the rest continued the play.

Colonel Mellesh was asked what were his feelings when he entered the battle of Vermeira. 'Precisely the same,' he replied, 'as those I used to feel when laying a tremendous stake at Macao.'[70] Hon. General Fitzpatrick once said: 'If I could coin my heart and drop my blood into drachms, I would do it to play, though by this time I should probably have neither heart nor blood left.'[71] It is not an uncommon thing for ruined gamblers to go and sit up night after night watching the play of others. Voltaire cites a case of an old woman, ruined by gambling, who offered to make soup *gratis* for the players provided she might look on the game.[72] Cotton in his *Compleat Gamester* writes of the passion as follows:

Gaming is an enchanting witchery, gotten between idleness and vice; an itching disease, that makes some scratch the head, whilst others, as if bitten by a tarantula, are laughing themselves to death; or, lastly it is a paralytic distemper, which seizing the arm, the man cannot chuse but shake the elbow. It hath this ill property above all other vices, that it renders a man incapable of prosecuting any serious action, and makes him always unsatisfied with his own condition; he is either lifted to the top of mad joy with success, or plunged to the bottom of despair by misfortune; always in extremes, always in a storm; this minute the gamester's countenance is so serene and calm that one would think that nothing could disturb it, and the next minute so stormy and tempestuous that it threatens distruction to itself and others; and, as he is transported as he wins, so losing, is he tost upon the billows of a high swelling passion, till he hath lost sight of both sense and reason.[73]

La Placette says: 'In order to conceive clearly the state in which the soul of the gambler finds itself, it is not sufficient simply to represent a sea always agitated; it is necessary to imagine that these agitations come from five or six opposite vents, which rule, each in its own course in such a way, that there is not one of them, which has not the advantage many times in the quarter of an hour.'[74] Barbeyrac writes: 'I do not know if there is any other passion which allows less of repose and which one has so much difficulty in reducing.' He cites anger as a passion of excessive violence, yet one which does not endure long in intensity; likewise ambition and love. Each of these has its moments of cessation and decrease in intensity.

But the passion of gambling gives no time for breathing; it is an enemy which gives neither quarter nor truce; it is a persecutor, furious and indefatigable. The more one plays the more one wishes to play; one never leaves it, and with difficulty, one resolves to leave off a little while from dice and cards to satisfy the needs of nature; all the time he is not playing, the time seems to him lost; he is tired (ennui). When he does anything else; it seems that gambling had acquired the right to occupy all his thoughts . . . Old age far from diminishing the ardor of this passion only results in reenforcing it.[75]

Steinmetz writes:

The gamester lives only for the sensation of gaming. Menage tells us of a gamester who never saw any other luminary on the horizon but the moon. St Evremond says: 'All the rays of the gambler's existence terminate in play; it is on this that the centre of his existence depends. He enjoys not an hour of calm serenity. During the day he longs for night, and during the night he dreads the return of day.'[76]

*

Section 3

Psychological theories of the gambling impulse are few in number and inadequate in treatment. What little the writer has found is summed up in the following. Steinmetz gives these points: (1) A desire for a stimulus to call forth the natural activity of the mind; indolence, vacuity being the cause. (2) Love of wealth. (3) It intensifies and gives rise to such feelings as vanity, curiosity, surprise.[77] Another writer[78] says that the passion is due (1) 'to avarice – as promising either a vast accession of wealth, or a short road to the possession of it'; (2) to a deficiency in what in physics is called a stimulus.

Ribot, speaking of plays and games in general, says:

This last item [games of chance] alone might prove a tempting one to a psychologist. It has a quasi-passive, somewhat blunted form which Pascal called a diversion (that which turns aside, dis-

---

*Section 2 is omitted. – Eds.

tracts), a way of pretending to work, or filling up the blanks in existence, of 'killing time'. It has an active form, the gambling passion whose tragedy is as old as humanity, and which is made up of attraction toward the unknown and hazardous, of daring, emulation, of the desire for victory, the love of gain, and the fascination of acquiring wealth wholesale, instantaneously, without effort. These and other elements show that in play, as in love, it is complexity which produces intensity.[79]

A writer in the *Spectator* takes up arms against those who attibute the impulse to avarice. (1) 'No really avaricious person ever gambles, for the pain of paying his losses overcomes both the pleasure of the game and the pleasure derived from winning.' (2) 'Nor is gaming a mark of inner effeminacy, of a desire for excitement to be gained without exertion.' He cites Bismarck and Count Cavour, men of the greatest energy – addicted to high play. (3) 'Nor is the gambler at heart a cheat.' (4) 'The true temptation is the desire which prompts most men to drink hard – love of excitement, a desire to forget self and be rid of the monotony of the commonplace.'[80] Apropos of the above is the observation of Drähms, who says: 'The professional gambler is prodigal and generous, especially towards those in distress, and for religious and moral purposes.'[81]

Professor Lazarus's treatment[82] contains the following points: (1) The state of tension (*schweben*) is sought, avarice being entirely subordinate. (2) Hope and fear are dominant states – with especial emphasis on hope. He thinks the state lottery partially justifiable because it gives the poor people something to hope for. 'Man can live without pleasure, but not without hope.' (3) Gambling satisfies the positive attraction for danger, present in many men. (4) It satisfies the feeling that we are lucky; emphasizes the efficacy of the idea of fate in overcoming the idea of blind chance; is the abandonment of reason and giving oneself up to superstition.

Mr Thomas, in a paper in the *American Journal of Sociology*,[83] gives some interesting points in regard to the gambling instinct. He bases the instinct primarily on what he calls the conflict interest, which will be best understood by quoting his own words: 'There could not have been developed an organism, depending on offensive and defensive movements for food and life, without interest in what we call a dangerous and precarious situation. A type without this interest would have been defective and would have dropped out in the course of development.' That this interest prevails he considers 'a sign of continued animal health and instinct in the race'. Thomas also lays stress on the desire to get rid of routine – pointing out that those professions in which there is an element of work and uncertainty are more popular and more often chosen, as competitive business, the Stock Market, the learned professions; and among the less intelligent – the callings of policemen, firemen, detectives, livery stablemen, barkeepers, barbers. He sums up: 'Gambling is a means of keeping up the conflict interest, and of securing all the pleasure–pain sensations of conflict activity with little effort and no drudgery; and, incidentally or habitually, it may be a means of securing money.' He believes 'the instinct is born in all normal persons. It is one expression of a powerful reflex, fixed far back in animal experience. The instinct is, in itself, right and indispensable, but we discriminate between its applications.' He holds that the gambler by profession is often of a high type of man – intelligent, and not degenerate. There is no special gambling type; at worst, he is but representative of a class of men who have not been 'weaned from their instincts'.

In the following the writer attempts to analyse the factors involved. His conclusions are based on questioning and correspondence with some twenty gamblers, on personal observations in gambling resorts, on a large amount of literature, historical and descriptive, on an analysis of over a hundred stories of gambling, written by gamblers,[84] and accounts of the lives of gamblers.[85]

The psychic attitude toward uncertainty – the state of suspense – is the most natural starting point.

Professor Lazarus says: 'The pleasure in all chance plays consists fundamentally in suspended activity; in dice, roulette and faro, nothing of more importance can be discovered than the mental tensity because of the question: "Will it be seven or eleven; a little or a great number?" This *"oder"* (either – or) is a mighty psychological force, an irresistible attracting magnet.'[86] We have here curiosity and something added – the feeling of expectation in which, as Wundt says, we outrun the impressions of the present and anticipate those the future will bring, and if the result is postponed there arises strained expectation, in which the muscles are held tensed like those of a runner awaiting the signal for the race, although very possibly the impression demands no motor response whatsoever.[87]

When the stake is added there arises all the pleasure of pursuit with increase of intensity, for as Bain says: 'An element of uncertainty increases the interest of pursuit by making it more exciting . . . absolute certainty unduly relaxes the bodily and mental strain that is needed for the maximum of gratification.'[88] 'The purest form of pleasurable excitement.' says Sully, 'is afforded by a set of circumstances which opens up a number of possible issues though we have not the knowledge to determine which is most probable.'[89] We have here ideal conditions for arousal and imagination.

A case is reported of a man who for many years was a spectator at one and the same table without participating in the play. A dispute arising, he was asked to make a decision, as he must know best the laws of the game. He replied that he did not know the game; that he had only looked on to observe where the best cards fell.[90]

At any gambling-table, where it is permitted, you will observe spectators watching with strained attention to see where the wheel will stop or which card will turn up. The writer has found it difficult to leave such a table after standing a few minutes merely to observe what number will win next. In any uncertain event there is the same attracting force, and although one may have no interest in either side, there is always a tendency to speculate on the outcome. This constitutes a large part of the philosophy of life, resolving the uncertainties into certainties. George Eliot writes:

So absolute is our souls' need of something hidden and uncertain for the maintenance of that doubt and hope and effort which are the breath of its life, that if the whole future were laid bare to us beyond today, the interest of all mankind would be bent on the hours that lie between; we should pant after the uncertainties of our one morning and our one afternoon; we should rush fiercely to the Exchange for our last possibility of speculation, of success, of disappointment: we should have a glut of political prophets foretelling a crisis or a no-crisis within the only twenty-four hours left open to prophecy.[91]

The race has been evolved in an environment of uncertainty, and it may be that such an environment has thus become indispensable. It cannot be doubted that the state of mental tension, of being on the alert with ears pricked and nose in the air, is a factor of high selective value. We have reason to believe that this state of expectation not only links together and sets in a condition of unstable equilibrium motor centres, but also that in the higher association centres there is a preparatory condition produced. On this assumption the metabolism of both brain and body would be increased, and consequently the potential efficiency of the given moment. Not only reflex action and muscular co-ordination, but also memory, imagination, and judgement-times would be quickened. Is it not thus that a condition of uncertainty holds the mind in a tonic and un-relaxed condition? As evidence that, as we approximate a dead-level certainty, we tend to lose in mental efficiency, we have the case of the arrested development of the Chinese. It is significant in the case of the Chinese that the passion for uncertainty, having no exercise in the serious side of life, shows itself in the form of play – they being the greatest gamblers in the world. It is then this need of mental tension, this 'either – or' state, which is one of the chief factors in chance games and gambling.

The addition of the stake brings in a whole train of added states centring about the feeling of power. Hope and fear, joy and sorrow are especially predominant. It is significant to note that hope must at the moment of action predominate over fear – a necessary biological condition of all action in uncertainty. Again in connection with this playing power, we find arising emulation, aggression, the instinct of domination, with the love of humiliating one's opponent, much allied to the bullying and teasing tendency, pugnacity – with all the resulting emotions.[92] Jealousy and envy are especially strong in the mind of the loser. In the great American game draw poker the battle element is especially predominant. It is here also that the 'bluff' plays so great a role – the attempt to beat your opponent by sheer boldness and self-confidence. The psychic effects of this are significant. It makes the man who bluffs play better and the opponent play worse. The psychic effects of the bluffer in everyday life only need to be mentioned.

There are many minor factors indispensable to the success of the gambler – the cultivation of a calm and dispassionate demeanor in moments of crisis, never displaying any emotion or hesitancy; the ability to recover quickly from defeat; being ever vigilant and attentive; acquiring the habit of studying your opponent most closely, few men being better 'sizers-up' of men than the gambler; a sufficient degree of caution tempering your boldness; the learning how to bear sanely good fortune, as well as bad. These fit closely the essentials of any active, exploiting life. But for its costliness and dangers, no better education for life among men could be devised than the gambling-table – especially the poker game.

The phase of gambling known as betting is important. The practice is very ancient. At one time in England it became a mania.[93] It has its basis in the tendency to make dogmatic statements on the outcome of uncertain events and the strong inclination to throw your lot in with one possibility. Dr Small in his monograph on certainty, in which he showed the tendency to make strong assertions regarding certain events, only stated half the truth. The whole history of partisanship, dogmatism and fanaticism is in point, for these are but an outcrop of this tendency plus some interest at stake. Its simplest form is the 'I'll bet you' one hears a dozen times a day. A man often will take either side, but after backing one he is apt to believe in it. The wide pedagogical and ethical bearings are evident.

The possibility of getting something for nothing, and that quickly, is another of the salient features in gambling. It is the basis of the Stock Exchange, of many exploring expeditions, the explanation of such phenomena as the Keeley motor, the Miller syndicate, Mrs Howe's bank, the Rev. Mr Jernegan's scheme of obtaining gold from sea water, etc. The credulity of people in the presence of such frauds is most wonderful. This speculating tendency has two or three times in the course of history manifested itself in an extraordinary degree. Two of these, the South Sea Company, better known as the South Sea Bubble, and John Law's Mississippi scheme all but financially wrecked England and France, respectively.

John Law, who in 1817 was in control of the French finances, issued bonds on large tracts of land along the Mississippi River. The paper was in the shape of stocks, bearing interest. The scheme worked so well, Law issued a second large amount. The whole French people went mad in speculating. McKay says:

People of every age and sex and condition in life speculated on the rise and fall of these bonds . . . There was not a person of note among the aristocracy, except the Duke of St Simon and Marshall Villars, who was not engaged in buying and selling stock. Gamblers with their roulette tables reaped a golden or rather a paper harvest from the throng.[94]

Wood says: 'The frenzy prevailed so far that the whole nation, clergy and laity, peers and plebeians, statesmen, princes, nay, even ladies . . . turned stockjobbers.'[95] It is worthy of note that Law was a Scotch adventurer, and had been for many years a gambler.[96]

About the same time in England the South Sea Company began to sell stocks, claiming the company had rich lands in the South Seas, and promising enormous dividends. McKay writes:

It seemed as if the whole nation had turned stock jobbers . . . The inordinate thirst for gain affected all ranks of society . . . Besides the South Sea, innumerable other companies started up everywhere. There were nearly a hundred of these projects or bubbles – extravagant to the last degree, yet the people were hypnotized by the craze of speculation . . . It has been computed that nearly one million and a half sterling were won and lost by these practices . . . In the heyday of its blood, during the progress of this dangerous delusion, the manners of the nation became sensibly corrupted . . . It is a deeply interesting study to investigate all the evils that were the result. Nations, like individuals, cannot become gamblers with impunity.[97]

Another of these great speculating crazes was the tulip mania in Holland in the seventeenth century.[98]

The following figures show how this speculating tendency pervades the commercial world as represented in the Stock Exchange. The legislative committee of New York reported that in the three years preceding 1882 the optional cash sales of wheat in the New York Produce Exchange amounted to $244,737,000, while the total of optional sales of all kinds during the same period rated up to the enormous sum of $1,154,367,000. The United States Cotton Commission, sent to investigate the New Orleans cotton deal, in 1892, reported 52,000,000 bales as being disposed of on the New York Exchange, and 16,000,000 in the New Orleans, or 68,000,000 in all. As a matter of fact but *seven and three-fourths* million bales all told were raised in the United States during that period, and a little over 400,000 of these were sent to New York. The surplus in both cases represent bogus sales. This is gambling on the largest scale, and that done in the name of legitimate business.[99]

Section 4

A feature closely allied with that of the state of tension, and largely influential in increasing it, pervades and permeates the whole fabric of the gambling impulse – that of luck. The term 'luck' is used here in a large sense to include a group of phenomena very significant in the study of chance. It is this group of phenomena which it is the purpose of the present section to attempt to explain in its biological origin and values. As a foreword, I would like to lay especial emphasis on the implications of natural selection in respect to the presence of long existing and strongly tenacious psychic manifestations – to wit, that such manifestations are based upon psychic variations which must have been of use in the biological economy and thus have been of high selective value. The greater their permanence, and the stronger their tendency to express themselves, we must conclude that proportionately great was their importance in determining the fitness and survival of their possessors. Bearing this in mind through the ensuing chapter let us glance at some of the phases of those psychic manifestations which we will group under the term 'luck'.

Father Lalemont, in describing gambling among the Indians, tells how they prepare for the game:

> They pass the night in shaking to find who is most adroit in spreading out their charms and exhorting them. They abstain from their wives, fast, sleep in the same cabin – all this to have a lucky dream. Everything they dream would bring them luck is brought to the game in bags. They also bring to the game any old men who are supposed to have charms. When the game begins every one sets to praying and muttering . . . with gestures and violent agitations of the hands, eyes and entire face, all for the purpose of attracting good fortune to themselves and exhorting their particular spirits to take courage and not let themselves be worried. Some are appointed to utter execrations and make contrary gestures for the purpose of forcing bad luck upon the other side and frightening the familiar spirits of the opposite party.[100]

This is a typical example among many to be found in the anthropological literature.

Richard Proctor[101] gives the following five things that gamblers hold: (1) Gamblers recognize some men as always lucky – as always 'in vein'.[102] (2) Gamblers recognize those who start on a gambling career with singular luck, retaining that luck long enough to learn to trust in it confidently, and then losing it once and for all. (3) Gamblers regard the great bulk of their community, as men of varying luck – sometimes 'in vein', sometimes not; men who, if they are successful, must, according to the superstitions of the gambling world, be most careful to watch the progress of events. If men will not withdraw when they are not 'in vein', gamblers believe they will join the crew of the unlucky. (4) There are those, according to the ideas of gamblers, who are pursued by constant ill luck. If they win in the first half of the evening, in the last half they will lose more. (5) Gamblers recognize a class who, having begun unfortunately, have had a change of luck later, and have become members of the lucky fraternity. This change they ascribe to some action or event. For instance, the luck changed when the man married, his wife being a shrew; or because he took to wearing waistcoats; or because 'So-and-So', who had been a sort of evil genius to the unlucky man, had gone abroad or died. Then there are especial phases in the belief in luck. Some believe that they are lucky on certain days of the week, unlucky on others. The skilful whist player, under the name of Pembridge, believes that he is lucky for five years; then unlucky for five years, and so on. Bulwer-Lytton believed that he always lost at whist when a certain man was at the same table, or in the same room, or even in the same house. Mr Proctor considers this belief in luck to be 'the very essence of the gambling spirit'. Robert Houdin gives the following maxims which he obtained from a gambler. The first three deal with the kind of game a man should play, that he should be calm and cool and not play for pleasure:

(4) A prudent player should put himself to the test to see if he is 'in vein'. In all cases of doubt you should abstain. (5) There are persons constantly pursued by bad luck. To such I say – 'Never play.' (6) Stubbornness at play is ruin. (7) Remember that fortune does not like people to be overjoyed at her favours, and that she prepares bitter deceptions for the imprudent who are intoxicated by success. Mr Houdin sums up: (8) 'Before risking your money at play you must deeply study

your "vein" and the different probabilities of the game'.[103] The following is a typical case of the superstitious gambler:

This man believed that his clothes had an influence on his luck. If luck followed him he would wear the same clothes whether they were adapted to the weather or not. The same man believed in cards and seats. He objected to anyone making a remark about his luck. He had the strongest objections to our backing him. He was distressed beyond measure if any touched his counters. His constant system of shuffling the cards was at times an annoyance. This was a great card-player.[104]

Miss Bergen found the following superstitions to be current among gamblers and card-players: (1) If your luck is poor walk around your chair three times, lift it, sit down and your luck is secured (general in U.S.). (2) It is bad to play against the grain of the table (general in U.S.). (3) It is unlucky to turn up your hand before the dealer is through (Alabama). (4) It is common to blow on the deal without looking at it for good luck (Providence, R. I., and Salem, Mass.).[105]

A's pet aversion is a man who puts his foot on his chair. He says, 'When I tilt my chair back and find a foot on the rung I feel like swearing, as I know I am hoodooed for that round anyway.' B will not play with a man standing behind him looking over his hand. C puts his stockings on wrong side out to bring him luck. Such cases as these might be multiplied indefinitely.

Rouge et Noir gives the following superstitions common among gamblers:

To turn your back to the moon when playing for money portends ill luck; to lend money, when so engaged, is unlucky; to play on borrowed money is unlucky; playing with money first laid on the altar Christmas night is lucky; some gamblers believe they can cheat luck by going from table to table, or playing at certain intervals. Beau Brummell believed that a crooked sixpence brought him luck and that, on losing it, his luck deserted him (*Raikes Journal*). In Germany the rhyme – 'Lirum, larum, broomsticks hot,/Aged women eat a lot' written on a piece of parchment and kept in the gambler's pocket, was supposed to enable him to win large quantities of gold. In 1897 little china or golden pigs were treasured as fetishes to bring luck. The approach or touch of a hunchback is held to be a sign of luck. In London about Throgmorton Street (the paradise of stock-brokers), there used to sit a man with a bag of nuts into which passers-by thrust a hand, and if they guessed correctly the number, they would be paid a penny for each, if wrong, the guesser paid a penny. Many a speculator regulated his 'bulling' and 'bearing' by his successful or unsuccessful dip into the bag.[106]

Rouge et Noir continues, by giving some of the superstitions of Chinese gamblers.

The forms which this belief takes – such as, for example, belief in seats, clothes, etc., may be largely accounted for by association. I lost two or three times when such a person was in the game; losing becomes associated with him. Further, a generalization is made on this basis from one or two particular cases. Professor Jastrow in a very interesting paper shows, also, that many of the forms of belief, and of superstitious practice, have their basis in the crude form of reasoning by analogy;[107] the clover on account of its trefoil form, suggesting trinity, is good against witches; the ill luck of thirteen and Friday – being probably due to religious associations, etc. This only explains why certain things come to have a lucky significance attached. It does not explain the belief itself. Let us consider this larger problem.

Professor Stuart Culin, in a most comprehensive study,[108] finds that the implements of gambling of primitive man have their origin in methods of divination, and gives many cases where the same methods and implements are used, now for gambling, now for divination. The following abridged abstract from Professor Tylor shows the same facts. He points out that divination by lot was a branch of savage philosophy of high rank; though with us it is a mere appeal to chance, it was not so with them. It was to no blind chance that appeal was made when Matthias was chosen by lot to become the twelfth apostle, or when the Moravian Brethren chose wives for their young men by lot, or the Maoris when they threw lots to find who among them was the thief,[109] or the Guinea Negroes' appeal to the bundle of little leather strips in the hands of the priest;[110] or the Greeks, the ancient Germans,[111] the ancient Italians,[112] or modern Hindus when they left decisions, etc., to be determined by lot.[113]

The uncivilized man thinks that lots or dice are adjusted in their fall with reference to the meaning he may choose to attach to it, and especially is he apt to suppose a spiritual being, standing over the diviner or gambler, shuffling the lots or turning up the dice to make them give their answers. This view held its place firmly in the Middle Ages, and later in history we still find games of chance looked on as results of supernatural operation.' Thomas Gataker in a work *Of the Nature and Use of Lots* (1619), shows that this view prevailed at that time. Jeremy Taylor, forty years later, seems to give credence to the view.[114] Tylor points out the vitality of this notion of super-natural interference as illustrated in the still flourishing art of the gambler's magic and the folklore of the day. 'Arts of divination and games of chance are so similar in principle that the very same instrument passes from one use to the other . . . In the Tonga Islands the cocoanut is now spun to see if a sick person will recover, now spun for amusement.[115] In Samoa the spinning of the nut was formerly used as an art of divination to discover thieves, but now they only keep it as a way of casting lots and as a game of forfeits[116] . . . The connection between gambling and divination is shown by more familiar instruments.[117] The huckle-bones or astragali were used in divination in ancient Rome, being converted into rude dice by numbering the four sides, and even when the Roman gam-bler used the 'tali' for gambling he would invoke a god or his mistress before the throw . . . 'The Chinese gamble by lots for cash and sweetmeats, whilst they also seriously take omens by solemn appeal to lots, kept in the temple, and professional diviners sit in the market-place.[118] Playing cards are still used in Europe for divination. If it is a rule to be relied on that serious precedes the playful, then games of chance may be considered survivals in principle or detail from corresponding processes of magic – as divination in sport made gambling in earnest.[119]

Space will not permit the writer to give here the mass of material that pertains to the belief in luck – the lucky days, numbers, proverbs, the thousand-and-one charms and methods of avoiding bad, and bringing good luck. A volume has been written on the horseshoe alone. Suffice it to say that we have to do with a belief that was almost the guiding philosophy of action for centuries, and one that is not yet dead.

Miss Bergen has collected a volume of such beliefs still prevalent throughout the United States. She points out clearly that they are not merely 'survivals', that these things only survive as long as endures that state of mind which originated them, that as thoughtless habits such phenomena would not long persist, maintaining that her collection emphasizes the doctrine that the essential elements of human nature continue to exist; and that 'we can see the inclination has not disappeared however checked by meditation or through complex experience, and however counteracted by the weight of later maxims. The examiner finds that he himself shares the mental state of the superstitious person.'[120]

That the belief in luck still prevails was shown by a bit of recent Boston history – the 'Lucky Box' craze of February 1900 – initiated by one Henry Parker. Large, conspicuous advertisements appeared for weeks in the daily papers – stating the wonderful powers of the lucky box, giving testimonials of those who had obtained marvellous success after having purchased one. It is estimated that Mr Parker made $75,000 out of the scheme before his mail was stopped by the post office department, a period of three to five weeks. Though he had originally a plant, turning out a thousand boxes a day, he could not supply the demand. Twenty thousand letters addressed to Parker were held up at the Boston post office. An employee of a big transfer company said that he bought five boxes and enjoyed great luck. He said he knew a man who had won $1,000,000 after he purchased a box.[121]

*

The following letter from a man of culture who visited Monte Carlo (and who played only once for the experience) is of value, as it is a faithful introspective account of his feelings on this subject.

And what was my experience? This chiefly – that I was distinctly conscious of partially attributing to some defect or stupidity in my own mind, every venture on an issue that proved a failure; that I groped about within me for something in me like an anticipation or warning (which of course was not to be found) of what the next event was to be, and generally hit upon some vague impulse in my own mind which determined me; that when I succeeded I raked up my gains, with a half impression that I had been a clever fellow, and had made a judicious stake, just as if I had really moved a skilful move at chess; and that when I failed, I thought to myself, 'Ah, I knew all the time I was going wrong in selecting that number, and yet I was fool enough to stick to it,' which was, of course, a pure illusion, for all that I did know the chance was even, or much more than even, against me. But this illusion followed me throughout. I had a sense of *deserving* success when I succeeded, or of having failed through my own willfulness, or wrong-headed caprice, when I failed. When, as not infrequently happened, I put a coin on the corner between

*A passage is omitted. – Eds.

four numbers, receiving eight times my stake, if any of the four numbers turned up, I was conscious of an honest glow of self-applause. I could see the same flickering impressions around me. One man, who was a great winner, evidently thought exceedingly well of his own sagacity of head, and others also, for they were very apt to follow his lead as to stakes, and looked upon him with a sort of temporary and provisional, though partially intellectual, respect. But what quite convinced me of the strength of this curious fallacy of the mind was that when I heard that the youngest of my companions had actually come off a slight winner, having at the last moment retrieved his previous losses by putting his sole remaining two-franc piece, out of the 125 francs he was willing to risk, on the number which represented his age, and gained in consequence thirty-two times his stake, my respect for his shrewdness distinctly rose, and I became sensible of obscure self-reproaches for not having made use of like arbitrary reasons for the selections of the various numbers on which I staked my money. It was true that there was no number high enough for that which would have represented my own age, so I could not have staked on that – but then, why not have selected numbers whereon to stake that had some relation to my own life, the day of the month which gave me birth, or the number of the abode in which I work in town? Evidently, in spite of the clearest understanding of the chances of the game, the moral fallacy which attributes luck or ill luck to something of capacity and deficiency in the individual player, must be profoundly ingrained in us. I am convinced that the shadow of merit and demerit is thrown by the mind over multitudes of actions which have no possibility of wisdom or folly in them – granted, of course, the folly in gambling at all – as in the selection of the particular chance on which you win or lose. When you win at one time and lose at another the mind is almost unable to realize that there was no reason accessible to yourself why you won and why you lost. And so you invent what you know perfectly well to be a fiction – the conception of *some sort of inward divining rod* which guided you right, when you used it properly, and failed only because you did not attend adequately to its indications.

We have here two important factors, one – the very essence of the belief in luck – and especially that phase of the belief represented by guardian angels, etc. – a semi-conscious feeling of a guiding power which gives us a cue to the result; second, we have an exaggerated feeling of our own skill. Both of these are closely allied, both have their basis in a feeling of self-confidence, and both are common to men playing games of chance or

entering on chance adventures. These inner feelings or premonitions are very strong in gamblers – the 'hunch',[122] as it is
called and, like the inner voice of Socrates, it is followed most
religiously.

Closely allied to this is the role played by the imagination.
Professor Lazarus says: 'The particular seductiveness of luck,
the sirens, who in winning or losing entice from stake to stake,
is *"die Phantasie"*. The player hears in roulette the ball rolling,
sees it fall and beholds himself a winner – 'not as though it
were a hope but as a living reality, does he perceive it with the
inner eye and ear of the imagination'. At first he puts no faith
in the inner voice, but later he comes to believe in the phantom
and wishes he had trusted in it.

The above facts, as well as those previously presented in the
returns to the questioner, seem to point to one conclusion, viz.,
that one important element involved is a strong passion for
certainty, a longing for the firm conviction of assurance for
safety. The uncertain state is desired and entered upon, but
ever with the dénouement focal in mind. In fact, so strong is
the passion for the conviction of certainty that one is impelled
again and again to enter upon the uncertain in order to put
one's safety to the test. Thus, if successful, is the conviction of
safety fostered and strengthened, and if unsuccessful, more
prurient is the desire to try again to attain to success, and thus
the general feeling of certitude, a little success tapping the whole
hereditary reservoir in which the feeling of certitude lies latent.
The feeling is thus out of proportion – either in success or
failure to the stimulus. Thus, paradoxical as it may sound,
gambling is a struggle for the certain and sure, i.e. the feeling
of certainty. It is not merely a desire for uncertainty.

We are here dealing with that same great passion for certitude
which is the cornerstone of science, philosophy and religion –
the desire to put the element of chance out of the game. We
cannot do business with it. Take any game of chance, the
player is pitted against a force which is different from a personal opponent. Here is a dark, inscrutable power which decides
for or against him. As Lazarus says, the battle in chance games
is not one of person against person, I against you; but now a
new factor is present. This is *lawless chance* which determines the
issue. There is no possibility of measuring the strength of the
opponent; no means of estimating whether I will be a winner

or loser.[123] It is because of this obscurity, because of the utter impossibility of prevision, that the player feels so utterly helpless before the unknown, in which there is no conception but that of chance as a deciding factor. On the side of chance is all the power and activity; on the side of the player all is impotence and passivity.

Such would be the condition of things when one acts in a game of chance or any chance environment, if there were no other psychic factors entering in to modify this. There is probably no case in which there are not other psychic factors, else a man could scarce bring himself to the point of action. But the equalizing force, which always enters, is that of belief in luck or something akin. It is not blind chance which now decides, but there is a willing power. Lawlessness is put aside for fate, law or will. This is the very meaning of luck, the substitution of a conscious, determining force or will, for an indeterminable, precarious, headless chance – law in place of lawlessness. The contest now becomes one between the players, each man's luck against each other man's. It is not now a question of blind chance, but this – do you or I stand better with the deciding power, who wills? This, says Brinton, is the one feature underlying all religions – viz., that the great force of the world is a personal will.[124] This also is the feature which lies deepest in the gambler's consciousness. The attraction toward this dark, inscrutable power, plus a personal interest, is the background motive. One hopes by gripping the very ground of things to obtain the conviction of certitude. It so fascinates, one is impelled to experiment with it, test its relation to one's own personality. It is a semi-unconscious desire – one ventures when one could not explain the reason. It is due to this same desire for a feeling of certitude that science, philosophy, religion and all endeavor have derived one of their chief motives – to fathom the fascinating unknown – to get the relief, the psychic 'let-down' from tension, a relief which the feeling of certainty always affords.

The significant fact, however, which the study of the gambler's consciousness, as well as that of men acting in uncertainty in general, impresses upon us is that the feeling of certitude frequently exists even in a state of great uncertainty.

We see men having the same feeling of surety under the most precarious conditions. The conditions do not allow of prevision, but the subject feels and believes in himself, and in the favorable outcome of events, just as if prevision were possible. This conviction of safety, expressing itself in the more or less definite objective forms of luck, guardian angels, etc., is a definite biological product. Its effectiveness as a force in evolution in the increasing of action is enormous. It is, we believe, an instinct-feeling as well defined as fear, its direct opposite, and like other similar psychoses is a result of natural selection. We must remember that the state of doubt bred by fear is ever and anon present in force – but still the opposite feeling holds its own, and must be in the ascendant at the moment of action. These two states so strongly counteracting each other are intermittent; now one is focal in consciousness, now the other. And this is precisely the economic value of these anthropomorphic forms of belief – as luck totems, ceremonies and formulas – to hold the faith-state focal.

We will term this feeling – faith – as directly opposite to fear; using faith in a much larger sense than in its general religious connotation. It has its physiological concomitants – the increase of blood-flow and general vital feeling, and is the underpinning of all such states of consciousness as those of the gambler who believes that he will win next time, of the lottery-player that he will be the holder of the winning number, of the soldier that the other man will be shot, of each of us who believes that he is born under a lucky star; it accounts for those 'inner voices' which tell us to do this or that, and we will win, those voices which led men into the belief in guardian angels, etc.; it also accounts for the gambler's 'hunch', those strange premonitions – 'Do this' or 'Avoid that' – and the belief in a special guiding Providence.

It is more definite than what we in general term self-confidence. It is the feeling: I have a special tip, a cue in touch with the very ground principle, who wills. It is the natural result in a race which has been evolved in an environment where to succeed and survive ventures and risks were necessary, and where those who did survive had been successful in their risks. Let us consider this.

McGee[125] in a very interesting account takes the position of a two-sided cosmos among animals and primitive man – 'the danger side in the van; the safety side in the rear – with self as an all important center'; and speaking of primitive man he writes: 'Only religious adherence to experience-shaped instincts, enabled his survival and permitted his tribe to increase.' Further he says:

Nearly all animals manifest a constant realization of three overshadowing factors in nature as they know it – factors expressed by danger, safety, self, or by death and life to self, or in general terms the *evil* of the largely unknown, and the *good* of the fully known – co-ordinated in the vaguely defined subject of badness and goodness; and the chief social activities of animal mates and parents are exercised in gathering their kind into the brightness of the known and educating their native dread of all outer darkness. So, too, the more timid tribesmen . . . betray, in conduct and speech, a dominant intuition of a terrible unknown opposed through self to a small but kindly known. This intuition is not born of inter-tribal strife – it is merely the subjective reflection of implacable environment . . . Over against this appalling evil there is a less complete personified good, reflecting the small nucleus of confident knowledge with its far-reaching penumbra of faith . . . A vague yet persistent placement of the two sides is clearly displayed in the conduct of men and animals – the evil side is outward, the good side at the place or domicile of the individual, and especially of the group . . . In general among the lower and more timid, the back stands for or toward the evil, the face toward the good, and among the higher and more aggressive, the face is set toward danger, e.g., defensively birds and sheep huddle with heads together, savages sleep with heads toward the fire, and timid tribesmen tattoo talismans on their backs, while litters of young carnivora lie facing in two or more directions, self-confident campers sleep with feet toward the fire, and higher soldiery think only of facing the foe.

The early development of self-confidence and faith no doubt began in some such conditions. Only through the exploiting of this terrible *unknown* could knowledge be acquired and advancement gained. It is thus clearly seen how all variations in men along the line of faith in self, feelings of safety in danger and uncertainty would be of the highest selective value. Men with such a characteristic would in consequence be inclined to take greater risks, and those of them that were successful would be much favored in survival through their newly acquired knowledge. Thus the exploiting type of man with great interest in the unknown, with a feeling of immunity from harm, with a strong feeling of coming success, was developed. In its early manifestations this feeling of safety was propped and strengthened by its objectification in such anthropomorphic forms as are exemplified in the complex structure of beliefs in luck, favoring deities, guardian angels, etc. The value of this feeling of certitude in an environment of uncertainty cannot be overestimated. It is a biological device to procure from men the greatest amount of activity – a device which takes no account of the safety of the individual. Antipodal to this feeling is that of fear. The two are ever in conflict. Character is largely determined by the relative strength in the individual of each. Every game of chance, every risk which a man runs, is an interrogation of his feeling – a question put to the powers that be, whether or no such a feeling is warrantable. Do I stand in with the deciding will or no? Fear says, 'No.' By being successful one gets a warrant, an assurance that one is lucky. Man will not believe that the deciding power is impartial to *him*. Who of us does not believe in his very soul, in the face of all evidence to the contrary, that *he* is 'born under a lucky star'? It is one of the chief encouragements in life – this more or less vague feeling that a kindly fate is pulling our way. Each of us believes himself *sui generis* and that the mighty will behind things is especially behind *him*. To men entering upon great enterprises such a feeling is indispensable. It made a Napoleon – the child of destiny – possible to the world. It also gave the Christian world its Christ.

Montesquieu and Diderot both were of the opinion that the gratifying self-reliance in the feeling that I am a special favorite of fortune was the one particular motive of hazard plays.[126] For one who does not believe in blind chance, a pure game of chance, or any risk, is the purest form of obtaining an expression from the guiding power, or favor or disfavor. A phenomenon closely allied is the desire to have one's fortune told. It is a very indefinite notion of somehow getting a clue to how I stand in relation to the universal mechanism. This is the central problem in an environment of uncertainty.

Thus we see how closely the gambling impulse approximates the philosophical and religious motive. With the savage, as we have seen, gambling and religion are almost identical. The one chief incentive to the savage for gambling is to see how he stands with his favoring or disfavoring deities. The very implements he uses are developments from divinatory implements and often the same devices are used, now in divination, now in gambling. In deciding any specific case as to whether he will go to war, or as to which direction he shall proceed to forage for food, he trusts to the answer from his deities, as given by the fall of his divinatory implements. Has a theft been committed, his deities reveal the guilty man through the same means. In all fortuitous circumstances he trusts implicitly to these same divinatory means. And with these he gambles in his time of recreation. Is it not clear why gambling is of the most serious moment to him? Now he is not seeking encouragement or direction in a specific case but in a general case. He feels that the fall of these implements, directly guided by the deity, is pregnant with meaning respecting his general status with that being. Thus it is the savage is so desperate a gambler, regarding his whole fortune, aye, even his wives and children, as insignificant in comparison with this decision for or against him. So also in a less intense degree is it with the modern believer in luck. This explains much of the almost inaccountable states of emotional frenzy gamblers display, and their tenacity in play.

Lucky or unlucky, that is the paramount issue with them both. No matter how much a man may understand of the calculus of probabilities, when he sits in the game, like the observer above quoted, he feels somehow he has in him a divining rod pointing the way to success if only he would be guided. The step to absolute superstition is a short and easy one. Men need sorely the assurance of their being a vital part in the universal economy. Hence the unfailing interest in the transcendent. The philosopher seeks by reason to get a grip on the ground principle; the religious man seeks it by faith; the gambler by faith strengthened by the favoring fall of the die.

Significant in this connection is the fact that there seems to be a correlation between the extensity and intensity of the gambling passion and the religious life of certain races. Professor Lazarus, remarking on this, says:

That race which shows the deepest religious development of all races up to the present, that has built up and developed the richest and most sincere spiritual life, the Teutonic, showed in earliest times a passionate inclination towards chance plays . . . The property so clearly conspicuous in the course of the history of the Teutonic peoples for the transcendent, the abstract and idealistic shows itself also in the inclination towards those plays in which the idea of fate in dark form and figure is represented. Stern moralists might object to see the highest ideas placed in connection with immoral plays themselves; but psychological facts must be investigated without prejudice where it has to do with tracing back a historically believed universal property in the innate character of a folk spirit.[127]

To realize the enormous role which this factor that we have termed faith, i.e. the feeling of safety under circumstances of great uncertainty and risk, has played in the development of civilizations, a glance at one or two significant cases in history is necessary. The Jews in an environment of uncertainty, i.e., wandering in the desert – with this feeling as a basis – created that system of monotheism which has been adopted by the whole Christian world. As the gambler must have the conviction of safety in his staking in games of chance, and so, on this feeling of faith as a basis, creates the objective forms of luck, etc., so the Jew under the same stress created the most effective of all confidence-producing agents – one omnipotent God – *who especially favored him.* In each case the principle is the same – that biological factor selected in the race – to instil confidence in the face of danger, that device to put chance out of the game. So wherever we find men acting under circumstances of great risk, we find this feeling asserting itself. Also it is where this conviction of immunity from danger is especially strong that we find races and individuals of the exploiting type. The Romans had it to an extraordinary degree. And as Tylor says: 'In the Roman world the doctrine of guardian angels came to be accepted as a philosophy of human life. Each man had his *"genius natalis"* associated with him from birth to death – influencing his action and fate.' We have here the backbone of individualism and optimism.

Just as this state of mind was strong in the Jew and Roman – the two great exploiting individualistic races of the ancient world – so it is one of the chief factors in the Anglo-Saxon mind. As a prop to this feeling of certainty and safety, he also has his religion. The Anglo-Saxon race believes as firmly that it is the favored people of the one great God as the Jew did two thousand years ago. And each individual believes that *he* is especially favored. His faith in his own ultimate safety and good fortune is something stupendous. If a great gambling enterprise, as in the case of the Philippine Islands, presents itself – a whole nation cries 'Manifest Destiny', and nearly every preacher in the land proclaims it to be the will of God. The gambler's faith in his luck – his constant belief that next time he will win – is but a fact similar to this.

It must be remembered, however, that though in every case the religion seems to give man this faith, it is the feeling of faith, this conviction of safety and certainty, which gave rise to this particular form of religious belief. On our thesis this feeling is one which has been selected in the course of evolution as a necessary factor in an environment of risk and uncertainty. It may have no objectification in religious or superstitious forms at all. In the case of men of genius this is often exemplified – as seen in the man who perceives a work to be done, precarious and uncertain in its outcome, yet who in his soul feels he is the man to accomplish that work and has little fear or doubt. This, says G. Stanley Hall, is the essence of genius. At root it is the same feeling or conviction of safety and certainty as gave rise to such beliefs as luck, guardian spirits and a special Providence. The only difference is that the man does not necessarily account for it by attributing its source to something external to himself, though often this is true as in the case of Napoleon, 'the child of destiny'. From this standpoint we may expect a race in whom a large part of what we now call religious belief and motive will be identical with normal life motives.

This factor of faith in self safety is often of a deleterious influence in cases of abnormal optimism where the individual trusts entirely to luck and not at all to his own effort. It is only too true that favorable chance is the goddess of the idle, the criminal and the desperate. On the other hand, this element of faith has additional value in that it places all the favorable things that happen to a man in italics. A horseshoe hung over your door is equivalent to underscoring everything fortunate which happens to you. The man who believes that he is lucky selects and isolates the happy things which happen to him. Further, the belief that you will succeed in an uncertain and difficult undertaking is often half the battle.

Conclusion

1. In the preceding we have attempted to study the psychic attitude and reaction of man in the face of one of the great

conditioning factors in life – that of chance and risk. Study shows two opposite feelings arising, fear and faith, i.e. a fluctuating feeling of certitude. The one tends to make man withdraw or at least remain inactive; the other to throw aside the idea of a blind chance and to replace it by one of law or order, i.e. a favoring will, and in consequence leads to taking risks and, in general, increased activity. In gambling this latter feeling expresses itself predominantly, as in this play the faith type of man is selected. His belief in his immunity from harm, in his final success, is his most marked characteristic. This feeling of certitude is the great biological organ which functions to suppress the idea of chance and to minimize the respect for the danger in risk. It is closely in touch with the philosophical question which is the paramount issue of every life – 'How do I stand in relation to the deciding will?' It is not surprising that this factor should be central in that great species of adult play which we have attempted to analyse in this study.

2. The preceding study also suggests that an environment of uncertain content may be necessary to the human species, in as much as it has been evolved therein; that it is an essential condition to give that state of suspense which is the ideal condition of all forms of pursuit. This need of tension, together with the feeling of faith in one's safety, is perhaps one of the most effective of all agents reacting against the great psychic tendency towards fixity, a tendency which expresses itself in the formation of habits and in the accepting of absolute standards – the natural end being arrest of development.

3. A third point worthy of emphasis is the emotional intensity incident to gambling – arising from the presence of many of the strongest egoistic instinctive feelings. We find that this is one of the chief incentives to gamble. To seek intense states of consciousness seems, as many writers have pointed out, a normal tendency. This tendency, which seems on the increase, may be of high selective value. The influence of intense emotional states on the bodily metabolism is now well recognized. The Indians realized their therapeutic value when, in cases of sickness, large gambling parties were assembled in which all present became intensely excited, often nearly wild. To these conventions the sick were brought. This is very suggestive. The race has probably nearly reached its limit in evolution along anatomical development. But physiologically, the possibilities

are unbounded. May it not be that this increasing tendency to seek emotional states is an attempt, through natural selection, to put man on a higher metabolic level? The psychology of excess of all kinds becomes a large problem in this light.

It is significant to note that we find gambling very prevalent in the early formative periods of society, and in newly exploited countries. Under these circumstances, the will to live increases with the increase of danger and uncertainty. Hence, intense emotional states which increase the feeling of the reality of self as well as the bodily metabolism are sought. This, together with the exercise of the feelings of hope and faith in self that gambling affords, makes it in early states of society attractive. So in later periods gambling is indulged in as an outlet, a channelling of the pent-up biological forces which a narrow specialized life does not afford. Man's biological heredity in the manifold form of various egoistic impulses cannot be ignored. They demand expression. There is, so to speak, a katabolic imperative. This outlet gambling furnishes in that it so well simulates the environment of primitive man. Again, a man in a narrow specialty feels his restrictions. He may be making needles and feel that he can make a machine. But give him strong emotional excitation, which increases the entire bodily metabolism, and he is on the metabolic level that he would be on were he making machines. He has all the enthusiasm and feeling of genius for the moment, though he may not be doing the work. Such results gambling excitations, alcoholic intoxications and the like produce. The problem is how to give normal emotional channeling the safety-valve of this biological heredity.

4. The study of the gambling impulse further emphasizes the fact that man easily gives up the intellectual for the instinctive life; that he has not learned, as well as many writers would have us believe, the lesson of work and the power of sustained voluntary attention. This has been considered one of the great achievements of civilization. One of the chief motives for gambling, as we have seen above, is to obtain the rewards of labor without laboring. This is one of its chief pleasures, to have acquired a dollar without sustained toil. It is also worthy of note that often the gambler expends as much energy in obtaining his dollar as if he labored for it. In the one case, however, the attention is spontaneous, in the other voluntary.

5. In the light of this investigation a few words in regard to theories of play may be instructive. It is a fair question whether plays of adults must be put under a different category from plays of children. Let us take a retrospect. We have been dealing with a form of play found among all peoples. The following points are most significant. (*a*) Gambling has for one of its chief motives the acquisition of property – in other words, power. (*b*) Gambling calls forth some of the deepest of human instincts. It is a courting of fear – fear with which you must trifle if, as it has been so well expressed, you wish to taste the intensest joys of living. So, also, it is the seeking after feelings of faith in self-safety in the face of danger – a play upon the hereditary orchestration of success in the race; a feeling which is our legacy in being the progeny of the survivors and the fit in the struggle for existence. So also, as we have seen, gambling raises into consciousness many egoistic instinct-feelings – as the desire to dominate and humiliate your fellow, the love of conflict – your courage and power against mine – the satisfaction of being the object of jealousy, the pleasures derived from the exercise of cunning, deceit and concealment. (*c*) Gambling also excites the deepest of all interests in life – that in the transcendent, the dark obscure beyond. This, together with the general uncertainty of the environment, together with the fluctuations between faith and in self and ever-recurring fear – plus the ever-present seeking for material gain – gives that tension which to many is the very definition of life.

Can you find a half dozen deeper things in man than these, which form the very nucleus of this great play? It is, indeed, a simulation of life-feelings. But of life in which all pity and sympathy for man is absent; in which self is the all important center; in which to gain, to fight and to feel God is with you are all in all; in which each of these is intensified and exaggerated. Neither the theory of play set forth by Spencer nor that of Gross, nor any of the theories of play the writer has met, wholly satisfies these conditions. We meet here with an expression of instinct centres which no doubt are highly anabolic. But it is not necessarily a case of surplus energy in the organism which is the meaning of Spencer as I understand it. If these psychic phenomena be latent in some organic condition, and their manifestations depend on the cells of these organic centers being in an anabolic state, may it not be that those centers which are oldest, acquired first in the process of evolution, are first objects of nutrition, and that each organic center receives energy according to its priority of age, especially if for a long period it was required to function actively in the preservation of the species. Thus it might result, where the supply of energy was at any time insufficient for the whole organism, that these oldest organic centers would be nourished, while variations acquired later would not, even though these might be of more value at the time in fitting the organism for survival. One answers immediately that those old organic conditions, having ceased to be of value and having become rudimentary organs, are finally sloughed off. But is this the case in the psychic realm? Is it not true that organs only become rudimentary through disuse? Do psychic centers ever cease to function actively? Do not old instincts – though of no value at present – still receive exercise by thrusting themselves at every possible opportunity into activity – especially in moments of recreation – determining thus, as I have mentioned, the forms and nature of play? At least it is clear that this being the case, they tend to become rudimentary much less than is the case with other organs of the body. Even with these latter, may it not be that organs, such, for example, as the tail of the monkey, long resisted degeneration because, even after the establishment of the monkey in the terrestrial environment, the tail was used to swing the monkey in moments of recreation. Certain it is, there is a glow of satisfaction in using these once-valuable organs. So in the psychic realm, even though these instinct centres may in time become rudimentary, is it not at least clear that they resist degeneration a long time by thus expressing themselves in forms of play in moments of recreation? In the light of these considerations play, especially adult play, becomes a subject of not a little sociological and ethical importance. Thus in play, for a long time at least, a race would revive its psychic past, having created the stimuli prevalent in the primitive environment. Play would thus be an index to the history of the psychic life – a kind of historico-anthropological theater.

6. As to the contribution of this study to the subject of ethics, it seems to the writer there is much which speaks for itself. Conduct is the result of latent biological forces; much conduct being the forced expression of highly anabolic instinctive centers which have functioned through long previous

periods in preserving the species. These resist for a long time degeneration, do not tend readily to become rudimentary, and hence are ever on the threshhold of activity. Prohibition is impossible. If this activity is a menace to our present social conditions, substitutions must be offered. In other words these instinct-activities must be channeled into harmless courses. To accomplish this there is necessary a thorough study of these instincts in their biological and genetic origins. This gives us a hint of what ethics and also sociology may gain by leaning on their natural supporter – psychology.

Notes

1. John Ashton, *The History of Gambling in England* (London: Duckworth, 1898), p. 3.
2. Andrew Steinmetz, *The Gaming Table: Its Votaries and Victims*, 2 vols. (London: Tinsley, 1870), Vol. 1, p. 57.
3. Ashton, op. cit., p. 4.
4. J. Talboys Wheeler, *The History of India from the Earliest Days* (London, 1868), Vol. 1, pp. 175–85.
5. Steinmetz, loc. cit.
6. ibid., p. 59
7. Jean Barbeyrac, *Traité du Jeu*, 3 vols. (Amsterdam, 1737), Vol. 2, p. 345.
8. John Disney, *A View of Ancient Laws Against Sin, Morality, and Profaneness* (Cambridge: Crownfield, 1729). Quoted from Ashton, op. cit., p. 5.
9. Huc, *Chinese Empire*. Quoted from Rouge et Noir, *The Gambling World: Anecdotic Memories and Stories* (London: Hutchinson, 1898), op. 35–6.
10. S. Wills Williams, *The Middle Kingdom* (New York, 1900), Vol. 1, p. 825.
11. Steinmetz, op. cit., Vol. 1, pp. 59–61.
12. Ashton, op. cit., p. 7.
13. ibid., pp. 11–12.
14. ibid., Vol. 1, ch. 4.
15. Juvenal, *Satires*, I, 87. Cf. Steinmetz, op. cit., Vol. 1, p. 67.
16. Steinmetz, op. cit., Vol. 1, p. 68.
17. Tacitus, *Germania*, 24.
18. Steinmetz, op. cit., Vol. 1, p. 157.
19. ibid., Vol. 1, p. 70.
20. ibid., Vol. 1, p. 78ff.
21. ibid., Vol. 1, p. 87–8.
22. Dusaulx, *De la Passion du Jeu* (1779). Quoted from Steinmetz, op. cit., Vol. 1, p. 105.
23. Rouge et Noir, op. cit., p. 259.
24. Ashton, op. cit., p. 12.

25. ibid., p. 13.
26. Theophilus Lucas, *Memoirs of the Lives, Intrigues and Comical Adventures of the Most Famous Gamesters and Celebrated Sharpers in the Reigns of Charles II, James II, William III, and Queen Anne* (London, 1714) [reprinted in Cyril Hughes Hartmann, *Games and Gamesters of the Restoration*, London: Routledge, 1930—eds.].
27. Ashton, op. cit., p. 41.
28. Quoted in ibid., pp. 45ff.
29. ibid., pp. 55ff.
30. ibid., pp. 76ff.
31. ibid., ch. 6, 'The Rise and Progress of Modern Gambling in England'.
32. ibid.
33. *Reminiscences*, Section 3. Quoted from Ashton, ibid., p. 99.
34. *Frazer's Magazine*, Vol. 8, pp. 191–206.
35. Ashton, op. cit., p. 128, ch. 8, on Crockford's Club.
36. Anyone interested in the history of the English turf is referred to Ashton's chapter on this, and that in Rouge et Noir, op. cit.
37. Rouge et Noir, op. cit., pp. 40–41. The reader who is interested will find in Steinmetz, op. cit., a chapter (Vol. 1, ch. 14) on the laws against gambling in various countries.
38. J. F. B. Lillard, ed., *Poker Stories* (New York: Francis P. Harper).
39. The reader is referred to Steinmetz, op. cit., Vol. 1, ch. 13; and 'Rouge et Noir', op. cit., ch. 8, for excellent accounts of lottery. Many excellent references may be obtained from Poole's index.
40. MacMaster, *History of the People of the United States* (New York, 1883), Vol. 1, pp. 587–8.
41. ibid., Vol. 2, p. 23.
42. ibid., Vol. 4, p. 529.
43. These figures are taken from 'Rouge et Noir', op. cit., pp. 254–5.
44. Most of these are taken from Steinmetz, op. cit., Vol. 2, ch. 11.
45. Bancroft, *Races and Peoples*, Vol. 1, pp. 113–14, 123, 219, 244, 353, 517, 587. See also a paper by Stuart Culin, 'Chess and Playing Cards': Catalogue of Games and Implements for Divination exhibited by the Natural Museum in connection with the Atlantic Exposition, 1895, *Smithsonian Institution Report* (1896), pp. 665–942.
46. Stevens in *Pac. R. R. Rep.*, Vol. 1, pp. 404, 412. Cf. Bancroft, op. cit., Vol. 1, p. 281n.
47. ibid., Vol. 2, pp. 299–301.
48. P. de Charlevoix, *Journal d'un voyage dans l'Amerique*, quoted in Culin, op. cit., pp. 721–2; and Brébeuf, 'Relations de Jésuites, Relations de l'année 1636', in Culin, op. cit., p. 722.
49. Morgan, *League of the Iroquois* (Rochester, New York, 1851).
50. J. G. Owens, *Popular Science Monthly*, Vol. 39, pp. 39–50.
51. Culin, op. cit., pp. 751–4; Bancroft, op. cit., Vol. 1, p. 244; Colonel R. S. Dodge, *Thirty-three Years among our Wild Indians*, pp. 325–33.
52. Americus Featherman, *Social History of the Races of Mankind* (London: Trubner, 1881–9), p. 302.
53. ibid., p. 325.
54. ibid., p. 382.

55. ibid., p. 404.
56. ibid., p. 416.
57. ibid., p. 448.
58. ibid. (1890), p. 16.
59. ibid., p. 489.
60. Arminius Vambéry, *Sketches of Central Asia* (London, 1868), p. 110.
61. Steinmetz, op. cit., Vol. 2, pp. 50ff.
62. ibid., p. 52.
63. Dusaulx, op. cit., Cf. Steinmetz, op. cit., Vol., 2, p. 54.
64. Steinmetz, op. cit., Vol. 2, p. 53.
65. ibid., pp. 54ff.
66. *Annual Register* (London: Longman, 1812).
67. Barbeyrac, op. cit., Vol. 2, pp. 338–9.
68. ibid., pp. 342ff.
69. ibid., p. 345.
70. Nimrod, 'Anatomy of Gaming', *Frazer's Magazine*, Vol. 16, p. 16.
71. Quoted in Steinmetz, op. cit., Vol. 1, p. 300.
72. ibid., p. 66.
73. Cotton, *Compleat Gamester* (1674). Quoted from Ashton, op. cit., pp. 1–2.
74. *Traité des Jeux de Hazard*, ch. 7, p. 225 (or ch. 9, p. 91, 2nd edn.) from Barbeyrac, op. cit., Vol. 2, p. 236.
75. ibid., pp. 336–8.
76. Steinmetz, op. cit., Vol. 2, ch. 3.
77. ibid., Vol. 1, p. 24.
78. Nimrod, 'The Anatomy of Gaming', pp. 9–24.
79. Ribot, *Psychology of the Emotions* (New York, 1897), p. 31n.
80. 'The Gambling Instinct', *Spectator*, Vol. 66, p. 286.
81. Drähms, *The Criminal* (New York, 1900), p. 119.
82. Moritz Lazarus, *Über die Reize des Spiels* (Berlin, 1883), pp. 58–88.
83. W. I. Thomas, 'The Gambling Instinct', *American Journal of Sociology*, Vol. 6, No. 2, (1901), pp. 750–63.
84. Curtis, *Queer Luck*; Lillard, op. cit., p. 231; Clarence L. Cullen, *Taking Chances* (New York, 1900), p. 269.
85. Lucas, op. cit.
86. Lazarus, op. cit., p. 59.
87. W. Wundt, *Lectures on Human and Animal Psychology* (London, 1897), p. 376.
88. Bain, *Emotions and Will* (London, 1899), pp. 220ff.
89. Sully, *Sensation and Intuition*, p. 298. Cf. Bain, op. cit., p. 222.
90. Lazarus, op. cit., p. 58.
91. George Eliot, *The Lifted Veil* (Oxford University Press, 1906; Hurst & Co.)
92. The reader is referred for a more lengthy account of the battle element to Thomas, op. cit., pp. 751ff.
93. i.e., the early part of the eighteenth century. Cf. Ashton, op. cit., chapter on betting.
94. McKay, *Memoirs of Extraordinary Delusions*, Vol. 1, p. 14.
95. J. P. Wood, *Memoirs of John Law* (Edinburgh, 1824), p. 44.

96. H. D. Adams, *Under Many Flags* (New York, 1896), p. 174; cf. also Wood, op. cit.
97. McKay, op. cit., Vol. 1, pp. 67–9.
98. ibid., p. 89.
99. Thomas, op. cit., speaks of this desire to get rid of routine and the interest in those forms of acquiring money based on speculation and hazard.
100. Culin, op. cit., p. 722.
101. 'Luck: Its Laws and Limits', *Longman's Magazine*, Vol. 8, pp. 256–69.
102. The term 'in vein' is difficult to translate. If a man is 'in vein', luck favours him and he is sure to win. When he loses it is thus always attributed to luck.
103. Steinmetz, op. cit., Vol. 2, pp. 253–9.
104. ibid., Vol. 1, p. 223.
105. Bergen, *Current Superstitions*, p. 79.
106. Rouge et Noir, op. cit., pp. 29–32.
107. J. Jastrow, *Fact and Fable in Psychology* (Boston and New York, 1900), pp. 236–74.
108. Culin, op. cit., pp. 665–942.
109. Edward B. Tylor, *Origins of Culture*, 2 vols. (London: John Murray), Vol. 1, p. 220.
110. Bosman, *Guinese Kust Letters*. English translation in Pinkerton, Vol. 16, p. 399.
111. Tacitus, *Germania*, 10.
112. *Smith's Dictionary of Greece and Rome*; art.; oraculum, sortes.
113. Roberts, *Oriental Illustrations*, p. 163.
114. Jeremy Taylor, *Ductor Dubitantium*, in *Works*, Vol. 14, p. 337.
115. Mariner, *Tonga Islands*, 2: 239.
116. Turner, *Polynesia*, p. 214; Williams, *Figi*, Vol. 1, p. 228. Cf. Cranz, *Grönland*, p. 231.
117. Cf. *Smith's Dictionary of Greece and Rome*; art.; 'Talus'.
118. Doolittle, *Chinese*, Vol. 2, pp. 108, 285–7, 384; Bastian, *Östliche Asien*.
119. Edward B. Tylor, *Primitive Culture*, 1, pp. 78–83.
120. Bergen, op. cit., p. 5 of Introduction.
121. *Boston Herald* (11 March, 1900), p. 8.
122. The term 'hunch' is very common among gamblers, and the religious strictness with which this 'hunch', or feeling in one of immediate coming success is followed is very significant.
123. Lazarus, op. cit., pp. 73ff.
124. Brinton, *Primitive Religions*, ch. 1.
125. J. W. McGee, 'The Beginnings of Mathematics', *American Anthropologist*, Vol. 1, No. 4, pp. 646–74.
126. Lazarus, op. cit., pp. 72, 73.
127. ibid., pp. 79–80.

Sigmund Freud

Dostoevsky and Parricide*

Four facets may be distinguished in the rich personality of
Dostoevsky: the creative artist, the neurotic, the moralist and
the sinner. How is one to find one's way in this bewildering
complexity?

The creative artist is the least doubtful: Dostoevsky's place
is not far behind Shakespeare. *The Brothers Karamazov* is the
most magnificent novel every written; the episode of the Grand
Inquisitor, one of the peaks in the literature of the world, can
hardly be valued too highly. Before the problem of the creative
artist analysis must, alas, lay down its arms.

The moralist in Dostoevsky is the most readily assailable. If
we seek to rank him high as a moralist on the plea that only a
man who has gone through the depths of sin can reach the
highest summit of morality, we are neglecting a doubt that
arises. A moral man is one who reacts to temptation as soon as
he feels it in his heart, without yielding to it. A man who
alternately sins and then in his remorse erects high moral
standards lays himself open to the reproach that he has made
things too easy for himself. He has not achieved the essence of
morality, renunciation, for the moral conduct of life is a
practical human interest. He reminds one of the barbarians of
the great migrations, who murdered and did penance for it, till
penance became an actual technique for enabling murder to be
done. Ivan the Terrible behaved in exactly this way; indeed
this compromise with morality is a characteristic Russian trait.
Nor was the final outcome of Dostoevsky's moral strivings any-

*From *The Standard Edition of the Complete Psychological Works of Sigmund
Freud*, ed. and trans. James Strachey, 23 vols. (London: Hogarth Press,
1953—); Vol. 21, pp. 177–94. Reprinted by permission of Sigmund Freud
Copyrights Ltd., The Institute of Psycho-Analysis, the Hogarth Press Ltd.
and Basic Books Inc.

thing very glorious. After the most violent struggles to reconcile the instinctual demands of the individual with the claims of the community, he landed in the retrograde position of submission both to temporal and spiritual authority, of veneration both for the Tsar and for the God of the Christians, and of a narrow Russian nationalism – a position which lesser minds have reached with smaller effort. This is the weak point in that great personality. Dostoevsky threw away the chance of becoming a teacher and liberator of humanity and made himself one with their gaolers. The future of human civilization will have little to thank him for. It seems probable that he was condemned to this failure by his neurosis. The greatness of his intelligence and the strength of his love for humanity might have opened to him another, an apostolic, way of life.

To consider Dostoevsky as a sinner or a criminal rouses violent opposition, which need not be based upon a philistine assessment of criminals. The real motive for this opposition soon becomes apparent. Two traits are essential in a criminal: boundless egoism and a strong destructive urge. Common to both of these, and a necessary condition for their expression, is absence of love, lack of an emotional appreciation of (human) objects. One at once recalls the contrast to this presented by Dostoevsky – his great need of love and his enormous capacity for love, which is to be seen in manifestations of exaggerated kindness and caused him to love and to help where he had a right to hate and to be revengeful, as, for example, in his relations with his first wife and her lover. That being so, it must be asked why there is any temptation to reckon Dostoevsky among the criminals. The answer is that it comes from his choice of material, which singles out from all others violent, murderous and egoistic characters, thus pointing to the existence of similar tendencies within himself, and also from certain facts in his life, like his passion for gambling and his possible confession to a sexual assault upon a young girl.[1] The contradiction is resolved by the realization that Dostoevsky's very strong destructive instinct, which might easily have made him a criminal, was in his actual life directed mainly against his own person (inward instead of outward) and thus found expression as masochism and a sense of guilt. Nevertheless, his personality retained sadistic traits in plenty, which show themselves in his irritability, his love of tormenting and his intolerance even towards

people he loved, and which appear also in the way in which, as an author, he treats his readers. Thus in little things he was a sadist towards others, and in bigger things a sadist towards himself, in fact a masochist – that is to say the mildest, kindliest, most helpful person possible.

We have selected three factors from Dostoevsky's complex personality, one quantitative and two qualitative: the extraordinary intensity of his emotional life, his perverse innate instinctual disposition, which inevitably marked him out to be a sado-masochist or a criminal, and his unanalysable artistic gift. This combination might very well exist without neurosis; there are people who are complete masochists without being neurotic. Nevertheless, the balance of forces between his instinctual demands and the inhibitions opposing them (plus the available methods of sublimation) would even so make it necessary to classify Dostoevsky as what is known as an 'instinctual character'. But the position is obscured by the simultaneous presence of neurosis, which, as we have said, was not in the circumstances inevitable, but which comes into being the more readily, the richer the complication which has to be mastered by the ego. For neurosis is after all only a sign that the ego has not succeeded in making a synthesis, that in attempting to do so it has forfeited its unity.

How then, strictly speaking, does his neurosis show itself? Dostoevsky called himself an epileptic, and was regarded as such by other people, on account of his severe attacks, which were accompanied by loss of consciousness, muscular convulsions and subsequent depression. Now it is highly probable that this so-called epilepsy was only a symptom of his neurosis and must accordingly be classified as hystero-epilepsy – that is, as severe hysteria. We cannot be completely certain on this point for two reasons – firstly, because the anamnestic data on Dostoevsky's alleged epilepsy are defective and untrustworthy, and secondly, because our understanding of pathological states combined with epileptiform attacks is imperfect.

To take the second point first. It is unnecessary here to reproduce the whole pathology of epilepsy, for it would throw no decisive light on the problem. But this may be said. The old *morbus sacer* is still in evidence as an ostensible clinical entity, the uncanny disease with its incalculable, apparently unprovoked convulsive attacks, its changing of the character into irritability and aggressiveness, and its progressive lowering of all the mental faculties. But the outlines of this picture are quite lacking in precision. The attacks, so savage in their onset, accompanied by biting of the tongue and incontinence of urine and working up to the dangerous *status epilepticus* with its risk of severe self-injuries, may, nevertheless, be reduced to brief periods of *absence*, or rapidly passing fits of vertigo or may be replaced by short spaces of time during which the patient does something out of character, as though he were under the control of his unconscious. These attacks, though as a rule determined, in a way we do not understand, by purely physical causes, may nevertheless owe their first appearance to some purely mental cause (a fright, for instance) or may react in other respects to mental excitations. However characteristic intellectual impairment may be in the overwhelming majority of cases, at least *one* case is known to us (that of Helmholtz) in which the affliction did not interfere with the highest intellectual achievement. (Other cases of which the same assertion has been made are either disputable or open to the same doubts as the case of Dostoevsky himself.) People who are victims of epilepsy may give an impression of dullness and arrested development just as the disease often accompanies the most palpable idiocy and the grossest cerebral defects, even though not as a necessary component of the clinical picture. But these attacks, with all their variations, also occur in other people who display complete mental development and, if anything, an excessive and as a rule insufficiently controlled emotional life. It is no wonder in these circumstances that it has been found impossible to maintain that 'epilepsy' is a single clinical entity. The similarity that we find in the manifest symptoms seems to call for a functional view of them. It is as though a mechanism for abnormal instinctual discharge had been laid down organically, which could be made use of in quite different circumstances – both in the case of disturbances of cerebral activity due to severe histolytic or toxic affections, and also in the case of inadequate control over the mental economy and at times when the activity of the energy operating in the mind reaches crisis-pitch. Behind this dichotomy we have a glimpse of the identity of the underlying mechanism of instinctual discharge. Nor can that mechanism stand remote from the sexual processes, which are fundamentally of toxic origin: the earliest physicians described coition as a minor epilepsy, and thus recognized in the sexual act a mitigation and adaptation of the epileptic method of discharging stimuli.[2]

The 'epileptic reaction', as this common element may be called, is also undoubtedly at the disposal of the neurosis whose essence it is to get rid by somatic means of amounts of excitation which it cannot deal with psychically. Thus the epileptic attack becomes a symptom of hysteria and is adapted and modified by it just as it is by the normal sexual process of discharge. It is therefore quite right to distinguish between an organic and an 'affective' epilepsy. The practical significance of this is that a person who suffers from the first kind has a disease of the brain, while a person who suffers from the second kind is a neurotic. In the first case his mental life is subjected to an alien disturbance from without, in the second case the disturbance is an expression of his mental life itself.

It is extremely probable that Dostoevsky's epilepsy was of the second kind. This cannot, strictly speaking, be proved. To do so we should have to be in a position to insert the first appearance of the attacks and their subsequent fluctuations into the thread of his mental life; and for that we know too little. The descriptions of the attacks themselves teach us nothing and our information about the relations between them and Dostoevsky's experiences is defective and often contradictory. The most probable assumption is that the attacks went back far into his childhood, that their place was taken to begin with by milder symptoms and that they did not assume an epileptic form until after the shattering experience of his eighteenth year – the murder of his father.[3] It would be very much to the point if it could be established that they ceased completely during his exile in Siberia, but other accounts contradict this.[4]

The unmistakable connection between the murder of the father in *The Brothers Karamazov* and the fate of Dostoevsky's own father has struck more than one of his biographers, and has led them to refer to 'a certain modern school of psychology'. From the standpoint of psycho-analysis (for that is what is meant), we are tempted to see in that event the severest trauma and to regard Dostoevsky's reaction to it as the turning-point of his neurosis. But if I undertake to substantiate this view psycho-analytically, I shall have to risk the danger of being unintelligible to all those readers who are unfamiliar with the language and theories of psychoanalysis.

We have one certain starting-point. We know the meaning of the first attacks from which Dostoevsky suffered in his early years, long before the incidence of the 'epilepsy'. These attacks had the significance of death: they were heralded by a fear of death and consisted of lethargic, somnolent states. The illness first came over him while he was still a boy, in the form of a sudden, groundless melancholy, a feeling, as he later told his friend Soloviev, as though he were going to die on the spot. And there in fact followed a state exactly similar to real death. His brother Andrei tells us that even when he was quite young Fyodor used to leave little notes about before he went to sleep, saying that he was afraid he might fall into this death-like sleep during the night and therefore begged that his burial should be postponed for five days.[5]

We know the meaning and intention of such deathlike attacks.[6] They signify an identification with a dead person, either with someone who is really dead or with someone who is still alive and whom the subject wishes dead. The latter case is the more significant. The attack then has the value of a punishment. One has wished another person dead, and now one *is* this other person and is dead oneself. At this point psycho-analytical theory brings in the assertion that for a boy this other person is usually his father and that the attack (which is termed hysterical) is thus a self-punishment for a death-wish against a hated father.

Parricide, according to a well-known view, is the principal and primal crime of humanity as well as of the individual. (See my *Totem and Taboo*.) It is in any case the main source of the sense of guilt, though we do not know if it is the only one: researches have not yet been able to establish with certainty the mental origin of guilt and the need for expiation. But it is not necessary for it to be the only one. The psychological situation is complicated and requires elucidation. The relation of a boy to his father is, as we say, an 'ambivalent' one. In addition to the hate which seeks to get rid of the father as a rival, a measure of tenderness for him is also habitually present. The two attitudes of mind combine to produce identification with the father; the boy wants to be in his father's place because he admires him and wants to be like him, and also because he wants to put him out of the way. This whole development now comes up against a powerful obstacle. At a certain moment the child comes to understand that an attempt to remove his father as a rival would be punished by him with castration. So from fear of castration – that is, in the interests of preserving his masculinity – he gives up his wish to possess his mother and get rid of his father. In so far as this wish remains in the unconscious it forms the basis of the sense of guilt. We believe that what we have here been describing are normal processes, the normal fate of the so-called 'Oedipus complex'; nevertheless it requires an important amplification.

A further complication arises when the constitutional factor we call bisexuality is comparatively strongly developed in a child. For then, under the threat to the boy's masculinity by castration, his inclination becomes strengthened to diverge in the direction of femininity, to put himself instead in his mother's place and take over her role as object of his father's love. But the fear of castration makes *this* solution impossible as well. The boy understands that he must also submit to castration if he wants to be loved by his father as a woman. Thus both impulses, hatred of the father and being in love with the father, undergo repression. There is a certain psychological distinction in the fact that the hatred of the father is given up on account of fear of an *external* danger (castration), while the being in love with the father is treated as an *internal* instinctual danger, though fundamentally it goes back to the same external danger.

What makes hatred of the father unacceptable is *fear* of the father; castration is terrible, whether as a punishment or as the price of love. Of the two factors which repress hatred of the father, the first, the direct fear of punishment and castration, may be called the normal one; its pathogenic intensification seems to come only with the addition of the second factor, the fear of the feminine attitude. Thus a strong innate bisexual disposition becomes one of the preconditions or reinforcements of neurosis. Such a disposition must certainly be assumed in Dostoevsky, and it shows itself in a viable form (as latent homosexuality) in the important part played by male friendships in his life, in his strangely tender attitude towards rivals in love and in his remarkable understanding of situations which are explicable only by repressed homosexuality, as many examples from his novels show.

I am sorry, though I cannot alter the facts, if this exposition of the attitudes of hatred and love towards the father and their transformations under the influence of the threat of castration seems to readers unfamiliar with psycho-analysis unsavoury and incredible. I should myself expect that it is precisely the castration complex that would be bound to arouse the most general repudiation. But I can only insist that psycho-analytic experience has put these matters in particular beyond the reach of doubt and has taught us to recognize in them the key to every neurosis. This key, then, we must apply to our author's so-called epilepsy. So alien to our consciousness are the things by which our unconscious mental life is governed!

But what has been said so far does not exhaust the consequences of the repression of the hatred of the father in the Oedipus complex. There is something fresh to be added; namely that in spite of everything the identification with the father finally makes a permanent place for itself in the ego. It is received into the ego, but establishes itself there as a separate agency in contrast to the rest of the content of the ego. We then give it the name of super-ego and ascribe to it, the inheritor of the parental influence, the most important functions. If the father was hard, violent and cruel, the super-ego takes over those attributes from him and, in the relations between the ego and it, the passivity which was supposed to have been repressed is re-established. The super-ego has become sadistic, and the ego becomes masochistic – that is to say, at bottom passive in a feminine way. A great need for punishment develops in the ego, which in part offers itself as a victim to fate, and in part finds satisfaction in ill-treatment by the super-ego (that is, in the sense of guilt). For every punishment is ultimately castration and, as such, a fulfilment of the old passive attitude towards the father. Even fate is, in the last resort, only a later projection of the father.

The normal processes in the formation of conscience must be similar to the abnormal ones described here. We have not yet succeeded in fixing the boundary line between them. It will be observed that here the largest share in the outcome is ascribed to the passive component of repressed femininity. In addition, it must be of importance as an accidental factor whether the father, who is feared in any case, is also especially violent in reality. This was true in Dostoevsky's case, and we can trace back the fact of his extraordinary sense of guilt and of his masochistic conduct of life to a specially strong feminine component. Thus the formula for Dostoevsky is as follows: a person with a specially strong innate bisexual disposition, who can defend himself with special intensity against dependence on a specially severe father. This characteristic of bisexuality comes as an addition to the components of his nature that we have already recognized. His early symptoms of death-like attacks can thus be understood as a father-identification on the part of his ego, which is permitted by his super-ego as a punishment. 'You wanted to kill your father in order to be your father yourself. Now you *are* your father, but a dead father' – the regular mechanism of hysterical symptoms. And further: 'Now your father is killing *you*.' For the ego the death symptom is a satisfaction in phantasy of the masculine wish and at the same time a masochistic satisfaction; for the super-ego it is a punitive satisfaction – that is, a sadistic satisfaction. Both of them, the ego and the super-ego, carry on the role of father.

To sum up, the relation between the subject and his father-object, while retaining its content, has been transformed into a relation between the ego and the super-ego – a new setting on a fresh stage. Infantile reactions from the Oedipus complex such as these may disappear if reality gives them no further nourishment. But the father's character remained the same, or rather, it deteriorated with the years, and thus Dostoevsky's hatred for his father and his death-wish against that wicked father were maintained. Now it is a dangerous thing if reality fulfils such repressed wishes. The phantasy has become reality and all defensive measures are thereupon reinforced. Dostoevsky's attacks now assumed an epileptic character; they still undoubtedly signified an identification with his father as a punishment, but they had become terrible, like his father's frightful death itself. What further content they had absorbed, particularly what sexual content, escapes conjecture.

One thing is remarkable: in the aura of the epileptic attack, one moment of supreme bliss is experienced. This may very well be a record of the triumph and sense of liberation felt on hearing the news of the death, to be followed immediately by an all the more cruel punishment. We have divined just such a sequence of triumph and mourning, of festive joy and mourning, in the brothers of the primal horde who murdered their father, and we find it repeated in the ceremony of the totem meal.[7] If it proved to be the case that Dostoevsky was free from his attacks in Siberia, that would merely substantiate the view that they were his punishment. He did not need them any longer when he was being punished in another way. But that cannot be proved. Rather does this necessity for punishment on the part of Dostoevsky's mental economy explain the fact that he passed unbroken through these years of misery and humiliation. Dostoevsky's condemnation as a political prisoner was unjust and he must have known it, but he accepted the undeserved punishment at the hands of the Little Father, the Tsar, as a substitute for the punishment he deserved for his sin against his real father. Instead of punishing himself, he got himself punished by his father's deputy. Here we have a glimpse of the psychological justification of the punishments inflicted by society. It is a fact that large groups of criminals want to be punished. Their super-ego demands it and so saves itself the necessity for inflicting the punishment itself.[8]

Everyone who is familiar with the complicated transformation of meaning undergone by hysterical symptoms will understand that no attempt can be made here to follow out the meaning of Dostoevsky's attacks beyond this beginning.[9] It is enough that we may assume that their original meaning remained unchanged behind all later accretions. We can safely say that Dostoevsky never got free from the feelings of guilt arising from his intention of murdering his father. They also determined his attitude in the two other spheres in which the father-relation is the decisive factor, his attitude towards the authority of the state and towards belief in God. In the first of these he ended up with complete submission to his Little Father, the Tsar, who had once performed with him in *reality* the comedy of killing which his attacks had so often represented in *play*. Here penitence gained the upper hand. In the religious sphere he retained more freedom: according to apparently trustworthy reports he wavered, up to the last moment of his life, between faith and atheism. His great intellect made it impossible for him to overlook any of the intellectual difficulties to which faith leads. By an individual recapitulation of a development in world history he hoped to find a way out and a liberation from guilt in the Christ ideal, and even to make use of his sufferings as a claim to be playing a Christ-like role. If on the whole he did not achieve freedom and became a reactionary, that was because the filial guilt, which is present in human beings generally and on which religious feeling is built, had in him attained a super-individual intensity and remained insurmountable even to his great intelligence. In writing this we are laying ourselves open to the charge of having abandoned the impartiality of analysis and of subjecting Dostoevsky to judgements that can only be justified from the partisan standpoint of a particular *Weltanschauung*. A conservative would take the side of the Grand Inquisitor and would judge Dostoevsky differently. The objection is just; and one can only say in extenuation that Dostoevsky's decision has every appearance of having been determined by an intellectual inhibition due to his neurosis.

It can scarcely be owing to chance that three of the masterpieces of the literature of all time – the *Oedipus Rex* of Sophocles, Shakespeare's *Hamlet* and Dostoevsky's *The Brothers Karamazov* – should all deal with the same subject, parricide. In all three, moreover, the motive for the deed, sexual rivalry for a woman, is laid bare.

The most straightforward is certainly the representation in the drama derived from the Greek legend. In this it is still the hero himself who commits the crime. But poetic treatment is impossible without softening and disguise. The naked admission of an intention to commit parricide, as we arrive at it in analysis, seems intolerable without analytic preparation. The Greek drama, while retaining the crime, introduces the indispensable toning-down in a masterly fashion by projecting the hero's unconscious motive into reality in the form of a compulsion by a destiny which is alien to him. The hero commits the deed unintentionally and apparently uninfluenced by the woman; this latter element is however taken into account in the circumstance that the hero can only obtain possession of the queen mother after he has repeated his deed upon the monster who symbolizes the father. After his guilt has been revealed and made conscious, the hero makes no attempt to exculpate himself by appealing to the artificial expedient of the compulsion of destiny. His crime is acknowledged and punished as though it were a full and conscious one – which is bound to appear unjust to our reason, but which psychologically is perfectly correct.

In the English play the presentation is more indirect; the hero does not commit the crime himself; it is carried out by someone else, for whom it is not parricide. The forbidden motive of sexual rivalry for the woman does not need, therefore, to be disguised. Moreover, we see the hero's Oedipus complex, as it were, in a reflected light, by learning the effect upon him of the other's crime. He ought to avenge the crime, but finds himself, strangely enough, incapable of doing so. We know that it is his sense of guilt that is paralysing him; but, in a manner entirely in keeping with neurotic processes, the sense of guilt is displaced on to the perception of his inadequacy for fulfilling his task. There are signs that the hero feels this guilt as a super-individual one. He despises others no less than himself: 'Use every man after his desert, and who should 'scape whipping?'

The Russian novel goes a step further in the same direction. There also the murder is committed by someone else. This other person, however, stands to the murdered man in the same filial relation as the hero, Dmitri; in this other person's case the motive of sexual rivalry is openly admitted; he is a brother of the hero's, and it is a remarkable fact that Dostoevsky has attributed to him his own illness, the alleged epilepsy, as though he were seeking to confess that the epileptic, the neurotic, in himself was a parricide. Then, again, in the speech for the defence at the trial, there is the famous mockery of psychology – it is a 'knife that cuts both ways'[10]: a splendid piece of disguise, for we have only to reverse it in order to discover the deepest meaning of Dostoevsky's view of things. It is not psychology that deserves the mockery, but the procedure of judicial inquiry. It is a matter of indifference who actually committed the crime: psychology is only concerned to know who desired it emotionally and who welcomed it when it was done.[11] And for that reason all of the brothers, except the contrasted figure of Alyosha, are equally guilty – the impulsive sensualist, the sceptical cynic and the epileptic criminal. In *The Brothers Karamazov* there is one particularly revealing scene. In the course of his talk with Dmitri, Father Zossima recognizes that Dmitri is prepared to commit parricide, and he bows down at his feet. It is impossible that this can be meant as an expression of admiration; it must mean that the holy man is rejecting the temptation to despise or detest the murderer and for that reason humbles himself before him. Dostoevsky's sympathy for the criminal is, in fact, boundless; it goes far beyond the pity which the unhappy wretch has a right to, and reminds us of the 'holy awe' with which epileptics and lunatics were regarded in the past. A criminal is to him almost a Redeemer, who has taken on himself the guilt which must else have been borne by others. There is no longer any need for one to murder, since *he* has already murdered; and one must be grateful to him, for, except for him, one would have been obliged oneself to murder. That is not kindly pity alone, it is identification on the basis of similar murderous impulses – in fact, a slightly displaced narcissism. (In saying this, we are not disputing the ethical value of this kindliness.) This may perhaps be quite generally the mechanism of kindly sympathy with other people, a mechanism which one can discern with especial ease in this extreme case of a guilt-ridden novelist. There is no doubt that this sympathy by identification was a decisive factor in determining Dostoevsky's choice of material. He dealt first with the common criminal (whose motives are egotistical) and the political and religious criminal; and not until the end of his life did he come back to the primal criminal, the parricide, and use him, in a work of art, for making his confession.

The publication of Dostoevsky's posthumous papers and of his wife's diaries has thrown a glaring light on one episode in his life, namely the period in Germany when he was obsessed with a mania for gambling,[12] which no one could regard as anything but an unmistakable fit of pathological passion. There was no lack of rationalizations for this remarkable and unworthy behaviour. As often happens with neurotics, Dostoevsky's sense of guilt had taken a tangible shape as a burden of debt, and he was able to take refuge behind the pretext that he was trying by his winnings at the tables to make it possible for him to return to Russia without being arrested by his creditors. But this was no more than a pretext and Dostoevsky was acute enough to recognize the fact and honest enough to admit it. He knew that the chief thing was gambling for its own sake – *le jeu pour le jeu*.[13] All the details of his impulsively irrational conduct show this and something more besides. He never rested until he had lost everything. For him gambling was a method of self-punishment as well. Time after time he gave his young wife his promise or his word of honour not to play any more or not to play any more on that particular day; and, as she says, he almost always broke it. When his losses had reduced himself and her to the direst need, he derived a second pathological satisfaction from that. He could then scold and humiliate himself before her, invite her to despise him and to feel sorry that she had married such an old sinner; and when he had thus unburdened his conscience, the whole business would begin again next day. His young wife accustomed herself to this cycle, for she had noticed that the one thing which offered any real hope of salvation – his literary production – never went better than when they had lost everything and pawned their last possessions. Naturally she did not understand the connection. When his sense of guilt was satisfied by the punishments he had inflicted on himself, the inhibition upon his work became less severe and he allowed himself to take a few steps along the road to success.[14]

What part of a gambler's long-buried childhood is it that forces its way to repetition in his obsession for play? The answer may be divined without difficulty from a story by one of our younger writers. Stefan Zweig, who has incidentally devoted a study to Dostoevsky himself (*Three Masters*), has included in his collection of three stories *Die Verwirrung der Gefühle* [*Confusion of Feelings*] (1927) one which he calls 'Vierundzwanzig Stunden aus dem Leben einer Frau' ['Twenty-four Hours in a Woman's Life']. This little masterpiece ostensibly sets out only to show what an irresponsible creature woman is, and to what excesses, surprising even to herself, an unexpected experience may drive her. But the story tells far more than this. If it is subjected to an analytical interpretation, it will be found to represent (without any apologetic intent) something quite different, something universally human, or rather something masculine. And such an interpretation is so extremely obvious that it cannot be resisted. It is characteristic of the nature of artistic creation that the author, who is a personal friend of mine, was able to assure me, when I asked him, that the interpretation which I put to him had been completely strange to his knowledge and intention, although some of the details woven into the narrative seemed expressly designed to give a clue to the hidden secret.

In this story, an elderly lady of distinction tells the author about an experience she has had more than twenty years earlier. She has been left a widow when still young and is the mother of two sons, who no longer need her. In her forty-second year, expecting nothing further of life, she happens, on one of her aimless journeyings, to visit the Rooms at Monte Carlo. There, among all the remarkable impressions which the place produces, she is soon fascinated by the sight of a pair of hands which seem to betray all the feelings of the unlucky gambler with terrifying sincerity and intensity. These hands belong to a handsome young man – the author, as though unintentionally, makes him of the same age as the narrator's elder son – who, after losing everything, leaves the Rooms in the depth of despair, with the evident intention of ending his hopeless life in the Casino gardens. An inexplicable feeling of sympathy compels her to follow him and make every effort to save him. He takes her for one of the importunate women so common there and tries to shake her off; but she stays with him and finds herself obliged, in the most natural way possible, to join him in his apartment at the hotel, and finally to share his bed. After this improvised night of love, she exacts a most solemn vow from the young man, who has now apparently calmed down, that he will never play again, provides him with money for his journey home and promises to meet him at the station before the departure of his train. Now, however, she begins to feel a great tenderness for him, is ready to sacrifice all she has in order to keep him and makes up her mind to go with him instead of saying good-bye. Various mischances delay her, so that she misses the train. In her longing for the lost one she returns once more to the Rooms and there, to her horror, sees once more the hands which had first excited her sympathy: the faithless youth had gone back to his play. She reminds him of his promise, but obsessed by his passion, he calls her a spoil-sport, tells her to go, and flings back the money with which she has tried to rescue him. She hurries away in deep mortification and learns later that she has not succeeded in saving him from suicide.

The brilliantly told, faultlessly motivated story is of course complete in itself and is certain to make a deep effect upon the reader. But analysis shows us that its invention is based fundamentally upon a wishful phantasy belonging to the period of puberty, which a number of people actually remember consciously. The phantasy embodies a boy's wish that his mother should herself initiate him into sexual life in order to save him from the dreaded injuries caused by masturbation. (The numerous creative works that deal with the theme of redemption have the same origin.) The 'vice' of masturbation is replaced by the addiction to gambling[15]; and the emphasis laid upon the passionate activity of the hands betrays this derivation. Indeed, the passion for play is an equivalent of the old compulsion to masturbate; 'playing' is the actual word used in the nursery to describe the activity of the hands upon the genitals. The irresistible nature of the temptation, the solemn resolutions, which are nevertheless invariably broken, never to do it again, the stupefying pleasure and the bad conscience which tells the subject that he is ruining himself (committing suicide) – all these elements remain unaltered in the process of substitution. It is true that Zweig's story is told by the mother, not by the son. It must flatter the son to think: 'If my mother only knew what dangers masturbation involves me in, she would certainly save me from them by allowing me to lavish all my tenderness on her own body'. The equation of the mother with a prostitute, which is made by the young man in the story, is linked up with the same phantasy. It brings the unattainable woman within easy reach. The bad conscience which accompanies the phantasy brings about the unhappy ending of the story. It is also interesting to notice how the *façade* given to the story by its author seeks to disguise its analytic meaning. For it is extremely questionable whether the erotic life of women is dominated by sudden and mysterious impulses. On the contrary, analysis reveals an adequate motivation for the surprising behaviour of this woman who had hitherto turned away from love. Faithful to the memory of her dead husband, she had armed herself against all similar attractions; but – and here the son's phantasy is right – she did not, as a mother, escape her quite unconscious transference of love on to her son, and Fate was able to catch her at this undefended spot.

If the addiction to gambling, with the unsuccessful struggles to break the habit and the opportunities it affords for self-punishment, is a repetition of the compulsion to masturbate, we shall not be surprised to find that it occupied such a large space in Dostoevsky's life. After all, we find no cases of severe neurosis in which the auto-erotic satisfaction of early childhood and of puberty has not played a part; and the relation between efforts to suppress it and fear of the father are too well known to need more than a mention.[16]

Notes

1. See the discussion of this in René Fülöp-Miller and F. Eckstein, *Der Unbekannte Dostojewski (The Unknown Dostoyevsky)* (Munich, 1926). Stefan Zweig, *Three Masters* (New York, 1938), writes: 'He was not halted by the barriers of bourgeois morality; and no one can say exactly how far he transgressed the bounds of law in his own life or how much of the criminal instincts of his heroes was realized in himself.' For the intimate connection between Dostoevsky's characters and his own experiences, see the remarks in the introductory section of René Fülöp-Miller and F. Eckstein, eds., *Dostojewski am Roulette (Dostoyevsky at the Roulette Table)* (Munich, 1925), which are based upon N. Strakhov, 'Über Dostojewskis Leben und literarische Tätigkeit', ('On Dostoyevsky's Life and Literary Activity') in F. M. Dostojewski, *Literarische Schriften (Literary Writings)* (Munich, 1921). (The topic of a sexual assault on an immature girl appears several times in Dostoevsky's writings – especially in the posthumous *Stavrogin's Confession* and *The Life of a Great Sinner.*)

2. Cf. Freud, 'Some General Remarks on Hysterical Attacks', *The Standard Edition of the Complete Psychological Works of Sigmund Freud*, ed. and trans. James Strachey, 23 vols. (London, Hogarth Press, 1953), Vol. 9, pp. 229–234.

3. See René Fülöp-Miller, 'Dostojewskis Heilige Krankheit' ('Dostoyevsky's Holy Illness'), *Wissen und Leben*, Vols. 19 and 20. Cf. also the account given by Aimée Dostoevsky, *Fyodor Dostoyevsky* (Heineman, 1921). Of especial interest is the information that in the novelist's childhood 'something terrible, unforgettable and agonizing' happened, to which the first signs of his illness were to be traced (from an article by Suvorin in the newspaper *Novoe Vremya* [1881], and quoted in the introduction to Fülöp-Miller and Eckstein, *Dostojewski am Roulette*). See also Orest Miller, 'Zur Lebensgeschichte Dostojewskis', ('On the Life History of Dostoyevsky') in F. M. Dostojewski, *Autobiographische Schriften (Autobiographical Writings)* (Munich, 1921), p. 140: 'There is, however, another special piece of evidence about Fyodor Mikhailovich's illness, which relates to his earliest youth and brings the illness into connection with a tragic event in the family life of his parents. But, although this piece of evidence was given to me orally by one who was a close friend of Fyodor Mikhailovich, I cannot bring myself to reproduce it fully and precisely since I have had no confirmation of this rumour from any other quarter.' Biographers and scientific research workers cannot feel grateful for this discretion.

4. Most of the accounts, including Dostoevsky's own, assert on the contrary that the illness only assumed its final, epileptic character during the Siberian exile. Unfortunately there is reason to distrust the autobiographical statements of neurotics. Experience shows that their

memories introduce falsifications which are designed to interrupt disagreeable causal connections. Nevertheless, it appears certain that Dostoevsky's detention in the Siberian prison markedly altered his pathological condition. Cf. Fülöp-Miller, 'Dostojewskis Heilige Krankheit', p. 1186.

5. Fülöp-Miller and Eckstein, *Dostojewski am Roulette*.
6. The explanation was already given by Freud in a letter to Fliess of 8 February 1897. See Sigmund Freud, *The Origins of Psycho-Analysis* (London, Hogarth Press, 1954), letter 58.
7. Sigmund Freud, 'Totem and Taboo', *Standard Edition*, Vol. 13 (1955), p. 140.
8. Cf. 'Criminals from a Sense of Guilt', the third essay in Freud's 'Some Character-Types Met with in Psycho-Analytic Work', *Standard Edition*, Vol. 14, p. 332.
9. The best account of the meaning and content of his attacks was given by Dostoevsky himself, when he told his friend Strakhov that his irritability and depression after an epileptic attack were due to the fact that he had a burden of unknown guilt upon him, that he had committed some great misdeed, which oppressed him. See Fülöp-Miller, 'Dostojewskis Heilige Krankheit', p. 1188. In self-accusations like these psycho-analysis sees signs of a recognition of 'psychical reality', and it endeavours to make the unknown guilt known to consciousness.
10. In the German (and in the original Russian) the simile is 'a stick with two ends'. The 'knife that cuts both ways' is derived from Constance Garnett's English translation, Book 12, ch. 10.
11. A practical application of this to an actual criminal case is to be found in Freud's comments on the Halsmann Case, 'The Expert Opinion in the Halsmann Case', *Standard Edition*, Vol. 21, p. 251, where *The Brothers Karamozov* is again discussed.
12. Cf. Fülöp-Miller and Eckstein, *Dostojewski am Roulette*.
13. 'The main thing is the play itself,' he writes in one of his letters. 'I swear that greed for money has nothing to do with it, although Heaven knows I am sorely in need of money.'
14. 'He always remained at the gaming tables till he had lost everything and was totally ruined. It was only when the damage was quite complete that the demon at last retired from his soul and made way for the creative genius.' Fülöp-Miller and Eckstein, *Dostojewski am Roulette*, p. xxxvi.
15. In a letter to Fliess of 22 December 1897, Freud suggested that masturbation is the 'primal addiction', for which all later addictions are substitutes. See Freud, *The Origins of Psycho-Analysis*, letter 79.
16. Most of the views which are here expressed are also contained in an excellent book by Jolan Neufeld, *Dostojewski: Skizze zu seiner Psychoanalyse (Dostoyevsky: Outline of his Psychoanalysis)* (Vienna, 1923).

Edmund Bergler

The Psychology of Gambling*

Where logic ends, the unconscious takes over

The psychology of consciousness is a tool inadequate for the task of unraveling the complex personality of the gambler. If we remain on the conscious level, we soon reach an impasse of rationalizations and illogical reasoning. To take the gambler's own evaluation of his motives at face value is as naïve as the belief that a drop of water is the same to the naked eye as it is to the eye of a microscope. Just as the microscope reveals the millions of dangerous bacilli that may lurk in a drop of 'clean' water, the psychology of the *unconscious* exposes facts hidden in the gambler's psyche.

The best approach to the problem of the gambler's *un-conscious* psychology is, first, to examine his illogical, senseless certainty that he will win. A literary example of this may be found in a passage from the diary of a woman who was the victim of her famous husband's gambling. Fyodor Dostoyevsky's wife wrote:

Fedja took eighty gulden, gambled and lost. He took the same sum once more and lost . . . He fetched the last forty gulden and promised me *unconditionally* that he would bring home my earrings and my ring which he had pawned for 170 francs. He said that *in a tone of complete conviction, as if his winning or not winning depended on him alone.* Of course that conviction did not help him; he lost the last forty gulden too. [22 August 1867.]

It is virtually impossible to match this lordly self-assurance with an equivalent attitude on the part of an average person leading a 'normal' life. A phenomenon like this can be found

*From *The Psychology of Gambling* (New York: International Universities Press, Inc., 1970 edition), pp. 15–32, 78–100. Copyright © Edmund Bergler, 1958. Reprinted by permission of Mrs Edmund Bergler, International Universities Press, Inc. and Granada Publishing Ltd.

only among pathological fanatics. Fanaticism is a megalo-maniacal condition, and the gambler, in his optimism, is a fanatic too. The structure of this megalomania can best be understood by briefly examining a common phenomenon of the psychology of the child: the 'fiction of omnipotence'.

As Freud and Sándor Ferenczi have shown, the child lives in a sort of megalomania for a long period; he knows only one yardstick, and that is his own over-inflated ego. He conceives of the outside world as something over which he has complete control. This misconception of reality is fostered by his parents, who automatically attempt to fulfil his every wish for food, sleep, affection. This fulfillment of his physical and emotional desires the child regards, not as the result of his mother's love, but as the result of his own omnipotence. Real experience gradually destroys this fiction, an experience which is probably the deepest disappointment of childhood.

A beautiful example of this childhood megalomania is found in Romain Rolland's novel *Jean Christophe*. The author describes Christophe as a child:

He is a magician, too . . . He commands the clouds. He wants them to go to the right, but they continue to the left. He scolds them, and repeats his command more urgently. His heart beats more quickly as he watches to see if at least one little cloud obeys him. But they continue to move to the left. He stamps his foot, menaces them with his little stick, and changes his command. Now he wants them to go to the left, and this time the clouds obey. He is happy and proud of his power.

The novelist is describing a transitory phase in the child's development, just as if he were outlining a clinical case. Reality forces the child to acknowledge that he is not an omnipotent magician, but still he must save at least a small part of his cherished fiction. It is as if someone, glancing at his watch at one minute to six, were to command the watch to point to six in exactly one minute, and then – his 'command' obeyed – were to feel omnipotent.

To become an adult in the real sense of the word means to relinquish the 'pleasure principle' (Freud) for the 'reality principle'. The child is educated, through love, persuasion and threats, to realize that there is an objective reality outside the world of his private wishes. But no one accepts this harsh truth without inner protest, and the clinical fact remains that only with great reluctance and difficulty does the child give up his phantasies of omnipotence. In fact, we all have remnants of this fiction in our unconscious, no matter how 'grown-up' we are.

Further life experience convinces the child that certain facts are unchangeable. After he has tried it a few times, he learns that it does not pay to run his head into a stone wall; the wall, despite his command that it give way, remains unyielding. And in a form of protective mechanism, he learns to avoid battle when defeat is predictable. He 'gets wise', but without enthusiasm. Still buried, deep within him, is the old fiction of omnipotence, and under certain circumstances it can be resuscitated, just as Homer's dead heroes in Hades came alive again when they drank blood.

The power of the 'reality principle' lies in the fact that its acceptance by the child, and later the adult, eliminates many defeats. *There is one exceptional situation in life, however, in which the reality principle has no advantage over the pleasure principle*: that is gambling. There blind chance rules, chance which in games of 'pure' gambling cannot be influenced by logic or intelligence.

An old anecdote told by one of my patients is illustrative. A college student won $10,000 betting on a dark horse at the races. His mathematics teacher was curious to know how he had picked the winner. 'Very simple,' was the reply. 'I dreamed about the figures 2 and 3 and thought that 2×3 equalled 12, therefore I placed my money on number 12.' 'But 2×3 is not 12!' objected the professor. At this, the pupil became indignant. 'You want to teach me how much 2×3 is?' he expostulated. 'I won!'

In this particular instance, the student could afford to ignore facts, and give priority to his private, *a*logical system of mathematics. A continued flouting of reality, on the basis of one piece of good luck, would be sure to lead him to disaster.

Gambling unconsciously revives, therefore, the old childish phantasy of grandeur and megalomania. More important, it activates the *latent rebellion* against logic, intelligence, moderation, morality and renunciation. The 'pleasure principle' is never entirely relinquished; traces of it, strong or weak, always remain in the unconscious. From time to time the latent urge to surrender to it becomes a propelling tendency, which leads the individual to scoff ironically at all the rules of life he has learned from education and experience. Heavy inner retaliation is the result. Since the child has learned these rules from his parents and their representatives (teachers, priests, superiors, etc.), his rebellion activates a profound unconscious feeling of guilt.

In clinical terms, this is the psychic situation of the gambler: first, *unconscious aggression*; second, an unconscious tendency toward *self-punishment* because of that aggression. The self-punishing factor, which is always present, is almost never recognized except in psychoanalytic treatment. Thus, the childlike, unconscious, neurotic misunderstanding of the whole gambling process creates a vicious, and endless, circle. Hence the inner necessity to lose.

The act of gambling in itself is a denial of the 'reality principle'. In this act of denial the gambler is expressing his neurotic aggression against those who have taught him the 'reality principle', in most cases his parents. In losing, he is simply paying the penalty for this aggression. Long analytic experience teaches us that in neurotics all aggression is paid for by some form of self-punishment. The whole concept of neurosis is based on the knowledge that neurotics unconsciously transfer conflicts, originally experienced with their parents, to innocent persons whom they unconsciously identify with their parents. Since aggression towards the mother and father was forbidden, every aggression towards the substitutes is inwardly forbidden, too. If the aggression is actually performed, it is expiated by severe self-punishment. Here is one of the important differences between normal and pathological aggression. In normal aggression, hostility is directed at the real enemy, not the imaginary one (i.e. the parent). Normal aggression arouses no feeling of inner guilt, because it is used in self-defence; and, since the enemy is not unconsciously identified with a person who figured in childhood experiences, the feeling of righteous indignation has no aftermath of guilt.

It is on these psychoanalytic facts that I base my conviction that the gambler cannot win in the long run. For him, losing is essential to his psychic equilibrium. It is the price he pays for his neurotic aggression, and at the same time it makes it possible for him to continue gambling.

This unconscious attack on rationality and intelligence (an attack on reality, actually), which is activated – also unconsciously – in gambling, is vicious and not at all harmless. Quite the contrary. Although he never gives his thoughts conscious expression, the gambler is really saying: 'You, parents, taught me that every good deed would be rewarded, every bad one punished. But what happens instead? Honest men work hard and earn little. The crook gets money and fame. You preached that there is a moral order of things and that heavy retribution follows if the path of decency is abandoned. What is the reality? The racketeer triumphs, the decent man is pushed around. You instilled in me the foolish notion that only honest work brings success. At the gambling table the opposite is true – people get rich without working at all. You wanted me to believe that logic rules in this world and that justice and reason prevail in the end. All lies. In gambling all your logic and reason and justice are meaningless. None of your rules can explain how the roulette ball rolls, how the dice fall, how stocks climb, or cards are dealt. You claimed that in this best of all possible worlds nothing is left to blind chance. But what happens in gambling houses, on the stock exchange, or at the racetrack shows you up as fools or hypocrites. Blind chance does rule in many places, and I intend to take advantage of it!'

It is in the gambler's *unconscious*, it must be remembered, that this monologue is delivered. Unconscious motivation is a clinically proven fact, but experience has shown that the psychologically uninformed person is extremely sceptical of such clinical facts. However, he is often willing to accept the same facts when they are presented in a non-scientific medium; in a novel, for instance.

For this reason, I should like to compare, from time to time, actual case histories with examples from literature. There are many such 'matched pairs' available, in which the main outlines of the fictional and real-life situations are basically the same. The following example will illustrate a typical way in which the gambler uses his pseudo-aggressive tendencies.

Clinical case

A gambling patient, while playing roulette in a New Jersey casino, was caught by his senior partner. The older man lectured him, pointing out that gambling and business did not mix. My patient's retaliation was to make friends with his partner's son, whom he introduced first to homosexuality, then to gambling. This action constituted a conscious rejection of bourgeois values. 'I couldn't stand the old fool's moral nonsense.' The fact that the son of the highly moral father could be seduced to perversion and addiction represented, in my patient's words, 'one of the triumphs of my life'. What he did not even suspect was that, behind the pseudo-aggression was a hidden desire for self-punishment. The desire was fulfilled: his partner learned the truth and dismissed him under very humiliating circumstances. The patient suffered a nervous breakdown and later came for psychoanalytic treatment.

Literary example

In Otto Soyka's *Master in Gambling* the gambler, Wehlen, is in love with a young girl from a middle-class family. But she believes in stability, morality and financial security, as represented by her fiancé, Walter. Wehlen's revenge against the girl is to introduce her fiancé into gambling circles. Walter wins at first, then loses everything and ends saddled with a debt representing two years' salary. Further to reduce accepted rules of normality to absurdity, Wehlen teaches the girl's brother the 'pleasures' of insecurity and danger. He races his car recklessly, and even arranges an automobile accident. The youngster 'learns' fast and enjoys it. Then, together with a psychopathic inventor, Wehlen conceives the idea of a device that will cut through steel like paper. This is Wehlen's ironic way of proving the absurdity of the bourgeois faith in the 'safety of the safe'.

The gambler is quite a rebel. He is the organizer of a private tempest in a teapot. He is invariable in his individualism; his rebellions take place, not within a political party, but in splendid isolation. This *private* rebel fights with neither guns nor ballots; cards, stocks, dice, chips are his weapons and his invisible colors. Out of inner necessity, therefore, he becomes a specialist in reducing bourgeois values to absurdity, because all who hold such values are a source of inner reproach to him. At the same time, his neurosis forces him to follow his pattern of pseudo-aggression in an attempt to expose the hollowness and 'moral weakness' of the rest of the world.

The mysterious thrill in gambling

In approaching the gambler's unconscious the first salient fact we discover is his fanatical belief in infantile megalomania. Education has forced him to repress his conviction of his own omnipotence to some degree, but in the unconscious this belief retains its full dynamic force. Nowhere is this more clearly demonstrated than in the attitude the gambler displays while gambling. Just like a child, he expects that he will win because he *wants* to win. When a gambler places his stake on a card or a colour or a number he is not acting like a person who has adapted himself to reality; he is 'ordering' the next card to win for him, in the complete illusion that he is omnipotent.

Mentally, he has regressed to the earlier period in which he was, to all intents and purposes, omnipotent, that is, to infancy, when all his desires were automatically fulfilled. His present megalomaniacal attitude is an act of aggression against his parents and the other educators who forced him into the awareness that he was not omnipotent. And, as previously stated, there can be no neurotic aggression without guilt. The guilt is expiated by self-punishment. In the case of the gambler this takes the form of an unconscious desire to lose and a wish to be rejected by the outer world.

The unconscious wish to lose becomes, therefore, an integral part of the gambler's inner motivations.

Is this aggression an original motive, or is it, in the case of the gambler, only a *defense* against something else? It is only a defense. The gambler's rebellion against his parents represents merely a superficial – though also unconscious – level of his neurosis. When the deepest layer is plumbed, a condition is found that is clinically known as *stabilization on the rejection level* – in other words, *psychic masochism.*[1]

Psychic masochism denotes the unconscious craving for defeat, humiliation, rejection, pain. From the 'logical' point of view the psychic masochist cannot exist, for common sense teaches that everyone seeks pleasure and avoids pain. It would be convenient if this handy formula were true; unfortunately, it cannot be applied to neurotics, whose unconscious is regulated by irrational factors. And the most powerful of these subterranean forces is psychic masochism.

How is this self-damaging mechanism first set in operation?

Imagine a child confronted with some refusal, either thoroughly justified or not. Regardless of its justifications, the refusal automatically provokes fury, since it offends his sense of omnipotence. The child's anger is inhibited, first by external and later by internal forces. The strongest child is weaker than the weakest adult. Later, the external authorities, personified by parents and teachers, are internalized; this shift is the starting point for the development of the inner conscience.[2] Instead of the warning voice and chastising hand coming from the *outside*, the child encounters an *inner* voice and *inner* punishment. One of the functions of the inner conscience is to punish internally those aggressions against maternal and paternal authority which were originally punished externally.

Megalomania, it must be understood, is normal in the very young child. Also, the *normal* child is able to cope with the inevitable assaults life makes on this illusion of omnipotence. This is done by partially renouncing, repressing or shifting his desires, and by diplomatically adapting himself to his environment. The *neurotic* child cannot do this; therefore he is constantly faced with the fact that every 'forbidden' wish is paralleled by painful punishment, reproach and feelings of guilt.

Once the normal solution is abandoned there remains but one way out: to make the best of it. And the best way is to follow the 'pleasure principle', to produce *pleasure out of displeasure*. This is exactly what the psychic masochist does.

In the course of their lives psychic masochists interminably construct situations in which they can be refused, rejected, unjustly treated, humiliated. Although they are unaware of what they are doing, their conduct proves conclusively that displeasure is their real goal. Not displeasure pure and simple – certain rules must be observed. Enjoyment of the forbidden and dangerous 'pleasure' must always be paid for, and the penalty is inner guilt. Since 'pleasure in displeasure' secondarily becomes a pleasure, too, the internal voice of authority, conscience, eventually objects to that pleasure as well. On the other hand, psychic masochism is an ingenious device for the nullification of punishment: when punishment becomes pleasure, punishment itself is reduced to absurdity.

The conscience is like a sadistic jailer who drives his prisoner to such desperation that he beats his head against the wall. At first the jailer gloats, but at the first suspicion that his victim is deriving pleasure from this self-torture the jailer will force him to stop.

Thus the conscience denies its victim the pleasure he would get from his pain. The victim, therefore, is forced to establish an alibi: 'I am not masochistic. I am aggressive.' *It is precisely this defensive alibi-aggression (pseudo-aggression) which is visible in the gambler's rebellion.* But even the aggression serves a masochistic purpose; it is used secondarily by the psychic masochist to provoke defeats and rebuffs, which he enjoys masochistically.

Once the masochistic neurosis is established the unconscious becomes the scene of a drama, endlessly and monotonously repeated. It is a drama in three acts:

1. The psychic masochist unconsciously provokes or misuses situations in which he is defeated, rejected, denied.

2. Unaware that he himself has been responsible for these defeats and rejections, he strikes out in righteous indignation, and apparently in self-defence, against the world's cruelty and injustice.

3. Then follows profound self-pity; Fate has handed him a 'raw deal'.

This triad, which I call the 'mechanism of orality', was first described by me nearly twenty-five years ago. In its different ramifications, it has been exemplified in a long series of papers and books.[3] The term 'mechanism of orality' derives from the fact that the foundation for this type of behavior is laid at a time when the mouth is the child's main contact with reality. Neurotics who use this mechanism extensively are called 'orally' regressed. The term 'orality' alludes to the earliest psychic-developmental phase of the child, where the mouth is the main contact with reality – the 'gimme' phase.

In this triad, the provocation (1) and the masochistic enjoyment (part of 3) are completely unconscious. The pseudo-aggression (2), and the self-pity and the complaints (part of 3), are conscious.

In applying this pattern of self-punishment to gamblers it is clear that the 'adversary' (the poker partner, the roulette wheel, the Stock Exchange) is always unconsciously identified with the phantasy of the refusing mother and, later, father. Only one thing can be expected from this 'monster' – refusal, denial and defeat. The gambler's unconscious wish to lose assures this defeat.

Consciously, the gambler is *absolutely convinced* that he must win. But *in unconscious reality, he is convinced that the cruel mother or father will be exposed as a refuser, by making him lose*. This masochistic wish is concealed in the unconscious, and intrapsychically transformed and shifted to the conscious 'conviction' that he will win.

A great deal of the psychic masochist's psychic energy is expended in the process of supplying alibis for himself. The alibi is addressed to the inner conscience. A typical attempt to refute the inner reproach that the psychic masochist enjoys defeat and humiliation is the formula: 'I am not masochistic; the world is unjust to me.' To establish this 'innocent victim' alibi the gambler forces the representatives of authority (the elongated arm of parental authority) into the position of refusing him. Every losing streak, therefore, is an alibi, allegedly proving that the gambler is not masochistic, as the accusing 'inner district attorney' claims, but simply an innocent victim of circumstance. The gambler is always in need of a new excuse, a fact which further bolsters his unconscious wish to lose. *Losing becomes a 'moral' alibi!*

How can the enigmatic thrill of gambling be explained psychoanalytically?

The unconscious drive which produces the phenomenon known as the gambler springs from the unconscious resuscitation of childlike megalomania, with all its neurotic implications. In simple language, the gambler is a 'naughty child' who expects to be punished for his forbidden and aggressive acts. Basically, the *pleasant* component of the tension felt by the gambler is derived from the pleasure of aggressively used childish megalomania. The *painful* component arises from expectation of punishment for the 'crime'.

The whole psychic problem, however, is complicated by a masochistic superstructure. Frequently the tension *seems* to take on a sexual character. This is illustrated by the following incident. A patient I treated for gambling neurosis told me that the interim between the placing of his stake and the outcome of the game reminded him of an experience he once had in school. During a written examination, he was tortured by the thought that, because of insufficient time and inadequate preparation, he would fail. At that moment his fear changed into sexual excitement. 'Is it possible to experience sexual pleasure in a situation of anxiety?' he asked me.

My patient's analogy was only partially correct. However, the tension felt in gambling is of shorter duration. More than that, sexual excitement in itself is repressed and *not* at all of the *genital* type. The pleasure experienced is unconscious only, and is partly made up of psychic masochism.

This is the sequence of psychic events in the tension of gambling: aggression is directed against the mother and father; punishment is anticipated; the aggression boomerangs, producing feelings of guilt in the gambler himself; the punishment is sexualized as psychic masochism.

The last step may need further explanation. Where psychic masochism is the predominant factor in sexual feeling, the sexuality is not of the genital type. What is sought is not normal sexual release, but rather a feeling of being passively overwhelmed. Analysts are familiar with this phenomenon. Anyone who denies that fear can be unconsciously sexualized should observe people observing a mystery thriller in a movie theatre. These fans identify themselves deeply with the victims, and thereby enjoy the thrill of being overwhelmed. A similar example of this sexualization of suffering is the neurotic child who remains unchanged by punishment. Having provoked punishment, he promptly repeats the deed for which he was punished. It is logical and permissible to assume, therefore, that the child unconsciously likes his punishment.

The psychic masochism embedded in the gambler's actions is not merely a theoretical problem, as the following news item proves:

WINS FIRST HAND AT RUSSIAN ROULETTE
Then His Luck Runs Out as
Trigger Hits Loaded Cylinder

The game was 'Russian roulette', and the odds were 5-to-1. Tony R— won the first time. Then he tried it again and lost everything.

R—, 25, a laborer who shared a basement apartment at —, the Bronx, with the Frank O— family, was demonstrating the 'game' to young Anthony O— last night.

The game was to remove all but one of the six cartridges fom the revolver, spin the cylinder and pull the trigger while pointing the gun at his head. R— went through the routine once and the trigger clicked harmlessly.

'See? That's all there is to it,' he said. 'I'll show it to you again.' He did, and this time a shot rang out and R— died instantly.

The gun, incidentally, turned out to be a ·38 caliber police revolver stolen last July from a patrolman's locker in the 1st Division Headquarters Armory, where R— trained as a member of the New York Guard.[4]

The masochistic component definitely decreases the possibility of winning. Since the gambler unconsciously wants masochistic pleasure, his best way of achieving maximum pleasure is to lose. Of course his conscious wish is to win, but the conscious wish is dynamically ineffective.

But the gambler's unconscious masochistic pleasure is not a complete answer to the problem. Why, out of the thousands of possibilities, does he choose this particular means of obtaining such pleasure? Masochistic enjoyment contributes much to his thrill – that is obvious. But this does not explain the *specificity* of the problem of gambling. The answer is to be found elsewhere.

The first factor is the vicious circle already described, in which the gambler rebels against conventional standards of behavior and against reality (unconscious aggression against the parents) and then punishes himself for his aggression. But not everyone feels this need for constant rebellion in order to revive feelings of childlike megalomania. The gambler's perpetual-motion rebellion is a tool with which to deny the parents' attempt to impose the reality principle upon him, and to assert instead the pleasure principle – that is, his own omnipotence. This pattern of rebellion is a specific characteristic of the gambler.

Secondly, gamblers are only a specific sub-group within a specific group of neurotics. These people are regressed to the earliest level of psychic development – the oral stage – which defines that period in which the mouth is the main organ of contact with reality. Neurotics of this type consistently use the mechanism previously mentioned, which I call the 'mechanism of orality'. To recapitulate the three components of this mechanism: first, unconscious provocation of a situation in which they are rejected and defeated. Second, attack, full of hatred and seemingly in self-defense, aimed at their self-constructed enemies. Third, self-pity and the enjoyment of unconscious psychic masochistic pleasure. The feelings of righteous indignation and self-pity are the only ones that are conscious; there is no understanding of what they represent. The rest, especially the initial provocation, is repressed.

Not all neurotics who use this mechanism of orality are gamblers, but all gamblers employ it. In other words, gamblers represent a specific sub-group of orally regressed neurotics. The significant factor of the oral mechanism is that it provides masochistic pleasure behind a façade of pseudo-aggression.

These neurotics are typical *injustice collectors*; they are always on the alert for unconsciously self-created defeats. Unaware of what they are really doing, they constantly repeat the situation in which they are deprived, refused, rejected. This gluttony for punishment, which has been unconsciously self-provoked, explains, for instance, the behavior of the three patients mentioned in Chapter 2.*

The first patient, the advertising man, inevitably provoked his dismissal from every job, and then combined self-commiseration with bitter complaints about the injustice done him.

The second, the engineering student, provoked defeat by refusing to take his examinations. The aggression against his father was spurious, since his own self-damage was considerably more serious than his father's anger. He, too, complained about self-created difficulties, and pitied himself because of his 'foolishness' in having chosen 'so complicated a profession'.

The third patient, the book-store owner, attacked Fate and the world in general, and blamed his financial troubles on the existing order. He was not consciously aware of his misuse of an adverse reality for private, self-punitive purposes – and also, incidentally, for the purpose of attacking his fiancée, a mother-substitute, and reducing her to absurdity as a 'giving' person. Nor was he consciously aware that unconscious masochistic pleasure was hidden behind his constant whimpering.

These neurotics' self-constructed defeats are saturated with infantile megalomania. The 'bad' outer world is unconsciously identified with the 'bad', allegedly refusing mother. Other oral neurotics use various means to create this refusal situation, but the gambler chooses a specific device. When he gambles he relies on blind chance, and in so doing laughs at parental rules and moral principles. In effect, he says to the mother who first refused him: 'The rules of reality you tried to teach me are meaningless. I don't have to obey them. I am omnipotent.'

The mainspring of the gambler's unconscious mechanism, therefore, is his unconscious wish to lose, which is powerful and

* Of Bergler's book—not reproduced here. – Eds.

effective by comparison with his weak and ineffective conscious wish to win. The following points sum up the analytical facts that convinced me that the gambler is motivated by this unconscious desire to lose:

1. Losing is the penalty paid for trying to recreate omnipotence through aggression against parents and educators.
2. Losing satisfies the psychic masochistic urge, the end product of the infantile conflict.
3. Losing provides an alibi for the inner conscience. 'I am not masochistic. The world is unjust and I am an innocent victim.'
4. The anticipation of losing provides a thrill, secondarily desired for its painful–pleasurable tension per se.

* * *

Typology of gamblers

Within the gambler's personality, in a state of constant conflict, are two contradictory forces: the conscious wish to win and the unconscious wish to lose. In their dynamic effectiveness, these forces are by no means evenly matched. The wish to lose must ultimately prevail. Nor is this surprising. The relative strength of conscious and unconscious wishes may be compared with the power of a doorman, and the power of an owner, of a building. The doorman's braggadocio may be intimidating, but he has no real power. It is in the hands of the owner, even though he is not present in the lobby.

Genetically, the gambler is regressed to the earliest level of psychic development. His conflict centres around the mother of his earliest infancy, whom later – by means of projected surrogates – he reduces to absurdity as a giving person, allegedly exposing her as bad, malicious and a refusing 'monster'.

Reduced to the simplest possible terms, the background of his conflict can be illustrated as follows. A child asks for candy; his mother, for sound dietetic reasons, refuses. The normal child overcomes this disappointment; the neurotic child does not. He interprets the refusal as malice. What would be the summation of thousands of such minor refusals? In maturity, the neurotic does not try to compensate for these disappointments in a logical way; he does not, metaphorically speaking, eat all the candy he can stomach. Instead, without realizing it, he continues to play the role of the refused child. As it were, he stares hungrily through the window of the candy-store, but he buys nothing, even though he has money. Unconsciously, such a neurotic repeats the situation of being unjustly treated. By masochistically refusing himself, he shows his parents up as 'refusers', a process which for him is obviously more satisfying than real gratification of his original desire.

In real life, the candy-store is the Stock Exchange, the roulette wheel or the poker table. Every loss serves as corroboration for the inner alibi: 'I am not masochistic. It is my parents who are mean.' *Gambling is thus used to furnish an excuse for the gambler's main inner conflict: the constant reproach of psychic masochism.* Unfortunately for the gambler, this alibi is forthcoming only when he loses. And the need for it is stronger than the conscious wish to win.*

The above is a description of how the gambling neurosis functions at the deepest level of the unconscious. However, psychic development does not stop on this early (oral) plane. Every child tries to rescue himself from this oral danger by moving to a higher development level. At *one* of these rescue stations, there is a passivity-shift from mother to father. The result is *unconscious feminine identification*, a psychological phenomenon that plays an important role in certain types of gamblers. This shift takes place between the ages of two and a half and five. Here the boy identifies himself with his mother, and wishes to replace her in the father's affection.

In my clinical work I have encountered several distinct types of gambling neurotics, and on the basis of my observations have found it possible to attempt a typology of gamblers.

Type 1: The 'classical' gambler

The classical gambler's neurosis centers around infantile omnipotence and its masochistic elaboration. Characterologically, he is distinguished by the mechanism of orality, made up of the three parts previously described: unconscious construction of defeats; retaliative fury, seemingly for the purpose of self-defense; and finally, self-commiseration. In life, this type appears to want proof that he is loved, just as he apparently wants to win when he gambles. But unconsciously

*Bergler here has a long footnote (pp. 79–82) reviewing the existing literature on the psychology of gambling. We have dealt with the substantial points he raises about other authors in the introduction. – Eds.

he remains unsatisfied unless he receives his 'daily dose of injustice'.

A patient of this type stated ironically: 'For me, gambling is a question I ask of fate. The question is simple: "Am I your favorite?" It's a constant fight between me and my competitors – the other two billion people on the earth. When I'm winning, my feeling is that I'm the favorite; when I'm losing, I feel that my prayer for love will be heard some time.'

'Very well,' I replied. 'You believe that gambling is a way of testing fate. But how do you explain your not being satisfied when you win? Why do you pester fate for constant confirmation?'

His answer to this was that a 'repeatedly confirmed statement was more foolproof'. I did not accept this evasion; I asked him to explain why his pleasurable emotion when he won was never so deep as his unhappiness when he lost. 'My capacity for suffering is greater than my ability to enjoy success, that's true,' he admitted. 'I'm just made that way.'

'Isn't it more likely', I asked, 'that, under the disguise of wanting to be loved, you want exactly the opposite?'

He vigorously denied this, and when I told him that he could not speak for the unconscious side of his personality he became angry. 'You kill every argument with this trick of referring to the unconscious,' he concluded.

If one sees more than the emotionally involved patient can, it is typical for the patient to accuse the physician of trickery. The accusation is of course absurd. When a patient denies having had any contact whatever with women, and his doctor detects gonococci under the microscope, is the patient justified in dismissing the discovery as a trick?

The following literary example shows how psychic masochism – the diagnosis my patient so violently refused to accept – operates in gamblers. In *Vandover and the Brute* Frank Norris described a gambler in highly accurate detail, without, however, understanding his subject. But this lack of conscious understanding is the writer's privilege – his unconscious works under 'subterranean' pressure, while his consciousness furnishes weak and sometimes foolish rationalizations.[5] The psychic masochism of Vandover, the fictional hero, finds a striking parallel in the actual clinical case:

Clinical case

Twenty-eight years ago a twenty-eight-year-old pharmacist consulted me. His problem was his inability to cope with his sister-in-law, his brother's widow. The woman had 'invaded' his apartment, supposedly for a short visit. Instead, she stayed on and on, using the apartment shortage as an excuse. She had already been 'camping' for six months when the man consulted me. 'I have no privacy any more. I don't dare see my girl. But I love her children and that makes it hard for me to get tough with her. A friend told me that my inability to arrive at a decision constitutes a psychological problem. What do you think?'

It was obvious that the young man was an inwardly passive person who enjoyed being pushed around by an aggressive woman. He came from a once-wealthy family, had been well educated, but was unable to pass his final examinations. He worked for a pharmacist illegally, since he had no licence, at a minimum salary. He accepted my suggestion that he enter treatment as a 'tentative proposal', and said he would 'think it over'.

Two years later he came to my office again, this time complaining of 'terrible headaches' for which no neurological reason could be found. His appearance had deteriorated; he admitted that he lived in constant fear of being found out for 'selling drugs illegally' – a euphemism for stealing them from the pharmacy. First he denied, then admitted, that he was drinking and taking morphine. He said he now understood perfectly that he could not help himself, and wanted my assurance that I would back him up when asked for information by a wealthy uncle, from whom he wanted money to finance his treatment. His sister-in-law still lived in his apartment; he still did not 'have time' to study for his examinations. I asked what he did with the money he 'earned' peddling stolen drugs; he confessed that gambling 'devoured' all his money. 'The thrill of gambling gets a hold on me, and I am helpless.' He was of course very penitent; promised without being asked to stop gambling, stealing, etc. He looked like a man who had let himself down completely, and who, because of the quantity of his self-damaging tendencies, was a hopeless case.

The uncle never called. Later I learned that my prospective

patient had not even asked him for money. I heard nothing more from the 'patient' until one day, a few years later, he paid me an unexpected call. He was dirty and unwashed. He looked like a beggar. Tearfully, he told me the hard-luck story of the last five years. His drug-stealing had been discovered, he was discharged, he had left the country. In another country he continued to gamble, and 'made a living that way'. He continued drug-peddling, and became involved in the suicide of a wealthy young man; he went to jail 'completely innocent of the charge of extorting money from the suicide'. He regularly took the latter's money when gambling. He blamed gambling for his unhappy lot, claiming that this addiction had led to all his other troubles. Now he was the picture of hopeless masochistic destitution. He had come to me to beg for a suit.

His uncle came to his rescue with money to start a small business. He lost the money gambling. I once met him begging on a street corner. Later I read that he had been killed in a fight he had started in a gambling-house.

Literary example

Vandover begins life with all the advantages anyone could ask for. His parents are kind and loving, his home is comfortable and he has had a good education. He believes he would like to be an artist, but puts little effort into becoming one. Somehow, Vandover is always 'looking for trouble'. He begins to dissipate with a shady crowd, and seduces a young girl. She commits suicide. Vandover's father, who has always protected him, dies shortly after this scandal. Out of guilt and grief, Vandover again takes up with painting but his reform is short-lived. When the father of the girl he had seduced brings suit, Vandover is forced to buy him off by selling his property at a loss. He lets himself be cheated in the deal by a former friend, Geary.

Then follows a period of complete despair, boredom and inactivity. Gambling at first is only a diversion in which he is not much interested. Then one night in a game with two pro-fessionals, Dummy and Ellis, he plunges, losing much more than he ever had before. The gambling passion seizes him, and he knows that *this* is what he's been looking for. Only this fresh, violent excitement can rouse him from his apathy. Overnight, apparently, he becomes a confirmed addict.

Once in the grip of gambling, Vandover becomes completely reckless. In one year he runs through all his money, throwing it away on women, drinking sprees and, above all, on gambling. He is dumbfounded when he learns that his bank account is overdrawn – he has always had a 'feminine' aversion for figures.

Somehow he gets enough money to continue gambling. He has long since ceased to think about winning. He loses almost constantly, but now all that drives him is craving for the excitement of the moment. His moral sense deteriorates so completely that he does not hesitate to pass a bad cheque to his best friend in order to get money for gambling. He is too far gone even to care about losing his best – and last – friend.

Eventually, he is reduced to the status of a bum. He lives among the lowest types in a filthy flop-house. His father's lawyer gets him a job that pays barely enough for bed and board. But Vandover has degenerated too much even to stick to the simplest task.

When all the money he has in the world is $5 a week, the income from a few bonds, he risks even that small sum gambling with derelicts in his flop-house. On many days, the only food available to him is what he can get from free-lunch counters, but not even this semi-starvation can cure his gambling fever.

Finally, he begins to sell his bonds – not for food, but for money to gamble with. When the last is gone, he is at the end of his rope. Filthy, half-starved, utterly abject, he asks for help from his former friend, Geary, who is now a prosperous realtor. Geary enjoys Vandover's humiliation, and condescends to give him a job. The job is that of cleaning some cottages owned by Geary, which stand on the land which once was Vándover's.

But Vandover has sunk too low even to feel humiliation. Like a beaten animal, he slaves all day at the degrading job. He does not rebel when the new tenant treats him as if he were something less than human. All he wants now is to stay alive on the lowest level.

Type 2: The passive–feminine male gambler

This type displays the characteristics of the classical gambler, with the addition of a tendency toward unconscious feminine identification. This identification makes it possible for him to enjoy, in defeat, the emotional sensation of being overwhelmed.

When I explained this particular element in his psychic structure to one patient, he said indignantly, 'I resent that statement. To put it bluntly, you seem to be saying that losing means to me what being forced, willy-nilly, to have sexual intercourse means to a woman.'

The patient was on the right track, even though he did not understand the defensive reason for his deep indignation. This type of neurotic is often unjustly accused of being a homosexual pervert. He is not a homosexual, and never becomes one. The structure of perversion homosexuality is quite different.[6]

Passive–feminine gamblers consistently seek 'stronger' partners. The women they choose to marry are shrews; the men they choose for their friends are 'strong', 'superior' characters, who exploit or dominate them. Submissive, always on the lookout for someone to admire, they are the typical followers. They are of course unconscious of all this, since lack of initiative and absence of normal activity are easily rationalized. Only rarely do they react against their inner submissiveness; even then, the revolts are short-lived and quickly suppressed.[7]

When a Mr Milquetoast, with the personality just described, gets into a game with a more aggressive partner, his chances of winning are nil, because for him defeat means – in the vocabulary of the unconscious – sexual pleasure. He would be no worse off if he handed his money over to his opponent before the game began, so strong is his inner urge to lose, and in this way to enjoy the feeling of being overwhelmed.

The following passage from Otto Soyka's *Master in Gambling* is a good description of the behavior of this type of gambler:

John Auberg is the owner of a country estate. For three days now he has been in town. On the third evening he comes to me. He cannot hold out any longer. He always expects me to be surprised. Then he starts to play for the lowest stake. After the first loss, he gets *excited*; after the second, *belligerent*. If his losing streak continues, he reacts only with *exhaustion*. Now he increases his stake; he doubles, forcing the game. He has 4000 in his pocket. That's the quarterly income from his estate. I am informed about these details. After losing all the money he has on him, he grows rude and runs out, filled with suppressed hatred. The last minutes of the game are mildly interesting. Here I use my *ability to tame animals*. I know only too well that this is all I need and it compensates for the hours wasted. The next day, I invariably receive a polite letter in which the money he owes me is enclosed. *Never is there any change of program.*

'Shall we? Do you want to, Wehlen?' exclaims Auberg, rubbing his hands.

'Is it really necessary?' I ask. I am tired. 'We could just as well have dinner without touching cards.'

'By no means!' Auberg exclaims with fright in his voice.

I smile. 'Tell me the truth. *Can you even imagine that you could win when you gamble with me?* Think! Is this even a possibility?'

'What does that matter? Winning! Do I play for that purpose? Besides, why not?' The last sentence is spoken with *hesitation*. [Italics mine. E. B.]

These submissive losers, who are meek even when they protest, who always come back for more punishment, represent the typical suckers among gamblers. It is interesting, by the way, to note that in many languages there is a proverb to express the familiar idea: 'Unlucky at cards, lucky in love.' This folk saying embodies the idea that a man works off his psychic passivity in gambling, and can then assume the active role of the normal male and enjoy love. This intuitive formulation of a psychological idea, however, can be applied only to Sunday gamblers. *The real gambler is as masochistic in love as he is at the roulette wheel.* Fundamentally, he is not interested in normal love, although he often goes through the motions. But this is only a defense against his basic passivity.

The gambler's love life is pathological, and imbued with pronounced psychic masochism. The case of Chevalier Menars, already quoted*, is an illustration; the following juxtaposition is another. There is an amazing congruity between the experiences of my patient and those of the fictional character.

Clinical case

A lawyer–patient, in treatment because of personality difficulties, made a poor living despite the good start his wealthy family had given him in his profession. His 'technique of failure' was to antagonize senselessly his wealthy clients. Contributing further to his chronic financial difficulties were his constant losses at poker and horse-racing. Often he did not even put in an appearance at his office, but spent his days gambling. His sexual affairs were of two types: those with 'nice' girls (non-aggressive girls) who bored him but served as

* Pp. 48–55 of Bergler's book—not reproduced here.—Eds.

alibis, and 'bitches', for whom he had an inner predilection, covered by the 'alibi' type. The 'bitches' made him suffer, and he complained bitterly, but returned to them like a moth to a candle. One of these girls humiliated him no end: she spoke in public of his weak potency (meaning that her own frigidity made her insatiable), and ridiculed him for 'sticking to her, though she told him to go to hell'. She had an 'on-and-off' affair with a real 'he-man' and at times asked for the lawyer's apartment, so that she could entertain her married lover. The patient obliged her regularly! He came into treatment in one of his chronic depressions. Once more he had had to go to a hotel for the night, because the girl was entertaining her other lover in his apartment. His approach to his gambling addiction was strange: he considered losing natural. 'Aren't you supposed to pay for the pleasure?' he asked.

Literary example

The main character in Dostoyevsky's *The Gambler* is a young tutor attached to the household of a tyrannical Russian general. The young man is hopelessly in love with the general's step-daughter, Polina, who treats him like dirt, and constantly humiliates him. She is herself in love with a sponging French-man. The tutor speaks of himself as her slave, and offers to commit suicide by jumping from a precipice to prove his love. In a complicated intrigue, Polina arranges a situation in which the young man is nearly beaten, physically, by an aristocrat. He endures even this gratuitous cruelty passively. When he wins a large sum at gambling, he gives it to his beloved 'to throw in the Frenchman's face'. What happens, however, is that the money is thrown in his own face – by Polina.

Finally, he becomes the prey of a prostitute who treats him exactly as he wishes to be treated. She kicks him in the face, literally, takes all his money, and generally makes a fool of him. In the end, she even makes him a 'present' of a few francs of his own money. All this the poor victim accepts with good grace!

Type 3: The defensive pseudo-superior gambler

Although he corresponds, genetically, to the passive–feminine type, this gambler's psychic structure is based, not on submissiveness itself, but on a defense against the wish to be overwhelmed. He operates on the theory that the stronger personality is bound to win. He gambles only with men, finding it boring to gamble with women. A similar type in another sphere is the Don Juan who uses promiscuity and an excess of virile aggressiveness as unconscious defenses against his femininity. So long as the defensive gambler can find a sucker (Type 2) to play with, the fiction of his toughness and superiority can be sustained, and his neurosis remains latent. Should the fantasy be endangered for any reason, neurotic symptoms begin to manifest themselves.

Type 4: The gambler motivated by unconscious guilt

In this type, inner guilt originating in psychic masochism is shifted to later masturbatory fantasies that have an Oedipal content. Here again Oedipal fantasies are used to conceal a guilt that is more deeply repressed. It may be of some significance that the word *play*, among its other meanings, connotes both masturbatory–sexual and gambling activities. Freud pointed this out in his paper on Dostoyevsky.[8]

However, my personal experience has led me to believe that the Oedipal content of the gambler's guilt is secondary, and that the real guilt pertains to the earlier oral level. In my clinical work I have not encountered a gambler with a real hysteria-neurosis. I have never cured a gambler by treating for an Oedipal neurosis, but have always found it necessary to pierce that defense and get down to the primitive oral roots of his guilt.

The factor of unconscious guilt, which is always related to psychic masochism and the omnipotence-wish, explains the curious phenomenon of beginner's luck. It is a well-known fact that beginners are frequently lucky in games. The apparent explanation is that some time must elapse before the pleasure-pain cycle is completed, and punishment overtakes the gambler for his masochistically tinged pseudo-aggression.

Another element is also involved: the gambler who needs his winnings is more likely to lose than the gambler whose need for money is less urgent. The inner conscience vehemently objects to the unconscious pleasure in gambling, and especially to the pseudo-aggression that conceals psychic masochism. Thus there seems to be irony in the fact that the gambler with limited financial resources – who is risking his money in exhibiting more pronounced masochism – is more heavily penalized than the gambler who can afford to lose. In other words, the greater the psychic masochism, the heavier the penalty exacted by the inner conscience.

Type 5: The 'unexcited' gambler

The 'unexcited' gambler is a legendary character. He exists only in the imaginations of those who would like to appear detached. In reality there are no detached gamblers; gambling is a business too uncertain to attract the man who does not feel the gambler's neurotic excitement. It is true that among the so-called 'superior' gamblers (Type 3) can be found people who seem to fit this description. They are the gamblers who play for a living, plunging only occasionally, and in the wildest games. Honoré de Balzac mentions this type in *La peau de chagrin*: 'Opposite the bankholder stood some of the smart speculators and specialists of gambling who, like old criminals, were no longer afraid of the galley. They came to play three stakes and disappeared immediately after having won their livelihood.'

Type 6: Female gamblers

The above descriptions have all been of male gamblers. Until the beginning of the nineteenth century, gambling was an exclusively male prerogative;[9] the emancipation of women has changed that – but not the genetic reasons for gambling. Analysis of women who are gamblers has convinced me that all of these come under the classification of the 'classical' gambler (Type 1). Nothing is added but a few hysteric trimmings. Such women often give the impression that other elements are involved; in other words, that winning is equated with masculinity. This, however, is a superficial palimpsest. Deeper analysis proves that these women are typical psychic masochists, fighting their 'battle of injustice' with the unconscious image of the 'cruel' mother.

In *The Gambler* Dostoyevsky gives an excellent description of the typically cold, impassive woman gambler:

Opposite us, a little to the left, I observed a young woman sitting next to a youth – some relation of hers, I think. I had often re-marked this lady before. She played every day at one o'clock and left the table again precisely at two; playing for exactly an hour each day. She was known, and at one o'clock every day her chair was ready for her. She used to take out her purse and stake a fixed sum, playing very carefully, and always calculating and noting each turn of the ball on a piece of paper at her side. This lady invariably used to win one or two thousand francs each day and then leave the tables.

Grandmother watched her for a long while. 'There – *she'll* never lose, *she'll* never lose. Look at that. Who is she, do you know?'

'French, I believe,' I whispered; 'she looks like it.'

'Yes, she looks like a regular bird of passage.'

One sometimes suspects that the wish to be pushed into a position of passivity – the wish of every gambler – meets with less resistance in women than in men. This is easily under-standable, since the inwardly more passive man must put up an 'active' front, a social compulsion which does not apply to women.[10]

Whatever the superficial trimmings, the psychic structure of the woman gambler does not differ from that of the male. Unless there is deep regression to the first stages of develop-ment (oral phase), the neurotic does not become a gambler.

The following case history exemplifies the woman gambler who uses hysteric symptoms as a defense against psychic masochism.

The patient came into analysis because of severe headaches, for which no organic cause could be found. She seemed cold and detached; her attitude toward men was decidedly cynical. She had been married and divorced twice; both marriages had been legalized excursions into blackmail. Both husbands had been wealthy weaklings, who eventually bought her off with cash settlements. She was totally frigid. Her only interest in life was gambling, but she did not consider gambling a neurotic problem. In fact, she was unwilling even to discuss it. 'You just concentrate on my headaches,' she ordered. I explained that the personality operates as a single unit that cannot be divided into separate sections; I emphasized the significance of exactly those 'sections' she wanted to declare taboo.

Her analysis proved that her neurosis corresponded only

superficially to hysteric regression. Her strong hatred of men, it is true, could be explained by the feeling of inferiority that grew out of her conflict with her older brother. She hated his privileges, hated the greater freedom he enjoyed because he was a boy and she was 'only a girl', as her autocratic father put it. A positive Oedipus complex could be reconstructed from these elements. The girl retired from that position at an early stage to construct the superficial defense: 'I don't love Father; I hate him.' That hatred was later directed at the pair of Milquetoasts she chose as her husbands.

Behind this façade, however, was a powerful oral regression. There was clinical proof that she re-enacted, with her husbands, the situation of being unjustly treated. She had conflicts centring around self-created injustices. Her husbands were weaklings, whom she mistreated, but in her version of the story she was always the aggrieved party. Neither man was capable of victimizing her; they were victimized themselves.

In reality, her hatred of men was only a superficial defense mechanism. Completely ignoring her husband's weaknesses, she turned the tables and made them into – sadists. The situation was grotesque: she accused these men of 'deliberately refusing' her sexual gratification, although both men suffered from potency-disturbance and she herself was totally frigid.

The differential diagnosis between this woman's superficial hysteric traits and the more deeply repressed oral regression could be clinically proven. Whenever we find an individual in whom the mechanism of orality operates (with its triad: unconscious construction of defeats, repression of the self-provoked defeat, pseudo-aggression, apparently in self-defense, and finally self-pity) we define that person as an orally regressed neurotic, however deceptive outward appearances may be.

The patient's gambling addiction had the typical characteristics: she felt 'queerly excited' when she gambled, and especially after she lost. And she lost constantly.

Basically, all gamblers are orally regressed, as described in the 'classical type', despite their various *superficial* disguises.

Notes

1. Psychic masochism is not to be confused with *perversion* masochism. where bodily pain is sought and consciously approved. The psychic

masochist is unaware of his longing for defeat and consciously rejects it, as does the normal person. Only unconsciously is he a glutton for punishment.

2. The development of inner conscience is of course more complicated. The reader is referred to the author's book *The Superego* (New York: Grune & Stratton, 1951).

3. For compilation, see my *The Basic Neurosis: Oral Regression and Psychic Masochism* (New York: Grune & Stratton, 1949).

4. *New York Post*, 23 October 1946. A similar case occurred more recently, involving an instructor at an Eastern university.

5. For elaboration, see my book *The Writer and Psychoanalysis*, 2nd enlarged edition (New York: Brunner's Psychiatric Books, 1954).

6. Summarized in my book *Homosexuality: Disease or Way of Life?* (New York: Hill & Wang, 1956).

7. See case Mr D., Chapter 10 [of Bergler's book—Eds.]. The 'negative Oedipus' is but a later and attenuated duplication of deeper repressed earlier masochistic vicissitudes; the 'power to damage' is shifted from mother to father. For elaboration see *The Basic Neurosis*.

8. Sigmund Freud, 'Dostoevsky and Parricide', *The Standard Edition of the Complete Psychological Works of Sigmund Freud*, ed. and trans. James Strachey, 23 vols. (Hogarth Press, 1953—), Vol. 21, pp. 177–94. (One might also quote the fact that the visible use of the hands in gambling provides an alibi for the inner reproach pertaining to their use in masturbation.)

9. The notable exception was the eighteenth-century Englishwoman of high society; see Austin Dobson's *Eighteenth-Century Vignettes* (New York: Dodd, Mead, 1892).

10. See the theory, 'The Hoax of the He-Man', in my book *Conflict in Marriage* (New York: Harper, 1949).

Ralph R. Greenson

On Gambling[*]

I

Gambling is a universally popular social institution. In our culture it enjoys a marginal position as an acceptable social activity. The shade of immorality varies in different countries and states, and in the various classes within those localities. The sociologists have described some aspects of gambling in different cultures. For example, Myrdal[1] has pointed out that the Negro in America finds gambling a favourite recreation because it offers the possibility of a quick monetary return for an economically repressed people. In addition, gambling is a form of entertainment which requires little paraphernalia and is particularly suited for those in monotonous occupations. Veblen[2] noted that the leisure class finds reckless gambling an enjoyable occasion for the need to demonstrate conspicuous waste. Rosten[3] has suggested that the prevalence of gambling in the movie colony may be due to the unpredictable and sudden changes of fortune in that industry which accentuate the importance of luck.

In our society, monetary rewards are morally justified only as the result of work, thrift and sacrifice. Easy money is considered ill-gotten. This sheds some light on the immoral connotation associated with gambling. On the other hand, several authors have pointed out the close association between gambling and religion. It is striking that in a Gallup Poll of 1938 it was found that 28 per cent of the adult American population have participated in church lotteries – a greater number than the 21 per cent who have played cards for money. Gambling has also been described in primitive cultures where it is intimately tied up with religious rituals.[4]

*Presented, in part, before the Los Angeles Psychoanalytic Study Group, 21 June 1946. From *American Imago*, Vol. 4, No. 2 (1947), pp. 61–77. Reprinted by permission of the author.

Some great literary artists have contributed to our knowledge of the unconscious motivations in gamblers. Dostoyevsky[5] portrays the character of the gambler as a sado-masochistically ridden individual who is unable to break himself of this addiction. Conrad's[6] gambler is a homosexual with a murderous hatred for all women.

Freud's contribution to the problem of gambling is to be found in his penetrating study of Dostoyevsky.[7] On the basis of the artist's writings, his wife's diary and communications from Dostoyevsky's personal friends, Freud formulated some of the basic concepts of gambling. Dostoyevsky's gambling was an irrational, instinct-like force. He played impulsively and could never stop until he had lost everything. This need to lose was a self-inflicted punishment. Only after Dostoyevsky had thus rid himself of guilt feelings was he able to return to creative writing. Freud pointed out how gambling is a substitute and derivative of masturbation. The emphasis on the exciting activity of the hands is the link which connects gambling and masturbation. The irresistibility of the urge, the oft-repeated resolutions, the intoxicating quality of the pleasure and the enormous guilt feelings are present in both gambling and masturbation. Furthermore, in both activities there are unconscious phantasies of being rescued by a mother-figure.

The psychoanalytic literature based on clinical material concerning gambling is very sparse.[8] It is the purpose of this paper to organize the available clinical material and to present some theoretical constructions concerning the essential psychodynamics of the gambler. My experience is limited to the analysis of five male patients who gambled. None of these patients, however, came for treatment with gambling as his main problem. In addition, I have had occasion to make observations on gambling in the U.S. Army from 1942 to 1946, primarily among officers, and in civilian life, primarily among physicians. Since these data are limited in scope, more research is necessary before definite conclusions can be drawn.

The decisive characteristic of gambling which differentiates it from other contests and speculations is the coexistence of a game-like quality and the importance of chance in determining success or failure. A game is a make-believe, a pretense, not to be taken seriously and not like real life. Chance refers to the unpredictability of the results, to the elements of risk and luck.

The more unpredictable a game is, the more it conforms to the definition of gambling. The more that skill is involved in a contest, the less it resembles gambling, and the more it resembles a sport or a business.

It is possible to classify superficially three different types of gamblers: (1) the normal person who gambles for diversion or distraction and who can stop gambling when he wants to; (2) the professional gambler who selects gambling as his means of earning a livelihood; (3) the neurotic gambler who gambles because he is driven by unconscious needs, and who is unable to stop gambling. These three types gamble for different conscious and unconscious reasons, nevertheless, some of the same motivations are found in all of them. The neurotic gambler caricatures the normal and professional gambler and the psychopathology is most vivid in him.

The following is a brief description of readily observable habits, customs and patterns found in watching a gambling game. The first striking characteristic is the atmosphere of excitement. This is visible in the tremor and sweating of the players, and in their motor restlessness. It is audible in the noise and in the hushed silences. There is a rhythm of tension–discharge, which is constantly repeated. At the beginning of play it is quiet, gradually there is a crescendo of excitement until a peak is reached, and finally there is a period of quiet. The excitement, the rhythm, the tension–discharge, and the final quiet bear an obvious similarity to sexual excitement. This seems to be borne out by the fact that the rolling of the dice is referred to as 'coming,' a slang expression for orgasm. It is further confirmed in the fact that the tension the players experience is a pleasurable one and the game ends with the players usually feeling spent.[9]

Another noteworthy observation is that in poker and in dice games usually only members of the same sex participate. When women take part they behave in an asexual manner, use masculine mannerisms and language, and seem to take the same position *vis-à-vis* the gamblers that the tomboy takes with boys. In bridge, where there is more skill and less gambling, there is usually an even distribution of the sexes and the women behave in a more feminine manner. In roulette, which is entirely a game of chance, women are present but psycho-sexual differences are barely recognizable; the women expect and receive no special courtesies or attention. There is no flirtation at the gambling table. The anti-feminine atmosphere of the gambling room is not only manifest in the exclusion of the opposite sex, but in the anti-feminine vocabulary of the players; for example, queens are often referred to as whores. (Women sense the anti-feminine atmosphere of the gambling hall and are usually antagonistic to their husbands' gambling.)

The vocabulary of the gamblers is very distinctive; it is profane, but not sexual, and it is highly aggressive. The stakes are always called 'the pot', the player refers to 'making a big pot' or to 'cleaning up'. Looking at one's hand slowly is called 'squeezing out a hand'. A lucky player is often referred to as one who has 'fallen into a barrel of shit', and dice are called 'craps'. Winning is referred to as 'making a killing'; losing as 'being cleaned out'. A specific maneuver in poker is designated 'sand-bagging'. When a player has a sure-fire winning hand he may refer to his position as having the others 'by the balls'. When one of the gamblers misses his turn, he is told that 'his nose is bleeding'.

Another characteristic of all gambling situations is the prevalence of superstitions and magical rituals. There are a great many colorful and varied practices which are used as attempts to bring good luck. The players change seats, walk around chairs, change decks of cards, have good-luck charms on the table or on their person, rub their cards or dice on various parts of their body, look at their cards in a certain prescribed order, wager high stakes on poor cards because of 'hunches' and bet little on good cards because certain cards are unlucky, etc. Many of them believe that concentration will influence the sequence of cards or the roll of the dice. The dice-player shouts as he throws the dice, exclaiming, 'Be good to me dicey,' or 'Come on Ada,' when he needs an eight. Some poker-players admit that they pray as they wait for a card.

Other behavior patterns of a stereotyped nature are readily observed among all players. Some constantly count, pile and sort their money or chips. Others have their money and the various colored chips carelessly scrambled before them. Expelling of gas by some of the players is accepted as part of the ritual of the poker game in some groups. Marked extremes in neatness and sloppiness of dress can be observed. Some players fondle their cards gently and others fling them on the table. Bluffing is a daring technique which some players frequently use, and which others always avoid. (It is one of the few occasions in our society where the act of deception is not merely permissible, but an enviable talent.)

There is an unusual amount of eating, drinking and smoking around the gambling tables. Most gamblers eat, drink and smoke more during the gambling than they do in any other comparative period of time.

Some of the phenomena described above are seen in all types of gambling and in all types of gamblers. All these activities are of a regressive nature; they are all derivatives of infantile partial instincts. The phallic and homosexual manifestations are apparent in the exclusion of women from a situation where sensual excitation is present. The vocabulary of the gambler abounds in anal, scatological and overtly sadistic expressions. Anal-sadistic derivatives are also seen in the extremes of neatness and sloppiness of dress, in the sorting and piling of chips and in the expelling of gas.[10] Oral drives are accentuated in the over-eating, drinking and smoking. Even the thinking of the gambler has regressed to a more infantile level, as is manifest in the superstitious, magical and ritualistic procedures. All these observations indicate very clearly that the gambling situation permits the discharge of pregenital impulses. Phallic, anal-sadistic and oral strivings may be discharged in this setting with a minimum of guilt feelings, since this behavior is accepted by the group and the guilt is shared by the other players. The regressive nature of these activities is confirmed by the archaic thinking and acting of the players in their attempts to influence luck. Since all people have remnants of pregenital instincts within them, and since our society imposes obstacles in the satisfaction of these instincts, and since gambling offers such a diversified opportunity for satisfaction of the many different partial instincts, it is understandable why almost everyone in our society can gamble.

II

Until now we have described and attempted to isolate phenomena which are common to all gambling situations and to all people who gamble. At this point, it shall be our task to formulate the specific conflicts which are decisive for the formation of a gambling neurosis. Here we refer to those people who must gamble, who cannot stop gambling, and who allow gambling to tyrannize and destroy their lives. There seem to be two crucial elements which are essential to the etiology of a gambling neurosis: (1) the neurotic gambler feels lucky and hopes each time he will be rewarded, despite all intellectualization to the contrary;[11] (2) the neurotic gambler is impelled to test out luck or fate. The normal and professional gambler may have either of these qualities, but the intensity of these drives is lacking. Feeling lucky and the need to challenge fate and chance are interwoven, yet it is possible to trace the genesis of these emotions separately.

The neurotic gambler hopes he is lucky and at times believes it. Consciously or unconsciously he believes in his right to ask fate for special privileges and protection. He hopes that fate will give proof that he is favored over all the others and he will be permitted to win. Winning is the proof that he is lucky. It is pleasurable not only for the money (some gamblers play for little or no money), but it is a token of special privilege and power. The neurotic gambler seeks a sign from fate that he is omnipotent. His longing for omnipotence is full of doubts and contradictions, yet it is this archaic ego feeling which makes gambling at all possible. He dares challenge the gods to give him a sign that will confirm this shaky belief in his omnipotence, yet he would never risk this challenge did he not, in part, already believe it. The neurotic gambler mistakes his strong yearnings for omnipotence for the feeling that he is omnipotent.[12] The regressive character of this state of affairs is in keeping with the infantile features of the neurotic gambler's thinking and actions which have a strikingly animistic, superstitious and magical quality. The neurotic gambler dares to gamble since he wants to convince himself that he is lucky, i.e. omnipotent, and needs constant reassurance from fate to calm his grave doubts.

The longing for omnipotence and the belief in one's omnipotence stem from early infantile life. Ferenczi[13] has presented the concept that all infants originally have a feeling of unlimited omnipotence. This is lost when hunger and pain destroy the infant's narcissism. The adults who assuage hunger and pain become the omnipotent ones. By introjection and identification the infant tries to participate in the omnipotence of the adults.

On this infantile level, hunger and need for love are undifferentiated, satisfaction and security are identical. In the infant, milk satisfies the hunger and brings about a reunion with the mother, which produces oceanic feelings and restores the lost omnipotence. It is this feeling which the neurotic gambler unconsciously is attempting to recapture.

The neurotic gambler is a personality on the brink of a severe depression. He deludes himself into feeling lucky and attempts to win from fate a sign of favor which will simultaneously gratify his urgent need for satisfaction and security.[14] We shall return to the question of why this attempt fails, but first let us examine the concept of fate and chance in this situation.

Who or what is luck or fate? Luck and fate are equivalent to God and to father. It is the powerful, omnipotent, protecting figure that can kill, castrate, abandon or love. The neurotic gambler's attitude toward this father-figure varies with the specific gambler and changes within him under certain circumstances. The gambling situation may represent:

1. A challenge or a testing-out of this father-figure.[15] If luck is good it means the father has accepted you and you may share in his omnipotence. If luck is bad, it means you have been rejected. Winning often results in transitory euphoria and losing in temporary depression, both inappropriate to the amount of money won or lost.

2. The game may represent a battle with fate. It is a sham battle for supremacy, an attempt to supplant the father as the omnipotent one.

3. Gambling may be felt as an act of extreme submissiveness in which the gambler places himself at the mercy of fate. The gambler's attitude is, 'Here I am, do with me what you will.'

4. Gambling may also represent an attempt to bribe this powerful father-figure. 'Here is my money, now am I allowed to enjoy certain forbidden pleasures?'

5. The game may also symbolize an occasion to court or woo the father-figure, according to the formula 'I have been a good boy and have done all my tasks, now will you reward me and let me win?'

Luck is also a mother-figure to some gamblers – Lady Luck. Here, the mother-figure is less frightening, but none the less powerful. Lady Luck is fickle, she is not to be trusted. She may deceive you, but she may also reward you. The demands of the gambler may be accepted or rejected, and he may challenge, battle, beg or woo. Bergler stressed aggressions against the mother as the most important unconscious motives in the gambler he studied.

In the patients I had occasion to analyze, the figure of luc was determined by the specific emotional conflicts of the patients which were in the foreground at the moment. The attitude of the gambler to this figure varied from battling to wooing, depending upon the drives involved in the patient's most pressing psychic conflicts. In any case, the image and attitude toward Luck was determined by the Oedipus constellation of the specific gambler. For example, a patient during the course of his analysis reacted to Luck as a father-figure he was battling, when he was reliving his hostility toward his father in his analysis. Later on Luck became 'Lady Luck', whom he wooed, when conflicts concerning his mother became the central point of his analysis.

To recapitulate: the neurotic gambler has regressed to infantile longings for omnipotence. He dares expose himself to Fate, since he has mistaken his longings for omnipotence, for the feeling that he is omnipotent. He enters this arena fearfully and hopefully, and expects a token from a parent-figure, Fate, which will prove that he is really the chosen one. Since strong longings for omnipotence and oceanic feelings are evidence of a failure of the ego to maintain a mature level, one would expect to find in the history of neurotic gamblers severe deprivation and/or over-gratification in childhood. This is confirmed by the clinical findings. One of my patients had a mother who never said no; he never learned to tolerate any rejection no matter how mild. It was significant that he gambled only when he was away from home – away from mother – as an attempt to prove that 'Lady Luck' (his phrase) was still with him. In the case of another patient, his father and mother each had their favorite child and he was not the favorite of either. Sent overseas to the C.B.I. Theatre, he became depressed and felt abandoned, and resorted to gambling, in part as a fight against Fate, father, for abandoning him and as a symbolic plea to Lady Luck, mother – a begging for a sign of love.

These attempts to recapture the lost feeling of omnipotence are unsuccessful. The neurotic gambler is unable to stop gambling because he cannot bear the feeling of abandonment and depression when he loses; nor can he bear the excitement of winning. In both cases, unresolved tensions require that he continue the game. The feelings aroused by winning and by losing are so interwoven with guilt feelings that full satisfaction is impossible and the frustrated wishes return again and again, seeking gratification. Our next task shall be to explore the sources of these guilt feelings involved in the neurosis of gambling.

For the neurotic gambler winning is equivalent to triumph. As Fenichel[16] pointed out, the feeling of triumph results from the removal of anxiety and inhibition by the winning of a trophy. Possession of the trophy brings with it 'oceanic' feelings, because it represents reunion with the omnipotent one. The trophy is a super-ego derivative since it is a symbol of parental power. The super-ego is a precipitate of the Oedipus complex which is internalized and serves as an authority over the ego. Since a trophy is also a representative of the authority once vested in the Oedipus figures, it, too, threatens the ego in the same way that the super-ego threatens the ego where unresolved Oedipus phantasies are at work. The winnings of the neurotic gambler resemble the trophy of the hunter and threaten the gambler in a similar way. 'Easy come, easy go' and 'hot money' typify the gambler's guilt-laden attitude towards his winnings.

The unconscious phantasies of the neurotic gambler are identical with the masturbation phantasies of the individual and are responsible in part for the guilt feelings in regard to gambling[17]. Masturbation and gambling both start out as play. A play begins as an attempt to discharge tension in a regulated dosage at a specific time. In masturbation and in gambling, the stirring up of unconscious Oedipal phantasies destroys the playful character of the act.[18] The ego is overwhelmed by anxiety and guilt, and what started out as play is no longer play nor pleasurable, but becomes a threat to the mental equilibrium. The neurotic gambler is conscious of his guilt feelings, but is unaware of the content of these guilt feelings. The forbidden nature of the phantasies stirred up in gambling are responsible for the fact that these phantasies must be maintained in repression. In gambling only distorted derivatives of these phantasies are permitted access to consciousness in the form of Fate and Luck phantasies. Since gambling allows only distorted derivatives of forbidden impulses to break through into consciousness, and since this is always accompanied by guilt feelings, the neurotic gambler's possibilities for complete gratification are nullified by these circumstances.

The neurotic gambler's constant losing is due in part to his inability to accept the dictates of the mathematical laws of chance. In part it is due to the fact that losing money can symbolize an anal orgasm for the pregenitally oriented gambler.[19] 'To be cleaned out' is a typical gambler's expression for losing. The unconscious guilt feelings are more important in explaining the need to lose of the neurotic gambler. Freud,[20] in describing the unconscious need for punishment, stated that some people act out forbidden phantasies in a distorted way in order to be apprehended. The unconscious guilt feelings of the neurotic gambler are responsible for the unconscious need for punishment.[21] This punishment, losing, bad as it is, is a lesser evil than the terrifying punishment of castration or total loss of love. The need to lose may also be an expression of masochistic strivings. Losing, i.e. being beaten, is eroticized, and becomes an appropriate vehicle for masochistic phantasies.

It was stated that the super-ego is a residue of the Oedipus complex. In the healthy individual the super-ego has been desexualized. In the pregenitally fixated person there is a resexualization of the super-ego. In keeping with the regression to sado-masochistic object relationships, there is also a sado-masochistic relationship between super-ego and ego. In manic-depressive states, euphoria and melancholia are manifestations of this special position of the super-ego.[22] In the euphoric state, super-ego and ego are united, and there is a minimum of tension between them. In melancholia, the super-ego takes great delight in cruelly tormenting the ego. Similar super-ego–ego relationships are found in drug addicts and in neurotic gamblers. A longitudinal survey of the clinical course in the addict and gambler reveals frequent sharp fluctuations of affect with recurring states of elation and depression.[23]

III

The discussion, thus far, has been concerned with analyzing what 'feeling lucky' means, what Fate represents and why the neurotic gambler is unable to stop gambling. All this would apply to the solitaire-players, the roulette-player, and those who play alone against Fate or Luck, rather than against other players. Competing against other players, as in cards or dice, had different meanings in the patients I studied. The fellow players served various purposes in the unconscious phantasies of the neurotic gamblers. The relationship of the neurotic gambler to his fellow gamblers may be schematized along the following lines.

1. The fellow gamblers are grown-ups and grant participation in the forbidden and exciting activities of adults.

2. The fellow gamblers are 'he-men'; sex and women are 'sissy stuff'. This is very reminiscent of the gang spirit of adolescence.[24] In the army, among personnel of late adolescent age (eighteen to twenty-one), gambling for high stakes was considered masculine.

3. The fellow gamblers are cohorts in homosexual activities. Gambling with other men was equivalent, in the unconscious, to comparing penises with other men; winning meant having the largest penis or being the most potent. Excitement together often represented masturbation together. In passive homosexual men who love the type of man they would like to have been, contact with strong men in a game had the significance of gaining additional manhood.[25] Unconscious homosexuality is demonstrated by the neurotic gambler in his sparse or Don Juan type of sexual life. Two of my patients had overt homosexual episodes and turned to gambling during periods of sexual abstinence. Another patient became a gambler only after developing premature ejaculation. His gambling, on the one hand, was a disguised homosexual substitute for heterosexual satisfaction, and on the other hand, it was an attempt to deny his impotence. The expression 'lucky in cards, unlucky in love' is a striking testimonial to the fact that neurotics with unresolved conflicts regarding homo- and heterosexuality find gambling an appropriate outlet for their frustrations.

4. The fellow gamblers may be reacted to as father or mother surrogates and therefore may also fulfill the same function as the figures in the unconscious fate phantasies. The neurotic gambler may act out in his card game a challenging, wooing, battling or submissive attitude in relation to the other players.

Many of the pregenital instinctual expressions are obvious to the onlooker at a gambling game, but in analysis one specific series of characteristics emerges with greater clarity. The waiting for fate to decide, the passive attitudes of the gambler as he waits for his cards, the inordinate dependence on this external image (Luck), all of these characteristics rooted in the oral-receptive phase of libidinal development were the most stubborn factors to overcome in the cases analysed.

The habitual kibitzer should be mentioned as a special type of neurotic gambler. He is a gambler without the courage to gamble. My clinical experience with chronic kibitzers has suggested that they are similar to that type of homosexual described by Freud[26] as those fixated to an older brother and who long to participate in his success. The kibitzer is afraid to participate in the game, but identifies himself with one of the players he would like to emulate. He avoids the risk of losing, but he also never achieves the satisfaction of having exposed himself successfully to danger. These men often go through life attached to some strong older brother figure and by identification with him enjoy and suffer in small doses the older brother's triumphs and sorrows.'

IV Summary

Neurotic gambling is based on an unconscious attempt to regain the lost feeling of omnipotence by fighting and/or wooing Luck or Fate. The gambler dares to expose himself to this situation because he already has regressed to a stage where the desire for this archaic ego feeling is misinterpreted for the feeling itself. Luck and Fate are derived from mother and/or father images and gambling offers an opportunity for the revival of unconscious Oedipal phantasies. In addition, gambling offers satisfaction possibilities for latent and unconscious homosexual, anal-sadistic, oral-receptive drives, and gratification of unconscious needs for punishment. Because of the diversity of opportunities and the social sanction, it is understandable why almost everyone in our society can gamble.[27] It is clear that neurotics with unresolved longings for omnipotence and oceanic feelings would be predisposed to fall ill with this disease.

Neurotic gambling belongs in the category of the impulse neuroses. It resembles the addictions and the perversions, in that the impulse to gamble is not felt as ego-alien, but ego-syntonic. Though it is not overtly sexual as in the perversions, nor is there the euphoric intoxication as in the addictions, yet the gambler likes his gambling – he feels forced to like it. The impulse to gamble is felt in the same way as normal people feel their instincts. It serves the purpose of denying an infantile sense of danger (i.e. abandonment) and simultaneously gratifies thinly distorted sexual and aggressive impulses. It has an irresistible quality: the tension has to be satisfied by action, not thinking, and immediately, not by postponement. (The gambler acts according to the pleasure principle, and in gambling games the pleasure principle is equally as valid as the reality principle.) The imperative demand for simultaneous instinct gratification and need to be loved indicates a regression to an early libidinal phase, where instinct satisfaction and striving for security were not differentiated from each other. To the neurotic gambler people are transformed into merely potential donors of narcissistic gratification, a characteristic of the orally oriented individual.

All these factors demonstrate the severely regressive character of the disease. This suggests that the gambling neurosis, like so many of the impulse neuroses, is an effort at defense against an impending severe depression.

The course of this illness is a very stormy one; these patients often require periods of institutionalization. The only adequate therapy is psychoanalysis. The prognosis is not favorable, since there are frequent relapses and often the secondary complications of gambling, namely legal and monetary difficulties interfere with the treatment. In general the course, prognosis, and treatment, is similar to that of the addictions and the perversions.

Notes

1. Gunnar Myrdal, *An American Dilemma* (New York: Harper, 1944), p. 985.
2. Thorstein Veblen, *The Theory of the Leisure Class* (London: Allen & Unwin, 1925; New York: Vanguard, 1932), pp. 68, 276.
3. Leo C. Rosten, *Hollywood, the Movie Colony, the Moviemakers* (New York: Harcourt, 1941), p. 222.
4. Collis Stocking, 'Gambling', *Encyclopedia of the Social Sciences* (New York: Macmillan, 1931), Vol. 6, pp. 555–8.
5. Fyodor Dostoyevsky, *The Gambler* (Harmondsworth: Penguin Books, 1971; New York: Macmillan, 1931).
6. Joseph Conrad, *Victory* (Methuen, 1924).

7. Sigmund Freud, 'Dostoevsky and Parricide', *The Standard Edition of the Complete Psychological Works of Sigmund Freud*, ed. and trans. James Strachey, 23 vols. (London: Hogarth Press, 1953—), Vol. 21, pp. 177–94.

8. Edmund Bergler, 'The Gambler: A Misunderstood Neurotic', *Journal of Criminal Psychopathology*, Vol. 4 (1943), pp. 379–93. Ernst Simmel, 'Zur Psychoanalyse des Spielers' ('On the Psychoanalysis of the Gambler'), *Internationale Zeitschrift für Psychoanalyse*, Vol. 6 (1920), p. 397.

9. René Laforgue, 'On the Eroticization of Anxiety', *International Journal of Psycho-Analysis*, Vol. 11 (1930), pp. 312–21.

10. Simmel, op. cit.

11. Otto Fenichel, *The Psychoanalytic Theory of Neurosis* (London: Kegan Paul, French & Trubner, 1946; New York: Norton, 1945), p. 372.

12. Dostoyevsky's Gambler: 'I only know that I must win, that it is the only resource left to me. Well, that's why, perhaps, I fancy I am bound to win.'

13. Sandor Ferenczi, *Contributions to Psycho-Analysis* (Boston: Richard G. Badger, 1916).

14. Sándor Rado, 'The Psychical Effects of Intoxication', *International Journal of Psycho-Analysis*, Vol. 9 (1928), p. 301.

15. Dostoyevsky's Gambler: 'A strange sensation rose up in me, a sort of defiance of fate, a desire to challenge it, to put out my tongue at it.'

16. Otto Fenichel, 'Trophy and Triumph', *The Collected Papers of Otto Fenichel*, 2nd series (New York: Norton, 1954), pp. 141–62.

17. ibid., p. 373.

18. Freud, 'Dostoevsky and Parricide'.

19. Ernst Simmel, personal communication.

20. Sigmund Freud, 'Some Character-Types Met with in Psycho-Analytic Work', *Standard Edition*, Vol. 14, pp. 309–33.

21. Freud, 'Dostoevsky and Parricide'.

22. Sigmund Freud, 'Mourning and Melancholia', *Standard Edition*, Vol. 14, pp. 239–58.

23. Sándor Rado, 'The Psychoanalysis of Pharmacothymia', *Psychoanalytic Quarterly*, Vol. 2, No. 1 (January 1933), p. 1.

24. It is interesting to note that gambling with others only starts after puberty. Prior to that the magical and animistic games are very common, but these are usually carried on alone. Gambling with others is a continuation of magical thinking and acting within the limits of an acceptable social institution. Luck replaces the secret oracles of the child.

25. Bergler points out that the need to be overwhelmed by Fate is the result of passive homosexual wishes toward the father and is especially true of those with the compulsive need to lose at gambling. In one of my patients, losing at cards meant for him the unconscious wish to be homosexually possessed by the father.

26. Sigmund Freud, 'Some Neurotic Mechanisms in Jealousy, Paranoia Homosexuality', *Standard Edition*, Vol. 18, pp. 223–32.

27. It would seem to be very worthwhile to study the relationship between economic and political frustrations and the tendency to gamble. More specifically, it would be interesting to have a sociological framework for studying the relationship between specific kinds of economic and political frustrations and the specific kinds of gambling in different societies.

Robert M. Lindner

The Psychodynamics of Gambling*

It is quite likely that gambling was recognized as an illness by
the laity long before it occupied the attention of behavior
specialists. The fact that the passion to risk possessions could
assume a pathological form characterized by symptoms related
to the various addictions, could marshal behind it compulsions
which were beyond reason, could overbear judgement to the
very last degree, seems always to have been common knowledge
among common folk everywhere.

The poet, too, and the artist have long since been aware of
the true nature of gambling. Indeed, with the insight of inspira-
tion so envied by the scientist – who, unlike the creative artist,
is constrained to walk the paths of knowledge more slowly out
of the necessity to gather and examine facts as he goes – the
wielders of pen and brush and song have correctly penetrated
to the core of this baffling phenomenon. For them, it has ever
been related to the emotions, and they have divined its intimate
connection with the excitements, the ecstasies, the pains,
pleasures, and perplexities of love and hate.

As an illness of mind, as a distortion of behaviour, gambling
has only very recently found a place within the compass of
concern of the psychological sciences and their arts of practice.
Beyond allusions and occasional obtuse references, nothing
appears on the topic prior to the current century. There exists,
on the subject, a startling paucity either of clinical or research
or speculative material before our own time; and even now,
only a handful of usable studies are available.

Perhaps the first paper of any value whatsoever as an aid
towards the understanding of gambling in any other than

* From the *Annals of the American Academy of Political and Social Science*,
Vol. 269 (May 1950), pp. 93–107. Reprinted by permission of the
publisher. As originally published Lindner's article was extensively inter-
spersed with sub-headings, which have been removed.

poetic terms was that of Ernst Simmel in 1920.[1] This psychoanalyst, following certain hints on the subject made by Freud, recognized the gambler as a seriously disturbed individual whose behavior bespoke a regression to the anal level of libidinous development. Simmel thought that the characteristics of the gambler (see below) derived from attempts to obtain, through the mechanism of reverting to earlier infantile ways of conduct, the 'narcissistic supplies' – i.e. food, love, comfort and attention – which were believed by the gambler to have been denied him. Gambling was thus a repetitive effort to force longed-for satisfactions by the use of primitive techniques, and its pathology lay in its hopeless reversion to outmoded and unsuitable modes of behavior and thought.

Simmel's formulation seems to have remained unquestioned until, in 1929, Sigmund Freud prepared, as a preface to a critical evaluation and compilation of sources of Dostoyevsky's *The Brothers Karamazov*, an essay entitled 'Dostoevsky and Parricide'.[2] In this acute psychological appraisal and analysis of the Russian novelist the founder of psychoanalysis sought, among other things, to interpret the great writer's passion for gambling. The theory the psychologist evolved relates the pathological compulsion to the pervasive conflict over masturbation. In the strength of desire to obtain onanistic gratification, in the heroic efforts to relinquish the habit, in the torment of self-castigation that follows upon giving in to the act, Freud finds amazing parallels with the experience of gambling; and for him it becomes a substitute – albeit an unconscious one and accompanied by exquisite self-punishment – for masturbation.

Soon after the appearance of this paper, the bare equation it proposed for the gambling passion as its psychodynamics was extended by Theodor Reik, Freud's eminent pupil and colleague. In a brilliant critical study of Freud's essay on Dostoyevsky, Reik related gambling to obsessional symptoms.[3] Taking as his clue the fact that it is the fear of the father that causes the boy to suppress the onanism, Reik went on to describe gambling as a 'kind of question addressed to destiny'. The astute and erudite Reik, more aware than most scholars of the oracular origins of gambling in the remote reaches of history (marked sticks and pebbles used by the seers and diviners who cast them to determine the will of the gods have been found by archaeologists), recognized it as a modern form of oracle through which the gambler seeks to penetrate the future and thereby to obtain an answer to the question that unconsciously plagues him: will I be punished or forgiven for my trespasses (masturbation)? Destiny, 'the ultimate father surrogate', is thus besought for an answer through the vicissitudes of the play and its chance-determined outcome.

Laforgue in France and Jones in England next made contributions towards understanding the psychology of gambling. The former dealt with the subject in terms of erotization of fear, while the latter considered it as a sublimation of Oedipal aggression towards the father.[4]

Not until the publication of the papers of Bergler, however, was the topic given the serious exploration it required. In two articles, the first appearing in 1936 and the second in 1943, Bergler tried to develop a comprehensive psychology of the gambling neurosis, to trace its origins on the basis of clinical material obtained directly from psychoanalytic–therapeutic work with gambling patients, and, finally, to develop a typology of gamblers.[5] Because his work represents the first thorough-going attempt in the entire literature of the psychological sciences to treat of this problem that now occupies us, it deserves elaboration.

Bergler begins with the amazing proposition that the gambler is a neurotic with the unconscious wish to lose, despite the overt behavior which seems directed upon winning. He substantiates this paradox by outlining the six symptoms or characteristics which, taken together, describe the gambler and his neurosis. They are:

1. 'The gambler habitually takes chances.' Here the determining factor is a quantitative one, the key being the word 'habitually'.

2. 'The game precludes all other interests.' A total investment of energy and time makes the gambler's preoccupation the center of his life and the focal point even of his phantasies and daydreams.

3. 'The gambler is full of optimism and never learns from defeat.' Despite losses and reversals, the mathematics of chance and all logic, he 'conveys the impression of a man who has signed a contract with Fate stipulating that persistence must be rewarded'.

4. 'The gambler never stops when winning.' The goal of the gambler, at least the conscious goal, is to win continuously, permanently, totally – or not at all.

5. 'Despite initial caution, the gambler eventually risks too large sums.' The conscience of the gambler requires continuous appeasement, and he consequently finds a conscious rationalization for every step towards total involvement even to complete degradation.

6. ' "Pleasurable–painful tension" (thrill) is experienced (by the gambler) between the time of betting and the outcome of the game.' Without the strange ingredient of 'thrill', no game is worth the candle to the gambler; it is a primary and necessary element which overshadows all else to be derived from the activity.

Following this inclusive symptomatology of the gambler, Bergler observes that, with this kind of neurotic a vicious circle of unconscious aggression and self-punishment has been set up. The activity of gambling in itself unconsciously activates the megalomania and grandiosity of childhood, reverting to the 'fiction of omnipotence'. This is combined with a latent rebellion against the reality principle in the guise of logic. Such aggression has to be paid for, according to the rigid economics of internal life, by feelings of guilt, and from this is derived the need for self-punishment. Obviously, then, the psychic equilibrium of the gambler depends upon his losing, so that the inner books may be balanced.

But beyond this, there occurs a sexualization of that punishment (Bergler here draws the apt parallel of the sexualization of fear as it can be observed in a culturally pure form among audiences attending mystery thrillers at motion-picture houses) as psychic masochism. To explain the term 'psychic masochism', Bergler draws upon his theory of the basic mechanism of all neuroses, the 'mechanism of orality', which need not concern us here.

Finally, Bergler distinguishes four types of gamblers: (1) the 'classical' gambler who demonstrates all of the six above-mentioned characteristics, rebels against the reality principle (logic, adult world), and pays through 'masochistically tinged' self-punishment; (2) a type of male gambler who has a strong feminine identification with his mother and seeks the sexual satisfaction of being overwhelmed; (3) a type of male gambler who seeks to defend against his feminine identification, throws up a defense of excessive masculinity behind which to hide, and maintains a façade of maleness; and (4) a 'fictitious type', the 'gambler without excitement', whose passion, Bergler believes, is there but hidden.

A final study by Greenson completes our survey of the available literature on the psychodynamics of gambling.[6] This author places the personality of the gambler among the impulse neurotics. He believes that the activity is resorted to in order to relieve tensions arising in an 'infantile sense of danger', denying it and at the same time gratifying distorted sexual and aggressive impulses for which it serves as a culturally accepted vehicle. He further regards the gambling neurosis as an attempt to ward off an impending severe depression, which apparently arises out of the threatened breakthrough into consciousness of such intolerable sexual and aggressive impulses.

Gambling is one among a number of neurotic syndromes that cannot be treated statistically. The number of patients who present themselves for treatment with the specific complaint as a main symptom must be exceedingly small, and perhaps only rarely does a clinician have the opportunity to study the illness in its pure form. On the other hand, gambling as one among many symptoms of a total neurotic pattern appears with considerable regularity, and perhaps in the same measure as alcoholism and drug dependency can be found. In an attempt at a solution of his essential conflict, a neurotic often resorts to alcohol or drugs, and for some persons gambling appears to serve a similar purpose. Here, however, we should be concerned only with those instances where gambling *is* the neurosis, or where the chief symptom in a neurotic pattern is the gambling. Therefore, I should like to report extensively on a relatively 'pure' case. As will be seen, this rather typical case may be of aid in carrying further our knowledge of the psychodynamics involved.

The man whom I shall call Paul was, during the period of our acquaintance, serving a three-year sentence in a federal prison for stealing government cheques and forging endorsements on them. He was forty-four years old when I met him. By training he was an engineer, but had abandoned his profession seventeen years previously, and since then he had made his home, quite literally, wherever 'a game' could be found – on ships at sea, in rented rooms, in hotels, aboard trains and at gambling resorts all over the world. The strain of these years was written on his face, which was otherwise handsome in a rather rugged fashion; and according to the prison physicians who had examined him, his body, too, had recorded the effects of the kind of life he had led. His manner was direct and simple. His visit to my office had been prefaced by a very formal note requesting an interview for the 'purpose of exploring the possibility of treatment by you for a condition that has ruined my life and brought disgrace to my family'.

Before seeing Paul I read through his case file, which revealed nothing of significance.

The interview began inauspiciously. Paul was late for his appointment – a sign of his reluctance, perhaps – and when he finally arrived it took longer than usual for us to find a cordial level of rapport. He expressed some regret that he had initiated the visit. He knew I was psychoanalytically trained, and he appeared very familiar with psychoanalysis, its literature, methods and aims. At the outset he expressed doubt that I could help him, and he spoke as if his problem were a rare one and beyond hope; at least he had never heard or read of anyone with his particular 'disease' who had benefited from psychotherapy. However, he responded to my reassurances that I would like to hear more about him and his problems, and he then began to tell me the following story, which I am here abbreviating in the interest of space.

Paul was the eldest of three sons. He described his mother, who was a minister's daughter, as a frail, shy but very beautiful woman who adored her husband and gave Paul the impression that the children were just chores to be got out of the way each day, so that she could devote all her time and effort to her husband's welfare. From Paul's present viewpoint, she seemed to have counted for very little in the lives of the children, especially his life, after childhood.

Paul's father was Professor of Religious Philosophy in a small college, and pastor of the local church of his denomination. Paul described his father as a modern version of an Old Testament prophet, aloof and austere. He said, 'I can remember nothing except my fear of him, and whatever I say about him is prejudiced and colored by that fear. At one time I thought he just hated us kids, especially me, and couldn't stand to have us around. When we were bad or had brought home poor marks from school, he would call us into his study, where we'd have to stand absolutely still while he lectured us about sin, the Devil, Hell and Heaven, and then whaled the tar out of us with his cane. I hated him with all my guts and was glad when I could get away from home.'

At the age of twelve Paul was placed by his father in a military school which he described as a hellhole with overbearing instructors and disagreeable older boys, where he 'learned everything there is to learn about nastiness and rottenness'.

At the age of eighteen Paul graduated from military school and went to college on a scholarship awarded because of his father's profession. He worked to meet his expenses, and occasionally received a few dollars from his father, accompanied by a grudging letter. He made occasional reluctant visits home at his father's insistence, and was glad when he was mustered into the Army, since for about two years he did not have to make excuses for not visiting the family.

On leaving college Paul secured a position in a city which was enlarging its port facilities. He apparently gave satisfaction, for when the first assignment was finished he was one of two engineers invited to remain with the city.

Meanwhile, Paul married a Catholic girl, for which his father forbade him ever to come to the house again, disinherited him, and forbade the mother and brothers ever to speak of him again in the father's presence. For about two years Paul corresponded with his mother and brothers through a post office box. Then his father died. Shortly afterwards Paul's daughter was born, and his mother visited the family for a few months.

About that time, Paul being twenty-five years old, he went with some of his friends one night to a fashionable club. He did not drink, and knew very little about such places. There was a gaming room, and rather out of boredom and curiosity he drifted over to a crap table and watched the game, which he understood, having played it in college for nickels a few times. While he watched he got a sudden impulse to play, and before he could check himself he was in the game. He won a little at first, then began to lose. He said, 'The whole thing was very unreal to me: I was excited and very much alive.' About one o'clock in the morning his friends went home. He was then low in funds, so he borrowed some money from one of his friends and played until the place closed at three o'clock, when he was well ahead. He walked home in a kind of dream, said nothing to his wife or mother about the matter, and the next day he returned the borrowed money. For the next few days he worked as usual and thought nothing of the incident. But contrary to his custom, he did not deposit his winnings in the joint account he had with his wife, but kept them in his pocket. Toward the end of the week Paul began to feel restless. He said, 'My mother was still visiting us and she'd been getting on my nerves – at least that's how I excused myself. Anyhow, before I knew it I was calling my wife to tell her I had to remain at work late. That night I ate alone in a restaurant and then walked to the speakeasy. I stood around a few moments and then started to play. I was very excited; my hands were so wet you'd think I was washing them, and my heart was going a mile a minute.'

That night Paul soon lost all his money and got home early. The next morning he drew from the bank half of the money there, and without calling his wife about coming home, he went straight to the speakeasy from work. He lost about a third of his money, but by midnight had almost recovered his losses. Another player suggested that they go to a larger establishment he knew, which was open all night and ran bigger games. They rode to a magnificent gambling house just outside the city limits, which was equipped with all sorts of devices and games that were new and exciting to Paul. He lost steadily, and about five o'clock in the morning he was cleaned out and the 'house' gave him cab fare home. He continued the story: 'The next day I went to work as usual, but before I left the house I took the small solitaire I had given my wife the year before that was her only piece of jewellery, a watch my father had given me when I graduated from college, and a few other odds and ends. These I pawned on my way to the office. That afternoon, around two o'clock, I pretended to be sick and left work [and went to the suburban house]. My intention, of course, was to recoup my losses and quit. I told myself that if I could once get even I'd never gamble again. All I wanted was to be able to get back the money I'd lost the night before, return it to the bank and take the jewellery out of hock. I soon had more than enough to do this, but of course I didn't quit. I got ambitious once I passed the mark I set myself and thought it wouldn't matter if I lost my winnings. I was running some real luck and wanted to stay with it. At first I kept winning, more and more, until I thought I was unbeatable. But then the tide turned again. To make a long story short, when I left that place at three in the morning I was cleaned out except for a few dollars I'd saved to get me home.

'When I got to my house I was *really* sick. I woke up my wife and confessed the whole thing. She cried a lot and carried on, but she forgave me when I promised I'd never gamble again. I swore all kinds of oaths, cried, asked her to believe me and finally felt clean enough to go to bed. The next day I spent at home with the family, did a few household chores and began to feel like a new man again, like someone getting over a sickness. My wife was wonderful to me. We told my mother, who offered to help us where she could if we needed her. Everything was fine – for about a week. Almost a week to the day after I had sworn off, I was back at it, this time with the rest of the money from the joint account. It went fast.

'For almost two years that's the way I lived. I ran through everything we ever had, what little my mother could give us, whatever I could beg or borrow. Sometimes I'd win and things would look brighter. At home, there were always tears, scenes, fights. I'd make promises and break them the next day. My wife always forgave me and I'd start out swearing I'd never look at a pair of dice or a card or a roulette wheel again. But it was no use. I had the fever and couldn't shake it. When I was winning I couldn't stop and when I was losing I couldn't stop. I realized what this was doing to my wife and kid, but nothing seemed to matter. Finally, I lost my job. They fired me for inefficiency because I was paying no attention to my work. When this happened I saw what I had to do. One day I left the house as usual, pretending to look for work – by the way, my wife was working at the time – and I just never went back.

'I've done nothing but gamble ever since then. I've been way up at the top and way down at the bottom. I make promises to myself and break them. I've never really been able to quit, no matter how far I've been ahead or how far I'm behind. Once, in the Far East, I swore off and managed to stay off for a few months – almost a whole year, as a matter of fact. I got a good job with an English outfit and thought I was out of it at last. But I was just kidding myself. Believe me, I hate it and hate myself. But what can I do?'

As I listened to Paul's hurried recital I was impressed with the fact that the story I had just heard was the story of Fyodor Dostoyevsky, at least in its skeletal structure. Word for word, point for point, character for character, pattern for pattern, this man was bringing to life, evoking as by witchcraft, the image of the brooding Russian novelist. (Even today, as I write this seven years after my last meeting with Paul, I am impressed with the parallels – so impressed that in order to check my data I have had to read another biography of the tortured creator of Raskolnikov, Stavrogin, Ivan Karamazov and Prince Myshkin.)

Here was the same stern father – Paul and his brothers, like Fyodor and Mikhail, even had to stand at attention while the patriarch thundered lessons and abuse at them – righteous, overbearing, miserly; the same frail mother – retiring, weak, worshipful; the same schooling, almost – military academy, engineering; and, of course, the same sick passion for gambling. But these were not all: the very words Paul had used evoked *The Gambler* and the much-maligned Anna Grigorievna's *Diary*.

Consequently, conscious only of these curious, challenging parallels, I offered to analyze Paul. He was reluctant and without hope, and our work together began with the handicap of his disbelief and despair after he had given his hesitant consent.

To recapitulate the psychoanalysis of the gambler, Paul, would be a lengthy and arduous task. Here, then, I shall do no more than touch on the highlights of the many hours we spent in that most intimate of all associations. In the following paragraphs are condensed almost two years of analysis.

Despite his initial resistance to the whole idea of analysis, Paul made a rapid and unequivocal transference. In analysing it, he recognized that he wanted me to forgive him, and that the inferred promise of absolution from the analyst accounted primarily for the fact that his original defenses against the analysis were so quickly overcome.

Behind the analyst soon emerged the figure of Paul's father: it was he from whom Paul wanted forgiveness. At first the trespasses remained vague, but a flood of memory relating to the sermons and lectures of the father, the ineffable boredom of Sunday afternoons, and the wretched feeling of always being 'under the all-seeing eye of God' gave body to the sense of sin. The very earliest trespass concerned the aggressive wish that the father would go away, disappear, be swallowed up or drowned.

Here it developed that Paul had been enuretic to his sixth year, and that his father's response to it had been a fastidious disgust. The design and aim of the enuresis had been to attract the mother from the marital bed. Because of her hearing defect, his cries when he soiled annoyed the father. As far as could be ascertained, it appeared that this led to scolding and punishment, and eventually a technique was worked out which required the mother to arise at intervals during the night to take care of Paul. An early competition with the father was thus initiated.

As for the 'swallowing up', this was projectively arrived at by the usual inversion of the hostile wish Klein has so well described.[7] But with the accumulation of knowledge, these at first vague notions collected into a powerful death-wish against the father and, under the impress of the obsessive religiosity that governed the entire household, this was a cardinal sin. In short, much of Paul's chronic psychic activity was concerned with poorly disguised wishes for his father's death, and he was consequently dominated by an all-pervading guilt.

Very early in his life Paul developed an obsessive pattern. He recalled how he used to employ his playtime activities in the service of his obsession by compulsive acts. His toys had to be arranged 'just so', and his smallest acts became disguised rituals conceived and executed to counter the obsessive ideas and wishes.

The second major trespass for which Paul sought forgiveness was of a sexual nature. It was a complex affair, interwoven with the first and yet separate and distinct from it. Infant and childhood masturbation had as its unconscious object the mother, who was later to be hidden behind screen figures as Paul grew older and as the masturbation continued into adult life, through and beyond his marriage. By organ association it was involved with the enuresis, and when the latter disappeared, self-manipulation substituted for bed-wetting. It evoked the mother and provoked the father, thus becoming an exceptionally powerful weapon in the psychic armamentarium, and one not lightly to be surrendered. More – by that curious and magic 'reasoning' peculiar to the psychic processes, the penis was endowed with very special qualities. It was an instrument for expressing Paul's hostility against his father and a means of punishing himself.

The last two ingredients in this potent sexual stew had been contributed first by Paul's own biology and morphology, and second by the character of the father as it reflected upon the boy. As with all bright children, Paul had been sexually precocious, and the expression of the precocity had become manifest earlier than in most. This fact was due to the enuretic–evocative use of his penis in combination with the aggressive–provocative and the usual self-indulgent–onanistic functions.

In any event, Paul's initial and tentative masturbating efforts were severely condemned, and thenceforward Paul interpreted his male parent's highly vocal preoccupation with the Devil, Sin, Badness and Company – whether it was so meant of not – as aimed specifically at his (Paul's) onanistic exercises and temptations. Now it will be seen how the aggressive–provocative potentiality of the organ was increased when it is considered that Paul actually used it in this fashion; that is, for hostile purposes and, as it were, in defiance. But still it served a self-punitive function, bringing the father's wrath down upon Paul when he was observed at masturbatory play or when he engaged in it with the very aim of calling down upon himself, for both the death wishes and the onanistic trespass, the thunder and lightning of disapproval.

The two themes – death-desires for the father and the masturbatory complex – emerged in the analysis of Paul as the basal responsible agents for the gambling. But, it must be remembered, neither of them is simple. If anything, they may be compared with the geneticist's chromosomes, each enclosing a full code-script of the destiny of Paul founded upon its characteristic genic components, and so complexly interwoven – internally and with each other – that two years of analysis were required merely to identify them and to indicate their possible effects.

The death-wishes Paul had nourished against his father from the tenderest years remained with him until his father actually died. Then it was as if all Paul's hopes and secret desires had been fulfilled. Yet, at the same time, it was also as if the child that Paul had unconsciously remained was indeed omnipotent, and this confirmation of omnipotence was hard to bear, since it involved an excess of guilt. So long as the wishes were there and his father remained alive, the burden of guilt was not so heavy; but when the father actually died, the death was unconsciously regarded as due to the wishes that had been such an important if unacknowledged part of Paul's life. Now, in the interest of his continued psychic equilibrium, it became necessary for Paul to put this omnipotence to the test.Obviously, the compulsions he had employed to counter the obsessive thoughts had not worked, for, after all, his father *had* died; and so a new series of compulsions were in order. But these had to have as their design, not the countering of the obsessive wish for death, but *the denial that the wish had caused the death*. The death could not be denied: to do that would have been to court insanity. Yet the question, 'Did I (my wishes) kill him?' tormented the young man; and this was one of the questions that took Paul to the gaming table and kept him there.

Paul had to know whether his wishes had been powerful enough to cause the death of his father. The secret obsessive idea that they had been effective tortured him, and he desperately wanted to be unconvinced. Yet, this involved a terrible dilemma, and one that could be resolved only when Paul was completely analyzed and so made aware of the unconscious question that was a link in the chain of his neurosis. With every cast of the dice, with every turn of the card, and with every spin of the wheel, Paul asked this question. Winning was a proof of his omnipotence: it meant that wishes came true, that one could influence the unseen powers by one's secret desires and hopes, that wishes could and did kill. Winning, in short, meant an affirmative answer to the question. Losing, on the other hand, meant the opposite, and with the negative answer came a great relief from guilt. But losing also meant the shattering of the fiction of omnipotence, a delusion so strong and so deeply embedded that the psychic pain consequent upon its loss is an acute one.

This, then, was a kind of Hobson's choice. Two immensely powerful, if unconscious, motives were at work here: one sought relief from guilt, the other sought the confirmation of omnipotence. It would be a mistake to say that they alternated. The fact is, they coexisted and formed a typical neurotic conflict.

Withal, however, Paul wanted to lose, even at the expense of his infantile omnipotence. As a matter of fact, it was of the utmost importance for his sanity that he did lose, since by this he was relieved of the burden of guilt and confirmed as to his innocence of causing his father's death. If he could have lost consistently – strange as this seems – he could have remained at peace. But the vicissitudes of chance are such that one occasionally wins, and thus, for the inner balance to be maintained, it becomes necessary that winning be paid for by losing. Nor is a single loss, even if it be of the same amount as a previous win, enough to balance the interior books, The answer to the question has to be clear and unequivocal. Thus and finally, *Paul gambled to lose.*

Paul not only addressed this unconscious question to the fortunes of the game – he also sought to influence its answer. The analysis disclosed that the money he invested in gambling had a significance beyond the obvious use of money as a possession to risk at betting. In his unconscious, *it represented a bribery.* It had the same meaning for him that the monetary gifts with which grace and absolution and other indulgences were purchased from ecclesiastical vendors before Protestantism had for the folk of that time. It bought for him – or, better, was meant to buy for him – the negative answer he so desired.

Beyond this, money unconsciously represented an atonement for the thought-crime of having desired the death of his father. When Paul could not obtain it readily, he would, as he tells us in his history, go to the most extreme lengths to get it, engaging in actual crime and degrading himself to the farthest depths. This was because it was not only his passport to the oracle of the game as the place where his unconscious question could be answered, but because both bribery and atonement became integral parts of his obsessive neurosis.

Lastly, money, by its very nature, is a remarkably apt tool with which to implement any compulsion; it can be handled, counted and distributed in a way that few other instruments for combating obsessive thoughts permit.[8] In Paul's case, because of his father's great concern with it during his lifetime and what Paul called his 'miserliness', its significance was increased.

It is time now to turn from the psychic chromosome of the death wish in the genesis of Paul's obsessive gambling neurosis to that of the masturbatory complex. It will be recalled that Paul's history as a masturbator began early and that many factors accounted for its persistence. It was a source of satisfaction on a number of scores, and when joined to the enuresis it became a definite means to an end. When, with repression, the mother as the prime sexual object was replaced in phantasy by substitute figures, and after onanism had completely displaced the enuresis the aims which both of these sought exerted great unconscious pressure. None of the tentative sexual excursions Paul made as a young man were as satisfactory to him as solo gratification, and even during his marriage he could never achieve full sexual satisfaction with his partner. In the analysis this much was revealed, as well as the very significant fact that the phantasies accompanying the act throughout the years before and after marriage were unquestionably maternal ones.

Therefore, despite Paul's objection to and rather summary treatment of his mother during the initial recital of his case – his dismissal of her as unimportant in his life – it appeared that she was not so lightly to be regarded. Indeed, the role she played was equally as strong as the part assigned to the father in the development of the gambling neurosis. Throughout his life Paul's mother represented the ultimate sexual temptation. That he competed for her with his father is well established; the enuresis, after all, was designed as a lure for her attention.

But beyond this, Paul feared that his father knew of his incestuous wishes, and that this also lay behind – was, in fact, the meaning of – the strong injunctions against sex inferred in each sermon and in the totality of the father's behavior toward him. An early reinforcement of the masturbatory drive reverted to an underlying fear of castration, with self-manipulation resorted to as continual reassurance that Paul had not, as he unconsciously feared, been deprived of his member.

Yet even this common form of reassurance was not enough for him. To divert his father's attention from Paul's incestuous preoccupations – which, I must again stress, he unconsciously believed his father to be aware of – Paul married his Catholic sweetheart. (This is not to say that he was not, when he married her, in love with his wife; but this motive certainly played no small part in his choice of just that girl.) He thus unconsciously meant this act as a kind of appeasement of his father, as if to say that by marrying a girl from a different faith – a faith against which his father had always expressed unreasonable and violent prejudice – he was making a public renunciation of his love for and designs upon his father's wife. Like all appeasements, however, this one miscarried: the father did not have the psychic perceptiveness attributed to him by his son; he chose instead to regard this act in its second or other aspect, that of simple defiance, and he forthwith disinherited and disowned Paul.

Now the disowning of Paul had an unintended and drastic effect on the young man's future. Paul related that until that time he had only infrequent contact with his mother; after this, and for the next two years, although distant from her, he was closer to her than at any previous time since he had left home to go to school. Unconsciously, the act of disinheritance, the public proclamation that 'he is no longer my son', had a secret meaning for Paul, which the reader can easily guess. The possibility was increased that the screen figures which had always served him for his masturbatory fancies would now be revealed in their true and horrible identity. So, in the period just prior to the death of his father, the young man was threatened by the return of what he had so long repressed.

The climax of the anxiety that was so strongly stirring within him came with his mother's visit. As a matter of fact, Paul told me in his first recitation that one of his rationalizations for returning to the gambling establishment the second time was because his mother was 'beginning to get on my nerves'. This meant more than the words themselves convey. Actually, his irritation with her was nothing more than the defense he erected to counter the temptation she presented.

Here we must pause to record a most curious and significant fact. Paul, who had been a chronic masturbator from earliest childhood through marriage, abruptly put a stop to this habit when he began to gamble. In the analysis he distinctly recalled this, stressing the fact that no effort was required to accomplish it, and stating, 'It just happened that way.' Now gambling and masturbation present a wide variety of parallels that spring to the attention with ease. Both are repetitive acts, both are compulsively driven, and the nervous and mental states accompanying the crucial stages in the performing of each are almost impossible to differentiate.

The parallels between the two are remarked upon consistently by patients under analysis. One, whom I am analyzing at this time, is a habitual slot-machine player. He has called my attention to the rhythmic–repetitive nature of his preoccupation with the 'one-armed bandits' and to the correspondence between his mental and physical states when indulging this pastime and his recollections from adolescence. This patient has also related 'hitting the jackpot' to orgasm, and believes the 'teasing' nature of each play is equivalent to the masturbating youth's manipulations of the genitals with the unexpressed question, How far can I go without having an ejaculation? Paul, too, remarked on the orgasmal nature of winning, and emphasized especially the mounting pleasurable tension of the interval between the bet and the outcome of the play. The current patient, who had also been enuretic, discussed the 'stream of coins' that was discharged from his machines; with Paul a similar but more involved symbolic equation was arrived at.

So we cannot avoid the conclusion that for Paul, gambling literally took the place of masturbation, in this case amounting to a transposition of the habit to a sphere and in a form removed from but related to the earlier compulsion, and undertaken with the design of minimizing the anxiety mobilized by the threat of the return of the repressed.

That this subterfuge did not work, however, is revealed by Paul's own statement that he required forgiveness for his activities when he returned from a session at the gaming tables. But – it should be carefully noted – he asked for this forgiveness *only when he had lost*. This must mean – and the analysis substantiates it beyond dispute – that losing had for him a special significance, apart from the social significance of gambling as a reprehensible activity and the superficial significance of the loss of goods and property.

The clue to what this might have been will be found in Paul's statement that when he had been forgiven, he 'felt clean again'. What it meant was, essentially, that losing was connected, in his unconscious, with disapproval for his masturbation. The disapproving agent was, of course, his father. The unverbalized formula that existed in Paul's mind was: if I win, it means that my father approves of my masturbation (sexual desire for my mother) and will reward me; if I lose, it means that my father disapproves of my masturbation and will punish me.

Therefore, when Paul lost, he understood by this that a punishment was in store for him, a punishment beyond the mere loss of his possessions. The analysis penetrated to the core of the expected punishment, which was castration, the ultimate unconscious fear. Made frantic by this fear, and desperately in need of forgiveness from some source, Paul had to turn to his wife; but the most she could provide – because, after all, she was not his father – was a kind of intermittent relief through her gracious pardoning of his transgressions. And this wiped the slate clean – for a brief while.

A final genic strand in the sexual chromosome remains to be considered. It will have been remarked by the reader that, contrary to the unconscious aim of Paul's gambling from the side of the death wish, *the orientation provided from the sexual side was toward winning*. By this time in Paul's analysis I understood why Paul had to lose, and also why he had to win. But I remained dissatisfied with the rewards of winning—or what I understood of them—for a personal reason.

I was then writing a book on crime and was collecting data on the role of alcoholism and drug addiction in criminal behaviour, and had uncovered what I believe to be a central feature of alcoholism, to which I have given the name 'the alcoholic phantasy'.[9] By this term I mean that the psychoanalytic exploration of the alcoholic (and the drug addict, too) never fails to disclose that he cherishes an infantile, megalomanic sort of daydream or reverie which it is one aim of his indulgence to evoke. This phantasy regularly stems from, and can be traced back to, the onmipotence experienced in infancy and early childhood, and is a characteristic of all addictions.

Gambling, in its structure, is also an addiction – although of a specific kind – and I suspected the presence of the phantasy here as well. But where, in this psychic puzzle, would it fit? Obviously it had to be related to the omnipotence, not only because this was itself a feature common to all addictions, but because omnipotence was the only genic element in the deathwish chromosome without its parallel in the sexual. Further reasoning localized the phantasy in connection with winning.

One of the rewards of gambling with which Paul now dealt

at great length and in detail was the phantasy, which was indeed megalomanic and omnipotent. In it Paul was a monarch unlimited in his power, unrestrained in his ambition. With the huge sums at his disposal he dispensed a fabulous largesse, conducted important philanthropies and won renown as a benefactor of the race. It was his money – won at the gaming table – that found the cure for polio, sheltered uncounted orphans, endowed great temples of religion and learning, and rescued the fallen. In this dream, this phantasy spun in the far reaches of the mind as it made bets, calculated odds and sought to penetrate the intentions of an opponent, Paul was everything and had everything he never was and never had.

With the revelation and examination of the phantasy, the last piece in the mosaic of Paul's gambling neurosis fell into place. The remainder of his analysis, the reintegrative part, is none of our concern here.

Through analysis, Paul entirely recovered from his illness. After leaving prison he eventually located his wife. He then learned that he had been declared legally dead about ten years after his unceremonious leave-taking, and that she had remarried. Paul is now a minor executive in a manufacturing company, has married, and has two small children. I get a card from him every Christmas.

I have presented the case of my former patient, Paul, chiefly because I believe that both his history and the dynamic study of his personality can serve as models for the careers and psychic structure of all gamblers. He represents a rather pure type, his complaint as he brought it to analysis uncomplicated by other major symptoms or distresses. In this sense, he is rather a *rara avis*. Bergler makes the significant observation that 'gambling is in every respect a losing proposition', especially for the analyst, since 'it rarely happens that a gambler of his free will seeks treatment'. I agree with this, completely. In a decade of psychoanalytic practice, in and out of institutions, Paul and the patient with whom I am presently working are the only two instances I have known where treatment has been freely sought.

On two additional occasions I have been consulted about gambling neurosis. One inquirer was a screen actor whose passion had involved him in unbelievable indebtedness; the other was a businessman facing total ruin because of his pre-occupation with cards. Both scoffed when I prescribed treat-ment, and I never saw either of them after the first interview. On the other hand, I have had many cases wherein gambling was one symptom among many in a neurosis, or where the passion had existed transiently, usually as a phase in the progressive development of an obsessional neurotic pattern. An agoraphobic woman who is under analysis with me now fits into this latter category. But in no case in my experience have the dynamics been different, to any marked degree, from those exhibited in the case of Paul.

The study of this 'pure' case enables us to advance somewhat the conclusions reached by former investigators. The first opinion that calls for revision is technical in nature. Current nosology places gambling among the so-called 'impulse neuroses'. Fenichel so classifies it in his classical work, although in the latter part of his brief discussion of the gambling syndrome he appears to be somewhat doubtful himself.[10] But I think that placement is in error and results from the fact that too little attention has been paid to the underlying obsessional content the passion discloses under analysis. Furthermore, at no time is the compulsion egosyntonic, that is, a thing which the gambler wants to do and in which he takes pleasure: it is always ego-alien or dystonic. The gambler is not a psychopath with a perversion, as the term 'impulse neurotic' suggests: he is an obsessional neurotic engaged in what might be called the making of magic. The proof of this lies in the course of the illness, and is best demonstrated in the instances where gambling is a tem-porary stage in the development of an obsessional neurotic pattern.

The oracular nature of gambling appears to be established beyond dispute. Reik, who first called attention to this, was not misled by his anthropological knowledge and clinical data, but I believe his formula was incomplete. The gambler does not ask one, but two questions of destiny: did I kill my father by wishing his death? (or, in the case of gamblers with living male parent: are my wishes powerful enough to cause the death of my father?) and, will I be punished or rewarded for my secret sexual desires (incest)?

Herein lies the great dilemma which literally chains the gambler to his place at the gaming table. If he wins, the omnipotence of his wishes is thereby proved and his incestuous aims condoned, *but* he is at the same time rendered and adjudged guilty of parricide and vulnerable to the tortures consequent thereon. If he loses, he is relieved of the burden of unconscious murder which is too much for sanity to bear, *but* he forfeits the omnipotence on which he has based his life and exposes himself to the terrible penalty to be exacted for his incestuous desires. We owe it to the astuteness of Bergler that the trenchant paradox – the gambler wants to lose – has been made comprehensible. But it now appears that the gambler must *win and lose at the same time*, for his sanity's sake, and this can never be done.

The role of money, too, has been clarified by our study. It appears to serve the function of bribery and is used to buy the favor of the fates, to influence the oracle. Unfortunately, coins and bills do not spontaneously stand on end, and this is what the gambler is, in a way, demanding of them, because he does not know what answer he wishes, and is made miserable by either. It is possible that if he could obtain, for his bribe, an equivocal reply such as the Delphic sibyls and their like were wont to give – a reply that could be interpreted either way at the same time and so satisfy both aims – the gambler would be content. But this also he cannot have. And apart from the unconscious use of money for bribery, its far-reaching symbolic uses are apparent. To win is to achieve an orgasm, to attain the potent manhood of ejaculation. Lastly, money unquestionably relates to the eliminative functions.

That a phantasy arising from the omnipotence was an important factor in the gambling of Paul is evident, and I have no doubt that it always exists. Like the carrot that dangles before the donkey's nose, it constitutes a call to futurity and promises a bright reward if captured. It is a lure, of course, and serves the function of insuring that the omnipotence – wished for and at the same time hoped against – will be recharged constantly in its magnetic attractiveness.

I believe the evidence speaks in favour of a number of common genetic factors in the morphology of gamblers. They seem all to be strongly aggressive persons with huge reservoirs of unconscious hostility and resentment upon which their neurosis feeds; and chronic masturbators to boot. Freud's remarkable discovery relating masturbation and gambling stands unimpeachable. The correspondence is so close that, as we have seen, the one can and does substitute for the other.

Now the aggression shared by gamblers appears rooted in the relationship toward the authoritarian figure in his family, the father, who in every case conforms to type. These fathers are strong, domineering, moralistic, sustained by their convictions of self-importance, lacking in warmth or the expression of warmth towards their offspring, and niggardly in money matters. They are the recipients of near-adoration from their weaker wives, and for this and for their personal qualities they are hated and feared by their children. The masturbation not only expresses the aggression borne against them, nor yet only the complementary and contrary feelings for the other and beloved parent, but in addition to these and the remaining ordinary gratifications from the habit, it serves as a transitional practice towards gambling itself. If the analogy is not too strained, we may regard it as the avenue of approach to the divinatory altar where the oracular sticks are thrown, the entrails examined and the omens read.

Thus the psychodynamics of gambling, that queer passion that with Erinyan fury has pursued some of the best – and some of the worst – of men.

Notes
1. Ernst Simmel, 'Zur Psychoanalyse des Spielers' ('On the Psychoanalysis of the Gambler'), *Internationale Zeitschrift für Psychoanalyse*, Vol. 6 (1920), p. 397.
2. Sigmund Freud, 'Dostoevsky and Parricide', *The Standard Edition of the Complete Psychological Works of Sigmund Freud*, ed. and trans. James Strachey, 23 vols. (London: Hogarth Press, 1953—), Vol. 21, pp. 177–96.
3. Theodor Reik, 'The Study on Dostoyevsky', in Reik, *From Thirty Years With Freud* (London: Hogarth Press, 1942).
4. René Laforgue, 'On the Eroticization of Anxiety', *International Journal of Psycho-Analysis*, Vol. 11 (1930), pp. 312–21; Ernest Jones, 'The Problem of Paul Morphy', *International Journal of Psycho-Analysis*, Vol. 12 (1931).
5. Edmund Bergler, 'On the Psychology of the Gambler', *Imago*, Vol. 22 (1936), pp. 409–41; 'The Gambler: A Misunderstood Neurotic', *Journal of Criminal Psychopathology*, Vol. 4 (1943), pp. 379–93.
6. Ralph Greenson, 'On Gambling' [this volume, pp. 202–16—Eds.].

7. Melanie Klein, *The Psycho-Analysis of Children* (London: Hogarth Press, 1959; New York: Norton, 1932).
8. A further significance of money for Paul and for all gamblers will be considered below.
9. Robert Lindner, *Stone Walls and Men* (New York: Odyssey, 1946).
10. Otto Fenichel, *The Psychoanalytic Theory of Neurosis* (London: Kegan Paul, Trench & Trubner, 1946; New York: Norton, 1945).

Ernest Jones

The Problem of Paul Morphy
A contribution to the psychoanalysis of chess*

Paul Morphy was born at New Orleans on 22 June 1837; he had a sister six and a half years older than himself, one two and a quarter years younger, and a brother two and a half years older.[1] His father was a Spaniard by nationality, but of Irish descent; his mother was of French extraction.

When Paul was ten years old his father, who was himself no mean player, taught him chess. In a year or two he proved himself the superior of his elder brother Edward, his father, his mother's father, and his father's brother who was at that time the chess king of New Orleans. A game is preserved which, according to an eye-witness, he is said to have played victoriously against his uncle on his twelfth birthday while blindfolded. At the same age he played against two masters of inter-national renown who happened to be in New Orleans at the time. One of these was the famous French player Rousseau, with whom he played some fifty games, winning fully nine tenths. The other was the Hungarian master Loewenthal, one of the half-dozen greatest living players; of the two games played the young Paul won one and the other was drawn. After this period little serious chess was played for some eight years while he was pursuing his studies; his father allowed him to play occasionally on Sundays, but with the exception of Judge Meek, the President of the American Chess Congress, against whom he played and won six games when he was seventeen years old, he encountered only much inferior opponents. His uncle had by then left New Orleans for the West, Rousseau was otherwise absorbed, and Paul's brother, father and grandfather had abandoned chess when he was in the teens, so the statement that

* Read before the British Psycho-Analytical Society, 19 November 1930. From *The International Journal of Psycho-Analysis*, Vol. 12, part 1 (January 1931), pp. 1–23. Reprinted by permission of Mrs Katherine Jones, the Hogarth Press Ltd and International Universities Press.

has been made is probably true that in these years he never met anyone to whom he could not give a rook, consequently no one from whose play he could learn anything. In 1851 the first International Chess Tournament had taken place, at which Anderssen emerged as victor, and in 1857, when Morphy was just twenty years old, one was held in New York. He easily gained the first place, losing only one game out of seventeen, and during his stay in New York played a hundred games with the best players there, losing only five of them. In circumstances which will engage our attention presently he visited London and Paris in the following year and his prodigious feats there read like a fairy-tale. He not only defeated every champion he could induce to meet him, including Anderssen himself, but also gave several astounding exhibitions of simultaneous blindfold play against eight picked players, winning the large majority of the games. Towards the end of his stay in Paris he defeated blindfold the whole of the Versailles Chess Club playing in consultation. On his return to New Orleans he issued a challenge to play anyone in the world at odds. On receiving no response to this he declared his career as a chess-player – which had lasted barely eighteen months, comprising actually only six months of public play – finally and definitely closed.

Of the actual quality of Morphy's play we shall have something to say later, but for the moment it will suffice to say that many of the most competent judges have pronounced him to have been the greatest chess-player of all time. After his extraordinarily premature retirement he took up the practice of law, his father's profession, but although he possessed much skill in the work he was unsuccessful in practice. He gradually relapsed into a state of seclusion and introversion which culminated in unmistakable paranoia. At the age of forty-seven he died suddenly of 'congestion of the brain', presumably apoplexy, as his father had before him.

The evident problem arises of what relation, if any, his tragic neurosis bore to the supreme activities of his life, activities for which his name will always be remembered in the world of chess. It was popularly believed that the excessive preoccupation had affected his brain, but his biographers, who were naturally chess enthusiasts and zealous for the credit of their beloved pursuit, asserted with conviction that this was in no way responsible. Nevertheless, with our present knowledge we should find it impossible to believe that there was not some intimate connection between the neurosis, which is necessarily concerned with the kernel of the personality, and the superb efforts of sublimation which have made Morphy's name immortal. In contemplating this problem let us begin with some reflections on the nature of the sublimation in question.

The slightest acquaintance with chess shows one that it is a play-substitute for the art of war and indeed it has been a favourite recreation of some of the greatest military leaders, from William the Conqueror to Napoleon. In the contest between the opposing armies the same principles of both strategy and tactics are displayed as in actual war, the same foresight and powers of calculation are necessary, the same capacity for divining the plans of the opponent, and the rigour with which decisions are followed by their consequences is, if anything, even more ruthless. More than that, it is plain that the unconscious motive actuating the players is not the mere love of pugnacity characteristic of all competitive games, but the grimmer one of father-murder. It is true that the original goal of capturing the king has been given up, but from the point of view of motive there is, except in respect of crudity, no appreciable change in the present goal of sterilizing him in immobility. The history of the game and the names for it are of confirmatory interest here. Authorities seem to be agreed that the game originated in India, passed from there to Persia, whose Arabian conquerors transmitted it to Europe nearly a thousand years ago. Its first name, from which all others are derived, was the Sanscrit one of *chaturanga*, literally 'four members'. This was also the Indian word for 'army', probably because of the four components of elephants, chariots, horse and foot. The old Persians shortened the name from *chaturanga* to *chatrang* and their Arabian successors, having neither the initial nor the final sound of this word in their language, modified it into *shatranj*. When it re-emerged into later Persian the unconscious must have been at work, for it had by then been shortened to *Schah*, an assimilation having evidently taken place with the Persian *Shah* = king; 'chess' thus means the royal game, or the game of kings. *Shah-mat*, our 'checkmate', German *'Schachmatt'*, French *'échec et mat'*, means literally 'the king is dead'. At least so the Arabian writers on chess thought, and most European authors copy them in this. Modern Orientalists, however, are of opinion that the word *'mat'* is of Persian, and not of Arabian, origin, and that *'Shah-mat'* means 'the king is paralysed, helpless and defeated'. Again from the point of view of the king it makes very little difference.

In the Middle Ages an interesting innovation was introduced into the rules of chess which deserves incidental mention. By the side of the king stands another piece who was originally his counsellor, Persian *firz* (Turkish *vizier*). As his main occupation was supposed to be not fighting, but advising and defending, he was in action the weakest piece on the board, his only move being one square diagonally. In the Middle Ages he gradually changed his sex, thus passing through the same evolution as the Holy Ghost, and came to be known as the *regina*, *dame*, queen, and so on. It is not known why this happened. It was suggested by Freret, an eighteenth-century writer on chess, that a confusion must have arisen between the words *'fierge'*, the French for *firz*, and *'vierge'*. It has more generally been thought that as this used to be the only piece for which a pawn could be exchanged on reaching the eighth square, when it was sometimes called *'un pion damé'*, this circumstance led to its being given the same name as the French one for draughts, i.e. *dames*. About the middle of the fifteenth century this change in sex was followed by a great increase in power, so that the piece is now stronger than any other two together. Whatever may be the truth, therefore, about the linguistic speculations I have just mentioned, it will not surprise the psycho-analyst when he learns the effect of the change: it is that in attacking the father the most potent assistance is afforded by the mother (= queen).

It is perhaps worth remarking further that the mathematical quality of the game gives it a peculiarly anal-sadistic nature. The exquisite purity and exactness of the right moves,[2] particularly in problem work, combine here with the unrelenting pressure exercised in the later stages which culminates in the merciless dénouement. The sense of overwhelming mastery on the one side matches that of unescapable helplessness on the other. It is doubtless this anal-sadistic feature that makes the game so well adapted to gratify at the same time both the homosexual and the antagonistic aspects of the son–father contest. In these circumstances it will be understood that a serious match places a considerable strain on the psychical integrity and is likely to reveal any imperfections of character development. All games are apt at times to be marred by unsportsmanlike behaviour, i.e. by the sublimation undergoing a regression to its asocial origins, but with chess the strain is exceptionally great and is complicated by the circumstance that a specially high standard of correct demeanour is exacted.

It is interesting to compare with these psychological considerations some historical data on the way in which the game has been variously received by religious authorities. Van der Linde and Murray, the two greatest authorities on the history of chess, discuss sympathetically the Indian tradition that the game was invented by the Buddhists. It is certainly suggestive that the first mention of it occurs in connection with a stronghold of Buddhists. According to their ideas, war and the slaying of one's fellow men, for any purpose whatever, is criminal, and the punishment of the warrior in the next world will be much worse than that of the simple murderer; hence – so runs the story – they invented chess as a substitute for war. In this they would appear to have anticipated William James's suggestion of providing war-like substitutes, one quite in accord with the psychoanalytical doctrine of the displacement of affects. In a similar vein St J. G. Scott narrates a Burmese story to the effect that chess was invented by a Talaing queen who was passing fond of her lord and hoped by this distraction to keep him out of war. Ambivalence runs through the whole story, however, for the view has also been put forward that chess was invented by a Chinese mandarin, Han-sing, who wanted to amuse his soldiers when in winter quarters. A Ceylon legend has it that the game was invented by Ravan, the wife of the King of Lanka, in order to distract that monarch when his metropolis was being besieged. On the other hand, about the year 1000 a puritanical regent of Egypt usually known as Mansar issued an edict forbidding chess. In medieval times chess became widely popular and the ecclesiastical attitude towards it appears to have been mainly negative. The statutes of the church of Elna, for example, lay down that clergy indulging in chess shall be *ipso facto* excommunicated. At the end of the twelfth century the Bishop of Paris forbade the clergy even to have a chess-board in their house, in 1212 the Council of Paris condemned it utterly, and some forty years later St Louis, the pious King of France, imposed a fine on whoever should play the game. John Huss, when in prison, deplored having played at chess and thereby run the risk of being subject to violent passions.

In returning to the problem of Paul Morphy I shall begin by giving some description of his personal attributes and the characteristics of his play. In appearance he was small, only five foot four in height, with preternaturally small hands and feet, a slim, graceful figure and a 'face like a young girl in her teens' (F. M. Edge). Falkbeer, who knew him, observed that he appeared younger than he really was, adding, 'One would certainly have taken him rather for a schoolboy on his vacation than for a chess adept who had crossed the Atlantic for the express purpose of defeating, one after another, the most eminent players the world then knew.' He had a very pleasing manner and a delightful smile. His demeanour was strikingly modest. On only two occasions was he known to invite anyone to play with him, and with an uncanny intuition he chose for these exceptions the two men, Staunton and Harrwitz, who were to exercise such a baleful influence on his life. He bore himself, even in the unpleasant controversy we shall presently relate, with the greatest courtesy and dignity. While playing he was very impassive, with his eyes fixed steadfastly on the board; opponents got to know that whenever he looked up, which he did without any exultation, it meant he could foresee the inevitable end. His patience seemed inexhaustible; Edge, his first biographer, records having watched the famous Paulsen spend an hour or two over a single move while Morphy sat calmly looking on without the slightest movement of uneasiness. He seemed insensitive to fatigue and I will recall a story which illustrates his powers of endurance as well as two other features: his astounding memory – which, incidentally, he possessed also for music – and his capacity for sensorial imagery, a quality which links chess-players with musicians and mathematicians. It is narrated by Edge, who was at the time acting as his secretary, and concerns an exhibition he was giving when just twenty-one at the Café de la Régence in Paris, then the Mecca of chess-players from all over the world. He played blindfold eight games simultaneously against powerful opponents who, incidentally, were freely helped by advice from a crowd of expert players. It was seven hours before the first of them was defeated and the match lasted ten consecutive hours, during the whole of which time Morphy abstained from taking either food or even water. At the close there was a scene of terrific excitement, and Morphy had the greatest difficulty in extricating himself from the ovation in the streets and escaping to his hotel. There he slept well, but at seven in the morning he called his secretary and dictated to him every move in all the games, at the same time discussing with him the possible consequences of hundreds of hypothetical variations. It will be agreed that only a mind working with exceptional ease could have accomplished such an astounding feat. Nor was it an isolated achievement sustained by excitement. There are few more exhausting occupations than serious chess, and the number of those who can continue for more than three or four hours on end without feeling the strain is not very great. Yet Morphy has been known to play continuously from nine in the morning until midnight on many successive days without his play weakening in the least and without his showing any signs of fatigue. In psychoanalytical terms this must signify a very exceptional level of sublimation, for a psychological situation of such a degree of freedom can only mean that there is no risk of its stimulating any unconscious conflict or guilt.

It is not easy to describe Morphy's qualities as a player in other than general terms without presupposing a knowledge of chess technique. I hope that the generalizations I shall venture on will be in some measure trustworthy; we possess, at all events, ample data on which to found generalizations, for there survive some four hundred of Morphy's games and an extensive literature has grown up of critical comments subsequent authorities have made on the individual moves.

To begin with, there are different styles of chess which depend partly on the temperament and aim of the player and partly on the conditions under which he is playing. Speaking very roughly, it depends on whether one sets more store on winning or on not losing. In tournaments, for instance, where defeats are heavily penalized it may pay to aim at a few victories and a number of draws rather than at more victories but more defeats. The two extremes are represented by a slashing but risky attack on the one hand and a tediously defensive stonewalling on the other. Naturally the ideal player combines the best from each attitude. He spends some time in fortifying his army, not so much for defensive reasons as to get them into the strongest position from which to deliver an attack. A player may excel in either of these activities, or his fortifying may have an almost purely defensive aim in which any opportunity for an attack comes rather as a piece of luck. In chess there are – if we omit the recent 'hyper-modern' play – two well-known styles, known as the combinational and the positional, which are sometimes said to correspond with the romantic and the classical temperaments respectively. At the period we are concerned with, about the middle of the last century, only the former existed and, indeed, the latter is essentially the product of the last fifty years. The main difference between the two methods, at least in its extreme form, may be likened to that between a cleverly designed attack in battle and a steady siege. The aim of the combinational method is to plan a skilful grouping of pieces to make a co-ordinated onslaught on the king, whereas that of the positional method is the more cautious – but in the end sounder – one of gradually building up a fortified position and taking advantage of the slightest weakness in the opponent's position, wherever this may happen to be.

Now Morphy certainly possessed in the highest degree the gifts necessary for a master of combinational play, those of foresight, calculation and power of divining his opponent's intentions. Some of his games are masterpieces in this respect which have rarely been equalled and indeed the popular impression of his style among chess-players is that of vehement and victorious onslaught. One would therefore have anticipated with assurance that someone possessing such gifts, and whose brilliant performances were at such an early age, would have owed his success to an unusual genius in the qualities of intuition and adventurousness that might naturally be expected to appeal to youth. Yet the interesting thing, and one that throws a good deal of light on Morphy's psychology, is that he passed beyond this style and, in fact, ranks as the first pioneer of positional play – though it was Steinitz who later developed the principles of it. It was a fortunate coincidence that the only player in history whose genius in combinational play has equalled Morphy's was not only just at that time at the height of his career, but actually met Morphy in combat: I refer to Anderssen, till that moment the foremost player of the day and virtually the world's champion – though this title was not formally employed till a decade later. Murray says of the two men: 'Both were players of rare imaginative gifts, and their play has never been equalled for brilliancy of style, beauty of conception, and depth of design. In Morphy these qualities blazed forth from sheer natural genius; in Anderssen they were the result of long practice and study.' Reti, in his *Modern Ideas in Chess*, has instructively explained that Morphy's famous victory over Anderssen was due not to greater brilliance in the sense just indicated, but to his establishing the method of brilliance on a basis of the more mature positional play. It must have been a memorable scene to witness this slim youth overpowering the huge, burly Teuton of forty, not in the traditional fashion of the young hero overcoming a giant by more audacious imagination – for in this quality they were equally matched and equally unsurpassable – but by more mature depth of understanding. The interest of this observation for our purpose is the indication it gives that in Morphy's mind chess must have signified a fully adult activity, and success in it the serious occupation of a man rather than the rebellious ambition of a boy. I shall submit later that being shaken in this matter was one of the factors that led to his mental catastrophe.

Morphy was master of all aspects of the game in such a high degree, and was so free of mannerisms and individual peculiarities of style, that it is not easy to single out any particular characteristics. Chess, it is true, like all other games, is replete with unconscious symbolism. One could, for instance, comment on the skill he showed in attacking the king from behind or in separating the opposing king and queen; the latter, by the way, is illustrated in the first of his games ever recorded, which was played against his own father. But such details are not to our purpose, for pre-eminence in chess depends on a broad synthesis of exceptional qualities rather than on skill in any particular device or method. Careful consideration of the whole of Morphy's manner of play yields, I think, the indubitable conclusion that the outstanding characteristic he exhibited in it was an almost unbelievably supreme *confidence*. He knew, as though it was a simple fact of nature, that he was bound to win, and he quietly acted on this knowledge. When the Americans who had seen him play prophesied that on meeting any European champion he would, in the manner of Raphael, 'bring the sweat into that brow of his', chess players in Europe scoffed at the prediction as mere American bombast, and the only question in their minds was whether it was worth their leaders' while to play such a youngster. To anyone who knows what years of assiduous practice and rich experience go to attaining any degree of prowess in chess nothing could seem more utterly unlikely than that a beginner embarking on this arduous path, as Paul Morphy was, should have the career he actually did on reaching Europe. Yet before he left his native town he calmly predicted his coming victories with the most complete assurance. Such presumption might reasonably be regarded as megalomania were it not for the awkward fact that it was justified. On his return home, far from being flushed with pride, he remarked that he had not done so well as he should have, and in a sense this also was true, for when playing on a few occasions in a state of indisposition he was guilty of some weak moves that fell below his usual standard of play and even cost him a few games. It is not surprising that endowed with such confidence in his powers his play was marked by a boldness and even audacity in his moves that give at first the impression of being over-adventurous, and perhaps even of hazarding risks, until one perceives the sureness of the calculation behind them. His intrepidity was naturally more manifest when he had to do with relatively inferior players. Here he could behave with apparent recklessness, extravagantly flinging away one after another of his pieces until with an unsuspected movement his small remaining force would suddenly deliver the *coup de grâce*; on one such occasion he achieved the extraordinary feat of effecting a mate by simply castling. His boldness and his sense of how important position is in chess-playing are shown in two other characteristics for which he is well known: the extent to which he appreciated the value of developing the pieces early and continuously, and his willingness to make sacrifices to gain a better position. There is a story, perhaps apocryphal, that when he was a child he was so eager to bring his pieces forward that he regarded his pawns as a nuisance to be got rid of as soon as possible: how different from the great Philidor, who had declared pawns to be the very soul of chess! It is at all events quite fitting that the name 'Morphy opening' in chess has been attached to the following device. What is called the Muzio opening is characterized by a bold attack in which a knight is sacrificed in the fifth move so as to obtain what is believed to be a commensurate advantage in position.

In the Morphy opening the same tactics are followed up by sacrificing a bishop also, so that it is sometimes known by the name of 'double Muzio'. Very few people indeed are to be found confident enough of their attack to be able to risk such grave initial losses. Even the defence named after him, the Morphy defence to the Ruy Lopez opening, one which is so valuable as to have been elaborated since into some twenty named variations, is the most aggressive of the manifold defences to this opening.

With Morphy chess sense, if one may use such an expression, was far more innate than acquired. He had read a good deal, but gave away the book as soon as he had looked through it. He said himself that no author had been of much value to him, and that 'he was astonished at finding various positions and solutions given as novel – certain moves producing certain results, etc., for that he had made the same deductions himself, as necessary consequences' (Edge). MacDonnell, who watched his play in London, wrote later of it in his *Chess Life-Pictures*: 'I fancy he always discerned the right move at a glance, and only paused before making it partly out of respect for his antagonist and partly to certify himself of its correctness, to make assurance doubly sure, and to accustom himself to sobriety of demeanour in all circumstances.' The following story raises the whole question of the method employed in mental calculation. In the famous seventeenth move in the Four Knights game played with Paulsen on 8 November 1857 Morphy offered to exchange his queen for his opponent's bishop. Paulsen was naturally suspicious of a trap and carefully investigated the possibilities. After pondering on the situation for more than an hour, and detecting no trap, he accepted the offer and after eleven more moves had to resign. Years afterwards Steinitz carried out a full analysis of the situation and maintained as a result of it that the future possibilities in the game were far too numerous and complicated for it to be conceivable that any human brain could calculate and predict them. It so happened that an onlooker had asked Morphy after the game was over whether he had been able to foresee the end of it from his famous move; to the question he returned the enigmatic answer: 'I knew it would give Paulsen a deal of trouble.' Steinitz was doubtless right in his conclusion so far as consciousness is concerned, but one wonders whether the so-called intuitive chess sense does not imply a special power of pre-conscious calculation. The experiments Milne Bramwell carried out showed that the subconscious capacity for arithmetical calculation, as tested in hypnosis, far exceeds the conscious capacity, and the same may well hold good for the computation of chess moves.

We may take it that this remarkable combination of capacity and confidence could not occur unless it was a direct representative of the main stream of the libido and was providing the best possible solution of any conflicts in the deepest trends of the personality. It follows that anything interfering with such an indispensable expression of the personality would be likely gravely to endanger its integrity, and so indeed events proved. Our knowledge of the unconscious motivation of chess-playing tells us that what it represented could only have been the wish to overcome the father in an acceptable way. For Morphy the conditions necessary for its acceptability were essentially three: that the act in question should be received in a friendly manner; that it should be ascribed to worthy motives; and that it should be regarded as a serious and grown-up activity. We shall see that each of these conditions was grossly violated on his fateful visit to Europe and shall try to trace the mental consequences of this. It is no doubt significant that Morphy's soaring odyssey into the higher realms of chess began just a year after the unexpectedly sudden death of his father,[3] which had been a great shock to him, and we may surmise that his brilliant effort of sublimation was, like Shakespeare's *Hamlet* and Freud's *Traumdeutung*, a reaction to this critical event.

I shall now consider the critical period of Morphy's life in more detail, and for this purpose shall find it necessary in the first place to introduce to those of you who are not conversant with the history of chess some of the most prominent figures of the day in that world. Six of these need to be mentioned in this context: four of them became friendly admirers of Morphy, the other two set him a psychological problem to which he was not equal.

First in order of time was Loewenthal, whom Morphy had already successfully encountered when a child. Loewenthal had made further progress since then and in the Birmingham tournament that took place during Morphy's visit to England, in which the latter did not participate, he won the first place, although both Staunton and Saint-Amant were also competitors. In a match arranged between the two Morphy decisively beat him, and Loewenthal became a firm friend and admirer, taking his side in the unfortunate controversy to which we shall presently have to refer. He foretold that after Morphy's games were published – a task which he himself successfully undertook later – the chess world would rank him above all other players, living or dead. The stakes in the Loewenthal match were £100, and after winning Morphy immediately presented Loewenthal with some furniture costing £120 for a new house he was taking. We shall repeatedly have occasion to note how fastidious Morphy was over the subject of money. Before he left America, for instance, when the New Orleans Chess Club offered to subscribe money to enable him to participate in the Birmingham tournament, he had refused – not wishing to travel as a professional chess-player. Next comes Paulsen, an American, famous at that time for his amazing exhibitions in blindfold chess and later for winning two matches against Anderssen as well as for his important contributions to chess theory. He was Morphy's only serious rival at the New York tournament and from reading a couple of his published games he predicted on that occasion that Morphy would beat him; just before the tournament they played three games blindfold, of which Morphy won two and drew one. Paulsen also became a devoted friend of Morphy's. Saint-Amant was at that time the foremost player in France. He did not play any single-handed games with Morphy, but lost five and drew two of seven consultation games against him. He also became a fervent admirer, and said of his blindfold play that it was enough to make the bones of Philidor and La Bourdonnais rattle in their grave, without doubt the handsomest compliment a Frenchman could pay. The genial Anderssen we have already met. He was the best player living and was generally recognized to be the world's champion until his defeat by Steinitz some years later; he obtained a prize at each of the twelve tournaments he took part in and won the first place in seven of them. Mongredien, the President of the London Chess Club, said of him that he was 'except Morphy, the most splendid and chivalrous player whom I ever encountered', and his treatment of Morphy certainly confirms this estimate of him. Although his colleagues brought the greatest possible pressure to bear to prevent his impairing German prestige by going abroad to play a match with a youngster of no official standing, and in spite of his having no opportunity to practise beforehand, Anderssen made no excuses but travelled to Paris to meet his fate at Morphy's hands. Reproached afterwards for not having played so brilliantly as he had in his famous match with Dufresne, he made the generous rejoinder, 'No, Morphy wouldn't let me.'

Morphy's relations with these four men contrast sadly with his experiences of the two who will next concern us. Of these the more important was Staunton, and to explain his significance for Morphy a word must be said about the position he occupied. He was a man with a greater prestige than his tournament record would lead one to suppose. It is true that by his victory over Saint-Amant, Horwitz and Harrwitz in the 1840s he could claim to be considered the leading player in the world, but he was not able to sustain this position, being beaten, for instance, in the London tournament of 1851 and the Birmingham one of 1858. He was, however, a great analyst; and the standard text-book that he wrote, together with his position as one of the first chess editors, made him the *doyen* of the English, if not of the European, chess world. In the middle of the last century England was easily paramount in chess, and perhaps this contributed to the reasons that made Morphy select Staunton as the antagonist he most wanted to meet; it was the wish to play against Staunton that was his main motive in crossing the Atlantic. In psycho-analytical language we may say that Staunton was the supreme father *imago* and that Morphy made the overcoming of him the test case of his capacity to play chess, and unconsciously of much else besides. A piece of evidence is extant which goes to show that this choice of father *imago* was far from being a recent one. At the age of fifteen Morphy had been presented with a copy of the games played at the first International Tournament of 1851, of which Staunton was the secretary. He took it on himself to write on the title page: 'By H. Staunton, Esq., author of the *Handbook of Chess*, *Chess-Player's Companion*, etc. (and some devilish bad games).' After Morphy's victory at the New York tournament some enthusiasts mooted the possibility of a European champion coming to America to play him. On hearing of this Staunton published a deprecatory paragraph in his weekly chess column and remarked that 'the best players in Europe are not chess professionals but have other and more serious avocations'. To hint that Morphy's chess was either a juvenile pastime or else a means of making money were innuendoes that must have wounded him to the quick, for there is ample evidence that he was morbidly sensitive to either suggestion. His New Orleans friends nevertheless issued a challenge to Staunton to come to America, which he not unnaturally refused, dropping, however, a broad hint that Morphy would find him at his disposal were he to come to Europe. Morphy crossed four months later and on being introduced to Staunton at once asked him for a game. Staunton pleaded an engagement and followed this by a course of such ungentlemanly behaviour as to be explicable only on the score of neurotic apprehension; it was in fact said of him that he suffered from what was called 'nervous irritability'. For three months, during his stay in England and after, Morphy endeavoured in the most dignified manner to arrange a match, to which Staunton responded by a series of evasions, postponements, broken promises and pretexts that his brain 'was overtaxed by more important pursuits' – not that the latter prevented him from participating in the Birmingham tournament in the very same month. Foiled in his hopes Morphy laid the whole matter before Lord Lyttelton, the President of the British Chess Association, who made a sympathetic reply, and the matter rested at that. During this time, however, Staunton kept up in his chess column a steady fire of criticism of the man he avoided meeting, deprecating his play, hinting that he was a monetary adventurer and so on. One sentence may be quoted from Morphy's final letter to him: 'Permit me to repeat what I have invariably declared in every chess community I have had the honor of entering, that I am not a professional player – that I never wished to make any skill I possess the means of pecuniary advancement.'[4] The whole episode led to an acrimonious wrangle in the chess world in which the large majority supported Morphy, and subsequent opinion almost unanimously regards Staunton's behaviour as totally unworthy of him. The effect on Morphy was immediate, and it showed itself in a strong revulsion against chess. As Sergeant, Morphy's latest and best biographer, writes, 'Morphy sickened of chess tactics – off the board. Is there any wonder?'

Towards the end of this episode Morphy crossed to Paris, where he at once approached Harrwitz, *le roi de la Régence*. This gentleman also does not appear in an amiable light in his dealings with Morphy, which were marked by morbid vanity and a total lack of chivalry (Sergeant). We need not go into the sordid details, which have been fully described by Edge, but the upshot was that Harrwitz withdrew from the match when he was being decisively beaten. Morphy at first refused to accept the stake, a sum of 290 francs, but on its being represented to him that other people would lose money unless his victory was officially sealed in this way he assented, but devoted the sum towards defraying Anderssen's travelling expenses to Paris. Morphy's neurosis increased after this, and it was only temporarily abrogated by the pleasant episode of the match with Anderssen, the final flare-up of his chess fever.

Something should now be said about the reception Morphy's successes met with, for they were of such a kind as to raise the question whether his subsequent collapse may not have been influenced through his perhaps belonging to the type that Freud has described under the name of *Die am Erfolge scheitern* ('Those wrecked by success'). I alluded earlier to the scene at the Café de la Régence on the occasion of the brilliant *tour de force* when Morphy successfully encountered eight strong players at once when blindfold; it was so tumultuous that soldiers ran up in the expectation that there was another revolution. Morphy became the lion of Parisian society, was entertained everywhere, politely allowed himself to be defeated at chess by duchesses and princesses, and finally left France in a blaze of glory, the culmination of which was a banquet at which his bust, made by a famous sculptor, was presented crowned with a laurel wreath. His reception on his return to New York, where patriotic fervour was added to the other enthusiasms, may well be imagined. It was widely felt that this was the first time in history in which an American had proved himself, not merely the equal, but the superior of any representative in his field drawn from the older countries, so that Morphy had added a cubit to the stature of American civilization. In the presence of a great assembly in the chapel of the university he was presented with a testimonial consisting of a chess-board with mother-of-pearl and ebony squares and a set of men in gold and silver; he also received a gold watch, on which coloured chess-pieces took the place of the numerals. An incident that occurred at this presentation may be mentioned as illustrating Morphy's sensitiveness. Colonel Mead, the chairman of the reception committee, alluded in his speech to chess as a profession, and referred to Morphy as its most brilliant exponent. 'Morphy took exception to be characterized as a professional player, even by implication, and he resented it in such a way as to overwhelm Colonel Mead with confusion. Such was his mortification at this untoward event that Colonel Mead withdrew from further participation in the Morphy demonstration' (Buck). At the Union Club of New York he was presented with a silver wreath of laurels. He then proceeded to Boston, where a banquet was given in his honour at which were present, among others, Agassiz, Oliver Wendell Holmes, Longfellow and Lowell; in a speech at this banquet Quincey made the witty remark: 'Morphy is greater than Caesar, because he came and without seeing conquered.' Shortly after this he was presented with a golden crown in Boston.

Adulation of this degree showered on a young man of twenty-one inevitably imposes a severe strain on his mental integrity, and one may well ask whether it did not play some part in the tragedy that followed. In this connection I should like to quote an interesting passage from the obituary notice written years later by Morphy's boyhood friend Maurian. Maurian ascribes the revulsion against chess – which, by the way, he does not associate with the subsequent mental derangement – to the completeness of Morphy's success, but in quite the opposite sense to that we have just indicated. He writes:

Paul Morphy was never so passionately fond, so inordinately devoted to chess as is generally believed. An intimate acquaintance and long observation enables us to state this positively. His only devotion to the game, if it may be so termed, lay in his ambition to meet and to defeat the best players and great masters of this country and of Europe. He felt his enormous strength, and never for a moment doubted the outcome. Indeed, before his first departure for Europe he privately and modestly, yet with perfect confidence, predicted to us his certain success, and when he returned he expressed the conviction that he had played poorly, rashly – that none of his opponents should have done so well as they did against him. But, this one ambition satisfied, he appeared to have lost all interest in the game.

Before attempting to answer the question just raised I think it well to finish the story itself and give some account of the later mental developments. On settling down in New Orleans Morphy's intention was to devote himself to the profession of law, of which he had an excellent knowledge. He found, however, that his now unwelcome fame as a chess-player prevented people from taking him seriously as a lawyer, and this injustice preyed greatly on his mind. Buck, who had the assistance of Morphy's relatives in compiling the story of his later years, states that 'he became enamoured of a wealthy and handsome young lady in New Orleans and informed a mutual friend of the fact, who broached the subject to the lady; but she scorned the idea of marrying "a mere chess-player".'

Within a year or two of his establishing himself in what he intended to be his serious permanent profession the Civil War broke out and Morphy was faced with the prospect of a real war interfering with his endeavour to substitute a peaceful occupation for his pastime of mock war.[5] His reaction was characteristic of the man who had built his mental integrity on converting hostile intentions into friendly ones – he hastened to Richmond, and in the midst of hostilities applied for a *diplomatic* appointment. This was refused and soon after his return to New Orleans, his mother-town, it was captured by the federal enemy. The Morphy family fled on a Spanish warship to Cuba, thence to Havana, Cadiz and Paris. He spent a year in Paris and then returned to Havana until the war was over.

Already at that time his mental state could not have been at all satisfactory, for within a couple of years of returning to New Orleans his mother persuaded him to spend eighteen months in Paris, his third visit there, in the hope that the change of environment would restore him. His aversion to chess was by now so complete that he did not go near the scenes of his former triumphs.

Before long there manifested itself unmistakable evidence of paranoia. He imagined himself persecuted by people who wished to render his life intolerable. His delusions centred on the husband of his elder sister, the administrator of his father's estate, who he believed was trying to rob him of his patrimony. He challenged him to a duel and then brought a law-suit against him, spending his time for years in preparing his case; in court it was easily shown that his accusations were quite baseless. He also thought that people, particularly his brother-in-law, were trying to poison him, and for a time refused to take food except at the hands of his mother or his (younger, unmarried) sister. Another delusion was that his brother-in-law and an intimate friend, Binder, were conspiring to destroy his clothes, of which he was very vain, and to kill him; on one occasion he called in the latter's office and unexpectedly assaulted him. He was given to stopping and staring at every pretty face in the street, which I should ascribe to feminine identification. He was also passionately fond of flowers. I will quote one habit from this time, on which, however, I am unable to throw any light. During a certain period, according to his niece's account, he had a mania for striding up and down the verandah declaiming the following words: '*Il plantera la bannière de Castille sur les murs de Madrid au cri de Ville gagnée, et le petit Roi s'en ira tout penaud.*' It sounds like a quotation, but if so I have not been able to trace it, nor can I explain the allusion. His mode of life was to take a walk every day, punctually at noon and most scrupulously attired, after which he would retire again until the evening when he would set out for the opera, never missing a single performance. He would see no one except his mother, and grew angry if she ventured to invite even intimates to the house. Two years before his death he was approached for his permission to include his life in a projected biographical work on famous Louisianians. He sent an indignant reply, in which he stated that his father, Judge Alonzo Morphy, of the High Court of Louisiana, had left at his death the sum of 146,162 dollars and 54 cents, while he himself had followed no profession and had nothing to do with biography. His talk was constantly of his father's fortune, and the mere mention of chess was usually sufficient to irritate him.

The problem we have set ourselves at the outset is what relation did Morphy's chess career bear to his later mental disorder? Sergeant is at pains to demonstrate that mere preoccupation with chess could not be held responsible, and every medical and psychological expert can only confirm this opinion. His summary of the pathogeny of the disorder is so clear as to merit full quotation.

Firstly, Morphy had some reason to be disgusted with, not chess, but chess-masters, whom he found of a very different character from himself. He set out, very young, generous, and high-spirited, recognizing, as he said himself, no incentive but reputation, and met not fellow-knights but tortuous acrobats of the pen, slingers of mud and chess-sharpers. Granted he also met very decent gentlemen such as Anderssen, Löwenthal and the majority of the leading amateurs in London and Paris. But the mean wounds inflicted by the other sort did not readily heal. Secondly, he always kept himself pure from any taint (as he rightly or wrongly imagined it to be) of professionalism in chess, yet was constantly being, if not called, at least looked on as a professional. And, lastly, he was ambitious in the career he had chosen for himself in life, and failing in that through an unfortunate combination of circumstances, laid the blame upon chess. The disappointed ambition was assuredly a cause of Morphy's sad fate . . . A super-sensitive nature like his was ill-fitted to stand such trials.

How much Morphy strove to conceal his wound from himself may be seen from the following passage from his speech at the presentation made to him on his return to New York: 'Of my European tour, I will only say that it has been pleasant in almost every respect. Of all the adversaries encountered in the peaceful jousts of the checkered field, I retain a lively and agreeable recollection. I found them gallant, chivalrous and gentlemanly, as well as true votaries of the kingly pastime.'

Let me put the problem in another way. Was Morphy's mental derangement brought on by his very success or by his failure and disappointment? Was his situation that of Browning's Pictor Ignotus, from whom the approach of supreme fame brought forth the cry:

> The thought grew frightful, 'twas so wildly dear!?

Did he say to himself, like Andrea:

> Too live the life grew, golden and not grey,
> And I'm the weak-eyed bat no sun should tempt
> Out of the grange whose four walls make his world?

Did he withdraw from the world with the disdainful consolation:

> At least no merchant traffics in my heart?

Couched in more psychological language, was Morphy affrighted at his own presumptuousness when the light of publicity was thrown on it? Freud has pointed out that the people who break under the strain of too great success do so because they can endure it only in imagination, not in reality. To castrate the father in a dream is a very different matter from doing it in reality. The real situation provokes the unconscious guilt in its full force, and the penalty may be mental collapse.

I do not think the full explanation can lie here. We have to remember that in the aim most vital to Morphy he had not succeeded, but failed. We have seen how Staunton must have been to him the arch *imago*, and he had not managed to bring him to book. It was all very well to have shown himself to be the best player in the world, with a good presumption that he could have defeated Staunton also. But the cold fact remains that this arch-opponent eluded him. The dreaded father was not merely still at large, but had himself shown signs of unmistakable hostility. Morphy's aim had miscarried of dealing with his repressed hostility towards his father – and the fear of his father's towards him – by converting this into a friendly homosexual encounter. The following consideration gives, I think, a hint that Morphy himself was partly conscious of the failure of his aim. When he returned to New York he declared he would not play any American again except at odds, and this was doubtless justified in the circumstances. But when, a few weeks later, he reached the safety of his home in New Orleans he issued a challenge to play anyone in the world at odds of pawn and move, the only instance in his whole chess career of his probably overestimating his powers.[6] I read this as indicating a psychological compensation for the underlying sense of having failed, and the anxiety this must have stirred in his unconscious.

There was, however, more than this. When Staunton eluded him he did so in a way that must have suggested to a sensitive person, as Morphy assuredly was, that his aim was a disreputable one. We know that mental integrity rests essentially on moral integrity, that mental stability can exist only so long as there is guiltlessness. It is impossible that Morphy could have displayed the capacities he did, had not his gifts and mental functioning been free to be wholly concentrated on the tasks he set them. But this was so only as long as he could be relieved from any possibility of the counter-forces in his unconscious being stirred. He was at the mercy of anything that might do this. I have pointed out earlier how abnormally sensitive he was to any hint that his aims might not be received in a friendly manner, i.e. that they might be treated as if they were unfriendly themselves; to any suggestion that they did not proceed from the purest incentives, and particularly to the possibility of their being tainted by mercenary motives; and to any attitude that betrayed disdain for their juvenile nature.[7] Staunton bitterly wounded him in each of these three respects. His treatment of him was certainly the reverse of friendly – it is hardly an exaggeration to call it scurrilous; he practically accused him of being a penniless adventurer; and he finally avoided him on the plea that he had more serious, i.e., grown-up, matters to attend to. In the face of these accusations Morphy's heart failed him, he succumbed and abandoned the wicked path of his chess career. It was as if the father had unmasked his evil intentions and was now adopting a similarly hostile attitude towards him in turn. What had appeared to be an innocent and laudable expression of his personality was now being shown to be actuated by the most childish and ignoble of wishes, the unconscious impulses to commit a sexual assault on the father and at the same time to maim him utterly: in short, to 'mate' him in both the English and the Persian senses of that word. Obedient to his actual father's wishes he now engaged in the grown-up profession of law and discarded what he had been told was the childish preoccupation of chess.[8] But it was too late: his 'sins' pursued him. In the two things that comprise manhood, a serious career among men and the love of women, his chess past dogged and thwarted him. He was never able to escape from the 'sins' of youth and to take his place among the world of men. Little wonder that his abandonment of chess became increasingly complete, until he loathed the very name of it. The only recourse left to him in attempting to deal with his burden of guilt was to project it. In the delusions of being poisoned and robbed we recognize the oral- and anal-sadistic phantasies projected on to his sister's husband. His homosexual friendliness to men had broken down, and the antagonism underlying it lay exposed. This emerged in the direction of his brother-in-law, evidently a substitute for his brother, while the last anecdote of his life related above, shows how he clung to the exaltation and veneration of his father, to whom was reserved the patriarchal privilege of 'making money'.

Perhaps a general conclusion emerges from contemplating this tragic story. It would seem to afford some clue to the well-recognized association between genius and mental instability. It may well be that Morphy's case is a general one. Genius is evidently the capacity to apply unusual gifts with intense, even if only temporary, concentration. I would suggest that this, in its turn, depends on a special capacity for discovering conditions under which the unconscious guilt can be held in complete abeyance. This is doubtless to be connected with the well-known rigour, the sincerity and the purity of the artistic conscience. It is purchased, however, at the cost of the psychical integrity being at the mercy of any disturbance of these indispensable conditions. And that would appear to be the secret of 'artistic sensitiveness'.

The story also lends itself to a discussion of some important psycho-analytical considerations which I have scarcely time here to adumbrate.

It will have been noticed that, for the sake of simplicity, I have throughout referred to Morphy's gifts as a mark of his capacity for sublimation, and the question may well be asked whether this is a just description of a disguised way of gratifying hostile, e.g., parricidal, impulses. In answer I would admit that the impulses behind the play are ultimately of a mixed nature, but the essential process seems to me to be a libidinal one. I conceive that the parricidal impulses were 'bound' by an erotic cathexis, actually a homosexual one, and that this in its turn was sublimated. The enormous value of the process to Morphy's mental health is evident from the considerations adduced above, and this I take to be an example of an important general law, namely that the process of sublimation has ultimately a defensive function.[9] By discharging id energy along a deflected path, and particularly by transforming a sexualized aggressivity it protects against the dangers to the ego which we know to proceed from excessive accumulation of that energy.

Finally, it is worth pointing out that when one speaks clinically of the 'breakdown of a sublimation' one really means the cessation of its defensive function. Morphy could play chess as well after as before his mental failure, as may be seen from his occasional games with Maurian: in most such cases, perhaps in all, the actual capacity acquired in the sublimating process remains intact in itself. What is lost is the ability to use this talent as a means of guarding against overwhelming id impulses, and this is really what patients are fearing when they express the anxiety lest 'psychoanalysis will take their sublimations away from them'.[10]

Notes

1. As the dates of their births are not given in any of the biographies I may usefully mention them here: Mahrina, 5 February 1830; Edward, 26 December 1834; Paul, 22 June 1837; Helena, 21 October 1839.
2. Chess may well be called the art of the intellect.
3. This occurred on 22 November 1856.
4. F. M. Edge, *The Exploits and Triumphs in Europe of Paul Morphy* (New York: Appleton, 1859).
5. In the discussion of this paper Dr Bryan and Miss Searl attached great importance to the effect of this episode on Morphy's mind, and I am inclined to agree with them; it may even have been the precipitating cause of the psychosis, as the London experiences certainly were of the neurosis.
6. Against this, I admit, the fact might be brought forward that no less a master than Saint-Amant had imagined that 'Paul Morphy must in future give odds to every opponent'.
7. How beautifully Morphy 'moralized' the pastime may be observed in the following passage from the speech already cited: 'It is not only the most delightful and scientific, but the most moral of amusements. Unlike other games in which lucre is the end and aim of the contestants, it recommends itself to the wise, by the fact that its mimic battles are fought for no prize nor honor. It is eminently and emphatically the philosopher's game. Let the chess board supersede the card table and a great improvement will be visible in the morals of the community.'
8. To quote again from the speech mentioned above: 'Chess never has been and never can be aught but a recreation. It should not be indulged in to the detriment of other and more serious avocations – should not absorb or engross the thoughts of those who worship at its shrine, but should be kept in the background, and restrained within its proper provinces. As a mere game, a relaxation from the severe pursuits of life, it is deserving of high commendations.'
9. Dr Glover expressed a similar conclusion in his recent paper before this Society: 'Sublimation, Substitution and Social Anxiety', October 1930.
10. The original material on which this essay is based can mostly be traced through the bibliographical references given in the *Encyclopaedia Britannica* (eleventh and fourteenth editions), and Philip W. Sergeant's *Morphy's Games of Chess* (New York: Dover Publications Inc., 1921). I am also greatly indebted to Mr Sergeant for his courtesy in placing at my disposal much unpublished material, including the manuscript of another forthcoming book by him on Paul Morphy. I am also obliged to Paul Morphy's niece, Mrs Morphy-Voitier, of New Orleans, for kindly furnishing me with much useful information about him and the family.

Sándor Ferenczi

The Ontogenesis of the Interest in Money*

The deeper psycho-analysis penetrates into the knowledge of social-psychological productions (myths, fairy-tales, folklore) the stronger becomes the confirmation of the phylogenetic origin of symbols, which stand out in the mental life of every individual as a precipitate of the experiences of previous generations. Analysis has still to perform the task of separately investigating the phylogenesis and ontogenesis of symbolism, and then establishing their mutual relation. The classical formula of 'Daimon kai Tyche' in Freud's application (the co-operation of heredity and experience in the genesis of individual strivings) will finally become applied also to the genesis of the psychical contents of these strivings, and this also brings to the front the old dispute about 'congenital ideas', though now no longer in the form of empty speculations. We may already, however, anticipate to this extent, namely, that for the production of a symbol individual experiences are necessary as well as the congenital disposition, these providing the real material for the construction of the symbol, while the congenital basis preceding experience has perhaps only the value of an inherited, but not yet functioning mechanism.

I wish here to examine the question of whether, and to what extent, individual experience favours the transformation of anal-erotic interest into interest in money.

Every psycho-analyst is familiar with the symbolic meaning of money that was discovered by Freud: 'Wherever the archaic way of thinking has prevailed or still prevails, in the old civilizations, in myths, fairy-tales, superstition, in unconscious

* From *First Contributions to Psycho-Analysis*, trans. Ernest Jones (London: Hogarth Press, 1952), pp. 319–31. Reprinted by permission of the Author's Literary Estate, the Hogarth Press Ltd., and Basic Books, Inc. First published in *Internationale Zeitschrift für ärztliche Psychoanalyse*, 1914.

thinking, in dreams and in neuroses, money has been brought into the closest connection with filth.'

As an individual–psychological phenomenon parallel with this fact Freud asserts that an intimate association exists between the strongly marked erogenicity of the anal zone in childhood and the character trait of miserliness that develops later. In the case of persons who later on were especially tidy, economical and obstinate, one learns from the analytic investigation of their early childhood that they were of that class of infants 'who refuse to empty the bowel because they obtain an accessory pleasure from defecation', who even in the later years of childhood 'enjoyed holding back the stools', and who recall 'having occupied themselves in their childhood in all sorts of unseemly ways with the evacuated material'. 'The most extensive connections seem to be those existing between the apparently so disparate complexes of defecation and interest in money.'[1]

Observation of the behaviour of children and analytic investigation of neurotics allow us now to establish some single points on the line along which the idea of the most valuable thing that a man possesses (money) is developed in the individual into a symbol 'of the most worthless thing, which a man casts aside as dejecta'.[2]

Experience gathered from these two sources shows that children originally devote their interest without any inhibition to the process of defecation, and that it affords them pleasure to hold back their stools. The excreta thus held back are really the first 'savings' of the growing being, and as such remain in a constant, unconscious interrelationship with every bodily activity or mental striving that has anything to do with collecting, hoarding and saving.

Faeces are also, however, one of the first toys of the child. The purely auto-erotic satisfaction afforded to the child by the pressing and squeezing of the faecal masses and the play of the sphincter muscles soon becomes – in part, at least – transformed into a sort of object-love, in that the interest gets displaced from the neutral sensations of certain organs on to the material itself that caused these feelings. The faeces are thus 'introjected', and in this stage of development – which is essentially characterised by sharpening of the sense of smell and an increasingly adroit use of the hands, with at the same time an inability to walk upright (creeping on all fours) – they count as a valuable toy, from which the child is to be weaned only through deterrents and threats of punishment.

The child's interest for dejecta experiences its first distortion through the smell of faeces becoming disagreeable, disgusting. This is probably related to the beginning of the upright gait.[3] The other attributes of this material – moistness, discolouration, stickiness, etc. – do not for the time being offend his sense of cleanliness. He still enjoys, therefore, playing with and manipulating moist street-mud whenever he has the chance, liking to collect it together into larger heaps. Such a heap of mud is already in a sense a symbol, distinguished from the real thing by its absence of smell. For the child, street-mud is, so to speak, deodorised dejecta.

As the child's sense of cleanliness increases – with the help of paedagogic measures – street-mud also becomes objectionable to him. Substances which on account of their stickiness, moistures and colour are apt to leave traces on the body and clothing become despised and avoided as 'dirty things'. The symbol of filth must therefore undergo a further distortion, a dehydration. The child turns its interest to sand, a substance which, while the colour of earth, is cleaner and dry. The instinctive joy of children in gathering up, massing together and shaping sand is subsequently rationalised and sanctioned by the adults, whom it suits to see an otherwise unruly child playing with sand for hours, and they declare this playing to be 'healthy', i.e., hygienic.[4] None the less this play-sand also is nothing other than a copro-symbol – deodorised and dehydrated filth.

Already in this stage of development, by the way, there occurs a 'return of the repressed'. It gives children endless pleasure to fill with water the holes they dig in the sand, and so to bring the material of their play nearer to the original watery stage. Boys not infrequently employ their own urine for this irrigation, as though they wanted in this way to emphasise quite clearly the relationship of the two materials. Even the interest for the specific odour of excrement does not cease at once, but is only displaced on to other odours that in any way resemble this. The children continue to show a liking for the smell of sticky materials with a characteristic odour, especially the strongly smelling degenerated product of cast-off epidermis cells which collects between the toes, nasal secretion, ear-wax and the dirt of the nails, while many children do not content themselves with the moulding and sniffing of these substances, but also take them into the mouth. The passionate enjoyment of children in moulding putty (colour, consistency, smell), tar and asphalt is well known. I knew a boy who had an intense passion for the characteristic smell of rubber materials, and who could sniff for hours at a piece of india-rubber.

The smell of stables and of illuminating gas greatly pleases children at this age – indeed, at much older ages even – and it is not chance that popular belief appreciates places having these smells as being 'healthy', even as being a cure for diseases. A special sublimation path of anal-erotism branches off from the smell of gas, asphalt and turpentine: the fondness for substances with an agreeable odour, for perfumes, by means of which the development of a reaction-formation – representation through the opposite – is concluded. People with whom this kind of sublimation occurs often develop in other respects as well into aesthetes, and there can be no question that aesthetics in general has its principal root in repressed anal-erotism.[5] The aesthetic and playful interest springing from this source not infrequently has a share in the developing pleasure in painting and sculpture.[6]

Already in the mud and sand periods of coprophilic interest it is striking how fond children are of fabricating objects out of this material – so far as their primitive artistic skill allows – or, more correctly, of imitating objects the possession of which has a special value for them. They make out of them different articles of diet, cakes, tarts, sweetmeats, etc. The reinforcement of purely egoistic instincts by coprophilia begins here.

Progress in the sense of cleanliness then gradually makes even sand unacceptable to the child, and the infantile stone age begins: the collecting of pebbles, as prettily shaped and coloured as possible, in which a higher stage in the development of replacement-formation is attained. The attributes of evil odour, moisture and softness are represented by those of absence of odour, dryness and now also hardness. We are reminded of the real origin of this hobby by the circumstance that stones – just as mud and sand – are gathered and collected from the *earth*. The capitalistic significance of stones is already quite considerable. (Children are 'stone-rich'[7] in the narrow sense of the word.)

After stones comes the turn of artificial products, and with these the detachment of the interest from the earth is complete. Glass marbles, buttons,[8] fruit pips, are eagerly collected – this time no longer only for the sake of their intrinsic value, but as measures of value, so to speak as primitive coins, converting the previous barter exchange of children into an enthusiastic money exchange. The character of capitalism, however, not purely practical and utilitarian, but libidinous and irrational, is betrayed in this stage also: the child decidedly enjoys the collecting in itself.[9]

It only needs one more step for the identification of faeces with gold to be complete. Soon even stones begin to wound the child's feeling of cleanliness – he longs for something purer – and this is offered to him in the shining pieces of money, the high appreciation of which is naturally also in part due to the respect in which they are held by adults, as well as to the seductive possibilities of obtaining through them everything that the child's heart can desire. Originally, however, it is not these purely practical considerations that are operative, enjoyment in the playful collecting, heaping up and gazing at the shining metal pieces being the chief thing, so that they are treasured even less for their economic value than for their own sake as pleasure-giving objects. The eye takes pleasure at the sight of their lustre and colour, the ear at their metallic clink, the sense of touch at play with the round smooth discs, only the sense of smell comes away empty, and the sense of taste also has to be satisfied with the weak but peculiar taste of the coins. With this the development of the money symbol is in its main outlines complete. Pleasure in the intestinal contents becomes enjoyment of money, which, however, after what has been said is seen to be nothing other than odourless, dehydrated filth that has been made to shine. *Pecunia non olet.*

In correspondence with the development of the organ of thought that in the meanwhile has been proceeding in the direction of logicality, the adult's symbolic interest in money gets extended not only to objects with similar physical attributes, but to all sorts of things that in any way signify value or possession (paper money, shares, bankbook, etc.). But whatever form may be assumed by money, the enjoyment at possessing it has its deepest and amplest source in coprophilia. Every sociologist and national economist who examines the facts without prejudice has to reckon with this irrational element. Social problems can be solved only by discovering the real psychology of human beings; speculations about economic conditions alone will never reach the goal.

A part of anal-erotism is not sublimated at all, but remains in its original form.[10] Even the most cultivated normal being displays an interest in his evacuation functions which stands in a curious contradiction to the abhorrence and disgust that he manifests when he sees or hears about anything of the kind in regard to other people. Foreign people and races, as is well known, cannot *'riechen'*[11] each other. In addition to the retention of the original form, however, there also exists a 'return' of what is actually concealed behind the money symbol. The intestinal disorders, first observed by Freud, that follow on a wounding of the money complex are examples of this.[12] A further instance is the curious fact, which I have noticed in countless cases, that people are economical as regards the changing of under-linen in a way quite out of proportion to their standard of living in other respects. Meanness finally, therefore, makes use of the anal character in order to gain once more a piece of anal-erotism (tolerance of dirt). The following is a still more striking example. A patient could not recall any kind of coprophilic manipulations, but soon after related without being asked that he took a special pleasure in brightly shining copper coins, and had invented an original procedure for making them shine; he swallowed the piece of money, and then searched his faeces until he found the piece of money, which during its passage through the alimentary canal had become beautifully shining.[13] Here the pleasure in the clean object became a cover for satisfaction of the most primitive anal-erotism. The curious thing is that the patient was able to deceive himself as to the real significance of his transparent behaviour.

Apart from striking examples of this sort, the erotic enjoyment of heaping in and gathering up gold and other money pieces, the pleasurable 'wallowing in money', can be observed countless times in daily life. Many people are ready enough to sign documents that bind them to pay large sums, and can easily expend large amounts in paper money, but are striking tardy in giving out gold coins or even the smallest copper coins. The coins seem to 'stick' to their fingers. (Cf. also the expression 'current capital', and the reverse of this, *'argent sec'*, which is used in the Franche-Comté.)[14]

The ontogenetic path of development of interest in money, as here sketched, while showing individual differences dependent on the conditions of life, is nevertheless on the whole among civilised people to be regarded as a psychical process which seeks realization under the most diverse circumstances in one way or another. It thus seems natural to regard this developmental tendency as a racial attribute, and to suppose that the biogenetic ground principle is also valid for the formation of the money symbol. It is to be expected that phylogenetic and historical comparison of the path of individual development here described will show a parallelism with the development of the money symbol in the human race in general. Perhaps the coloured stones of primitive men which have been found in cave excavations will then be capable of interpretation; observations concerning the anal-erotism of savages (the primitive men of today, who in many cases still live in the stage of barter exchange and of pebble or shell money) should considerably further this investigation of the history of civilisation.

After what has been communicated, however, it is already not improbable that the capitalistic interest, increasing in correlation with development, stands not only at the disposal of practical, egoistic aims – of the reality-principle, therefore – but also that the delight in gold and in the possession of money represents the symbolic replacement of, and the reaction-formation to, repressed anal-erotism, i.e. that it also satisfies the pleasure principle.

The capitalistic instinct thus contains, according to our conception, an egoistic and an anal-erotic component.

Notes

1. Sigmund Freud, 'Character and Anal Erotism', *The Standard Edition of the Complete Psychological Works of Sigmund Freud*, ed. and trans. James Strachey, 23 vols. (London: Hogarth Press, 1953—), Vol. 9, 1959, pp. 169–75.
2. ibid.
3. Freud conceives of the repression of anal-erotism and of the pleasure in smell together in the human race as a result of the upright posture, the erection from the earth.

4. The habit of euphemistically disguising coprophilic tendencies as 'hygienic' is very widespread. The fairly harmless behaviour of stool pedants is well-known, who devote to the regulation of their bowel activities a considerable part of the interest at their disposal; such persons, however, are rather prone to fall into what has been called 'stool hypochondria'. A whole series of analyses, by the way, has convinced me that in very many cases hypochondria is really a fermentation product of anal-erotism, a displacement of unsublimated coprophilic interests from their original objects on to other organs and products of the body with an alteration of the qualifying pleasure. The choice of the organ towards which the hypochondria is directed is determined by special factors (somatic disposition, pronounced erogenicity even in diseased organs, etc.).

5. Sándor Ferenczi, *Selected Papers of Sándor Ferenczi*, ed. Michael Balint, 3 vols. (New York: Basic Books, 1955), Vol. 3, pp. 295–9.

6. I have already in another connection pointed out the probable part played by the childish interest in flatus in later fondness for music. See 'On Obscene Words', *First Contributions to Psycho-Analysis* (London: Hogarth Press, 1952), p. 143.

7. A German idiom. – Trans.

8. Lou Andreas-Salomé, 'Vom frühen Gottesdienst', *Imago*, Vol. 2 (1913), pp. 457–67.

9. The German word *Besitz* (=possession) shows, by the way, that man tries even in his speech to represent by the idea of 'sitting on it' that which is valuable to him, which belongs to him. Rationalists evidently content themselves with the explanation of this simile to the effect that the sitting on is meant to express a concealing, protecting and guarding of the valued object. The fact, however, that it is the buttocks and not the hand – which would be more natural with men – that is used to represent protection and defence speaks rather in favour of the word *'Besitz'* being a copro-symbol. The final decision on the point must be reserved for a philologist who has had a psycho-analytic training.

10. The sum of anal-erotism present in the constitution is thus shared in adults among the most diverse psychical structures. Out of it develop: 1. The anal character traits in Freud's sense; 2. Contributions to aesthetics and to cultural interests; 3. To hypochondria. 4. The rest remains unsublimated. From the different proportion of the sublimated and the original parts, from the preference for this or that form of sublimation, the most variegated character types arise, which must naturally have their special conditional factors. Anal characteristics are specially suited for rapid characterological orientation concerning an individual, indeed concerning whole races. The anal character, with his cleanliness, love for order, defiance and miserliness, sharply deviates from the pronounced anal-erotic, who is tolerant on the matter of dirt, extravagant and easy going.

11. A German idiom, meaning 'cannot stand'. *'Riechen'* literally means to smell. – Trans.

12. Sándor Ferenczi, 'Transitory Symptom—Constructions During the

Analysis', *First Contributions to Psycho-Analysis* (London: Hogarth Press, 1952): section 'Temporary rectal troubles' (pp. 208–9), etc.

13. The case reminds one of the coprophilic joke in which the doctor who had succeeded in expelling by means of a purge a piece of money that a child had swallowed was told he could keep the money as his fee. As to the identification of money and faeces see also the fairy-tale of '*Eslein streck dich* (Donkey stretch yourself). The word '*Lösung*' (= deliverance) means proceeds of a sale (in business), but in hunting speech it means the faeces of wild animals.

14. To be '*à sec*' is French vernacular for 'hard up'. – Trans.

Elvio Fachinelli

Anal Money-time*

Mr K. was criticized on the grounds that too often in his case the
wish was father to the thought. Mr K. replied: 'There never was a
thought to which a wish was not father. The only thing you can
argue about is: What wish? You may suspect that it is difficult to
establish paternity, but that's no reason to suspect that a child has
no father at all.'
BERTOLT BRECHT, *Tales From the Calendar*

1. Let us start from one of Freud's most striking paradoxes. It
ranks among his most difficult and thought-provoking statements, and has received little attention since he made it:

Among those whom we try to help by our psycho-analytic efforts
we often come across a type of person who is marked by the
possession of a certain set of character-traits, while at the same time
our attention is drawn to the behaviour in his childhood of one of his
bodily functions and the organ concerned in it . . . The people I
am about to describe are noteworthy for a regular combination of
the three following characteristics. They are especially *orderly*,
parsimonious and *obstinate* . . . It is easy to gather from these people's
early childhood history that they took a comparatively long time
to overcome their infantile *incontinentia alvi* (faecal incontinence), and

* Elvio Fachinelli's article, 'Anal Money-time' ('Sul tempodenaro
anale'), was first published in the Italian review, *Il Corpo (The Body)*, Vol.
1, No. 2 (Milan, September 1965), pp. 92–107. (It is reprinted here
by permission of the author and publisher.) As with the question of gambling
itself, Freud did not 'complete' his theoretical work on money – yet
money clearly is an integral factor in gambling.
   Building on the work of Ferenczi, Fachinelli integrates the work of Marcel
Mauss in particular into his framework, and connects up the discoveries of
the psychoanalysts and anthropologists with those of Karl Marx, as well as
with the later work of Jacques Lacan. This provides a coherent base from
which further work on the whole subject (since gambling cannot be seen or
dealt with in isolation) can be carried out.

that even in later childhood they suffered from isolated failures of this function.[1]

This is the beginning of the short essay on 'Character and Anal Erotism', written in 1908, upon which virtually the whole of psychoanalytical characterology is founded.

Freud's clinical observation has an odd ring to it, and is presented to the reader very cautiously:

> I cannot say at this date what particular occasions began to give me an impression that there was some organic connection between this type of character and the behaviour of an organ, but I can assure the reader that no theoretical expectation played any part in that impression . . . I am venturing to make [my belief] the subject of a communication . . . The intrinsic necessity for this connection is not clear, of course, even to myself. But I can make some suggestions which may help towards an understanding of it . . . (pp. 169–172.)

Next let us consider the constituent parts of this cautious observation.

It seems clear right away that the 'bodily function' and 'the organ concerned in it', though apparently restricted in meaning, actually refer to a range of experiences wider than any one biological reflex. Referring back to his work three years earlier, *Three Essays on the Theory of Sexuality* (1905), Freud mentions a whole series of facts with quite various and contrasting meanings: as well as the difficulty of gaining control over *incontinentia alvi* there is a search for pleasurable excitation of the anal mucus, obtained through the retention of faeces, their subsequent violent expulsion and 'every manner of indecent interest in shit'. Furthermore, when repeating and enlarging upon what he had said in 'Three Essays' in his later 'Introduction to the Study of Psycho-Analysis' (first series, 1917), he writes:

> As Lou Andreas has pointed out, with fine intuition, the outer world first steps in as a hindrance at this point, a hostile force opposed to the child's desire for pleasure – the first hint he receives of external and internal conflicts to be experienced later on. He is not to pass his excretions whenever he likes but at times appointed by other people. To induce him to give up these sources of pleasure he is told that everything connected with these functions is 'improper' and must be kept concealed. In this way he is first required to exchange pleasure for value in the eyes of others. His

own attitude towards the excretions is at the outset very different. His own faeces produce no disgust in him; he values them as part of his own body and is unwilling to part with them, he uses them as the first 'present' by which he can mark out those people whom he values especially. (p. 265.)

2. One apparently marginal point in this account is worth underlining. In it Freud is drawing largely upon the work of Lou Andreas-Salomé, whom he commends soberly for her 'fine intuition'. May one not assume that this reference to a loyal colleague's labours, while of course emphasising the latter's worth, also (as often happens with Freud) implies a certain caution and a feeling of nagging doubt? The doubt does not lie in the account itself, which is if anything somewhat too clear and cut-and-dried. It ignores the fluid aspects of the situation it defines and tends to crystallize it from an over-adult point of view, so preventing the reader from grasping the germinal nature of what occurs, its necessary confusion and uncertainty. The reason for Freud's almost imperceptible hesitation must lie elsewhere. Salomé *observes* children and interprets their conduct from outside – that is, in a fashion quite distinct from Freud's own analytic method.

It is certainly true that in Freud extensive observational data are employed to support the data obtained through analysis, and vice-versa: one sometimes has the impression of a set of mutually reflecting mirrors where one order of facts finds direct confirmation in the other. Yet when some thematic emerges in analysis – the anal one, for instance – it is never really separable from the particular symptoms, the particular behaviour-pattern associated with it: it has an essentially historical and temporal nature, that is, from which there is no escape. The two orders of data are not genuinely commensurable, therefore – even though it is possible to accumulate them both and so discern trends and correspondences which allow the 'typical' character of this or that situation to be established. The temptation to try and 'prove' analytic insights by 'exact' naturalistic observation is undoubtedly a powerful one, which Freud did not avoid entirely. This was how the illusion of fixed biological 'stages' was born, with its inherent risk of reducing whole series of complex behavioural patterns to a one-dimensional biological–instinctive regularity actually quite incompatible with authentic Freudian description. Freud knew very well, no one better, that only the *internal* data from past experience which emerge within the neutrality of the analytic situation can be trusted and used in reconstructing a reliable history of events. All the rest was irrelevant, falling as it did (quite legitimately) within the realm of the measurable and the comparable, according to the rules of naturalistic observation.[2]

Though conscious of the essential diversity of these two kinds of fact, Freud was never to abandon the difficult task of trying to link them together. The reason seems clear enough. If, on the one hand, there is the risk of a 'natural history' of the instincts and their development, on the other there is no less of a risk associated with the exclusive use of pure analytic data. This is the risk of ignoring or by-passing the public *embodiment* of the motivation which analysis reveals; the latter may scarcely figure in the psychoanalytical dialogue, yet it clearly remains a possible object of observational science and cannot be ignored. Hence, Freud always tries to keep this difficult but decipherable unity in view – the total unity of a bodily development informed by a specific subjective history.

3. In this way the different facts to which Freud refers come together into a relationship that may be grasped in terms of a certain sort of development. Clearly this cannot be a mechanical succession of phases; it is, rather, a succession of attitudes that grow out of one another according to a distinct temporal rhythm. Consider again the obscure sequence of events: the pleasure initially associated with excretion as such grows more intense and complex, when the possibility of holding it in for a time is understood; at the same point interest in the product of the operation grows, and the latter turns into an object to be played with, and also (since it is part of one's body, therefore precious) a possession and a gift; then the mother intervenes to combat this anal complex, and it is prohibited.

We must not forget that this 'simple' account – taken largely for granted nowadays – was made possible by the uncovering of the anal thematic in the course of therapeutic treatment. Seen from outside the process appeared only as one stage of maturation among others in the child's evolution towards autonomy; it was the patient labour of analysis which transformed it into a significant unfolding of action in time, into a process open to quite different possible solutions and riddled with deeply contrasting and ambivalent meanings. Only in the latter context, precisely because it is playing a part in a particular personal experience, does each element in the situation appear as charged with antithetic and irreducible characteristics. The recital of seemingly elementary alternatives – to expel or to hold back, to give or not to give, to submit or to disobey – becomes a drama, a meaningful nexus. Within the nexus, a significant relationship of mutual tension and desire is gradually developed between the child and its mother. Moved by love for her and by the fear of losing her, by the pleasure of gratifying its desire or the pleasure of being compensated for not doing so, the child slowly renounces total control over its new-found power and agrees to produce the golden eggs only when and where she demands. But in order to re-exert some authority over her in turn, to win her recognition and some revenge for all the wrongs inflicted on it, it learns at the same time to postpone, to disappoint her, to make her wait . . . A pathetic, petty contest of wills, obscure and ridiculous. Yet this context concerns something which is 'our own body . . . transforming itself into an external object, the model for any and every object which can later be lost'.[3] Something created by us, that is, which in turn creates sensations for us, a plastic source of phantasy, and the very first object in which our relationship to others is concretized. No behaviourist psychology could ever have discovered this central position occupied by the training of the 'excretory functions' during one period of human life.

We are still far from having explored the whole corpus of meanings which emerge from analytic treatment here. But perhaps we have gone far enough to venture a preliminary definition that unites (with no pretensions to being exhaustive) the different strands in the ambivalent situation just described. Let us say simply that the anal situation appears to be an embryonic structure of struggle and exchange with the other person (the mother). Important implications of this are examined in greater detail below.

4. Next, let us look at the kind of relationship Freud posits between this situation and each of the characteristics he mentions. Orderliness (which 'covers the notion of bodily

cleanliness, as well as of conscientiousness in carrying out small duties and trustworthiness') is presented as 'a reaction-formation against an interest in what is unclean and disturbing and should not be part of the body'. Obstinacy (which 'can go over into defiance, to which rage and revengefulness are easily joined') can be related to 'infants who show self-will about parting with their stool', and also to maternal chastisement of the buttocks administered to break down such wilfulness. In adults one would naturally expect to find sado-masochistic tendencies related to this. Parsimony (which 'may appear in the exaggerated form of avarice') can be traced back to 'the connection between money and defecation' found wherever 'archaic modes of thought have predominated or persist'. In the individual, interest in money is supposed to represent the displacement of the former concern with excreta on to a new object, perhaps reinforced by the fact that 'the contrast between the most precious substance known to men and the most worthless, which they reject as waste matter ("refuse") has led to a specific identification of gold with faeces'. And so to his general conclusion that 'the permanent character-traits are either unchanged prolongations of the original instincts, or sublimations of those instincts, or reaction-formations against them.'

All later work on psychoanalytical characterology has followed a substantially similar interpretive schema, enriching Freud's account either by adding various other stages (so that it has become possible to speak about oral, urethral, phallic, genital characters, and so on), or else by refining the original analysis ever more closely and seeking out each nuance and transitional moment within it. Work of this sort tends to be endless, since there will always be an infinity of correlations and corrections to be added; also, it tends to dilute the significance of its own source by repetition, and by neglect of the latter's original overall suggestiveness. This is why, after the first flush of classificatory enthusiasm for the subject shown by Freud's early circle (Jones and Abraham, for instance) nearly all the interesting work on it has been mainly therapeutic and technical in orientation (Reich).

5. In this study I would prefer to go back to Freud's interpretive work at the grass-roots, so to speak, at the level of its original emergence from clinical observation.

It is clear at once that his judgements vary considerably in depth of penetration. For example, it is quite possible – indeed easy – to perceive the obstinacy trait (plus its sado-masochistic implications) as the continuation of an infantile stubbornness which finds new (but not unique) expression in the refusal to defecate. The latter would then be no more than the perfectly comprehensible sequel to a pre-existent situation, and it would be logical to suspect the existence of some basic disposition or constitutional tendency which passes unchanged through the anal phase. The 'obstinate' individual might well have been so *then*, as he is *now*: what need is there for any sort of functional relationship between his obstinacy and his anal experiences? Such a view placates the shades of the old masters of psychiatry, and Freud could only answer by making the problem one of why there should *not* have been any change at this stage – transposing the origins of the trait to an ever-earlier point in life, like Klein or Rank.

The cleanliness trait, as a reversal of the primitive concern with the 'filthy' into its opposite, could equally be understood in general (Jaspersian) terms, as simply one example of a general psychological mechanism at work – even although here, admittedly, the complexity of Freud's psychological schema does begin to appear in embryo at least (impulse, repression, counter-impulse).

Freud's third set of characteristics, however, parsimony-avarice, appears by contrast with these as far more complex. In it, the individual's displacement of interest in excreta to interest in money, although following a specific pattern that Freud tries to reconstruct, also does no more than re-enact faithfully a faeces–money connection *already present* in the unconscious. In this 1908 study, indeed, Freud's main effort is to come to terms with a nexus that apparently transcends the experience of the individual.

The insight is grounded in therapeutic practice, obviously:

Every doctor who has practised psycho-analysis knows that the most refractory and long-standing cases of what is described as habitual constipation in neurotics can be cured by that form of treatment . . . But in psycho-analysis one only achieves this result if one deals with the patients' money complex and induces them to bring it into consciousness with all its connections.

It must be admitted that, perhaps because of its extreme

generality, Freud's chosen example has a somewhat uncon-
vincing ring today. The generic constipation he speaks of would
now usually be interpreted as a psycho-somatic phenomenon.[4]
That is, as a functional change in the intestinal apparatus due
to psychic interference, but without any necessary relationship to this specific cause. However, if one delimits the scope of
his comment accordingly, its value remains: a certain sort of
faecal retention is cured the moment the patient becomes
aware of the corporeal meaning of his wish to retain money
(summarizing to the utmost). Hence, 'in this therapeutic
perspective, one might say that 'excreta = money'.

Freud's second and last clinical argument is an indirect one:

If there is any basis in fact for the relation posited here between
anal erotism and this triad of character-traits, one may expect to
find no very marked degree of 'anal character' in people who have
retained the anal zone's erotogenic character in adult life, as happens, for instance, with certain homosexuals. Unless I am much
mistaken, the evidence of experience tallies quite well on the whole
with this inference.

Turning to the first example again, it is rather curious that
Freud refers to a situation in which the repressed element is
money rather than excreta. Let us try to turn the argument the
other way round, equally schematically: suppose that parsimony–avarice is resolved the moment the patient realizes the
meaning of his retention of faeces – realizes, so to speak, that
'money = excreta'. One runs into clinical difficulty at once,
arising out of the difference between treating a hysterical-type
symptom (i.e. constipation) and dealing with a character-
trait (i.e. parsimony). Transition is easy from excreta to money,
therefore, but not the other way round. We must be content
for the moment simply to notice this clinical incompatibility,
which would seem to indicate – in view of its effects – a less
than perfect psychic equivalence between excreta and money.

It is also rather curious that Freud gives no other clinical
examples, and in particular none which would tend to demonstrate the contrary transition, from money to excreta. If I may
be permitted to offer an interpretation of this silence, I suspect
the only possible one is that, in 1908 no less than today, this
kind of case presented incomparably greater resistance to
treatment. So Freud was never in a position to state what
would have been the most conclusive proof of his thesis, a

resolution of the relevant symptoms in the course of analysis. He was forced, instead, to resort to an example at once over-general and too close to the pattern of somatic conversions (hysteria), outside the area in which anal characteristics typically reveal themselves.

6. At this point, Freud goes on to survey rapidly some data drawn from popular legends and history:

> We know that the gold which the devil gives his paramours turns into excrement after his departure, and the devil is certainly nothing else than the personification of the repressed unconscious instinctual life. We also know about the superstition which connects the finding of treasure with defaecation, and everyone is familiar with the figure of the 'shitter of ducats [*Dukatenscheisser*]'.* Indeed, even according to ancient Babylonian doctrine gold is 'the faeces of Hell'.

Perhaps. Yet the overall effect is hardly to clarify the faeces–money nexus, because Freud omits a mediating factor of the utmost importance: the one factor which will allow a connection between the anal situation and money to be established without trouble. This vital intermediary is the concept of the *gift*. Only by means of it does it become possible to grasp the entire logic of the displacement from excreta to money.

We saw how in the individual's experience faeces become the object of a sort of treatying, they are 'conceded' or 'denied' as part of a primordial struggle-cum-exchange which is the essence of the anal situation. Within the terms of this struggle, substitution of money for faeces as a result of repression presents no problem, if one imagines it as mediated by a gift relationship, and so as possessing the intrinsic necessity which is distinctly lacking from Freud's own account:

> The original erotic interest in defaecation is, as we know, destined to be extinguished in later years. In those years the interest in money makes its appearance as a new interest which had been absent in childhood. This makes it easier for the earlier impulsion, which is in process of losing its aim, to be carried over to the newly emerging aim.[5]

Nor is this all. We are now in a better position to comprehend fully the lesson which Freud draws from the 'archaic modes of thought'. If the devil 'is certainly nothing else than the personification of the repressed unconscious instinctual life', then

* A term vulgarly used for a wealthy spendthrift [note in original].

we may legitimately discern behind the legend a baby (at the anal stage) which makes a gift of gold to its mother, and only after 'her departure' (i.e. when repression has occurred) sees that the gold has turned to turds – the miserable precursors of real gold.

It is not necessary here to insist further on the point (a less obvious one than it might seem). There are familiar risks and temptations inherent in this kind of argument. It is more important to ask what it was that caused Freud's hesitation, and prevented him from including the logically required gift concept fully in his definition of the excreta–money nexus. Was it not the character of the Salomé description he relied on? All reconstructions of a remote period in life run the risk of adulterating its sense (that is, of almost literally 'adultifying' it) and perceiving it exclusively in function of a later perspective, eliminating all its 'irrelevant' aspects and its actual faults and failings. I would not claim that my own brief résumé of the anal situation given above avoided this peril, for example. Where the gift factor is given prominence in Freud's account, it expresses too intensely the emotions of an adult who is now re-discovering the fact and intuiting its presence in the infant's defecatory behaviour-pattern: the metaphorical dimension is almost certainly too rich. Hence one is bound to feel some doubt about its real existence in this sense. A 'present' in the adult meaning of the term probably has nothing to do with the problem. We are dealing with something wider and of more decisive import: with a part of the person which is yet external to him, and to which he can attribute values and meanings previously attached to his whole being, a part of himself whose production and presence become indispensable moments in his quest for autonomy.

7. Returning again to Freud's interpretive schema, the reader may have noted that I chose cleanliness rather than orderliness as an example of a reaction-formation against interest in dirt. Freud in fact does not hesitate to equate directly personal cleanliness, scrupulousness and punctiliousness, and neglects in this way a number of distinctions fairly obvious to common sense. Orderliness is certainly akin to cleanliness, and can be related to the struggle against dirt associated with anality. However, it is a kind of 'second-order' cleanliness; its implanta-

tion – undeniably an important feature of the total anal complex – involves the working of some mediating factor. The most evident factor uniting orderliness, conscientiousness (especially in small duties) and trustworthiness – to quote Freud's initial observations – is a certain attitude towards *time*. They all imply some way of employing, saving and producing time. The economic metaphor is no accident: it directly describes reality. Let us look to clinical experience again, the only thing which can give a basis for grasping the question concretely. Researchers who have tried to follow up Freud's original remarks on anal character are agreed on one fact: an anal character tries to treat time like money.[6] This means in the first place that the attitudes of parsimony–avarice are displaced on to time: in this form they range from fear of loss or of 'wasting' time to obsessive preoccupations about how to 'occupy' it, from Ferenczi's 'Sunday neurosis' to the accumulation of numerous contemporaneous jobs and occupations in order to 'save time'.

The list could be continued indefinitely. It is interesting to note in passing that (as Freud himself saw, and later observers were to confirm) this way of living out time – of *being* time – profoundly affects the possibility of therapeutic care. It is undoubtedly close to the source of the much-deplored *length* of psychoanalytic treatment.

In the case of time as in that of money – and even more strikingly so – there does not seem to be any exact correspondence with faeces from a clinical point of view. We must see why this is so.

8. At the present stage of the argument, we are dealing with an impulse or tension of the libido in the sadic-anal area which, when repressed, becomes displaced on to time and money through the mediation of the gift relationship. Thus is constituted what one might call 'money-time', which has then to be accumulated, divided up or shared out in exact portions.

It should be noted that we have now gone some way beyond Freud. His early disciples adventured on to this terrain, and spoke about objectified time in similar fashion, on the basis of empirical and irrefutable clinical experience. Yet Freud himself remained silent on the subject. Before long, most of those working within his inner circle had also lapsed into silence. It is advisable therefore to ask what the status of time is in Freud's thought generally.

This is perhaps one of the oddest and most contradictory aspects of Freud's whole system. It emerges most decidedly in Freud's attitude towards philosophy. He went to the lectures of Brentano in Vienna.[7] Most often he displays apparent disdain for 'philosophers' and 'philosophy', understood as a type of academic or professional activity. Nor is this attitude always an expression of mere impatience with the usual contemporary refusal to admit his concept of the unconscious mind. However, there are also comments on philosophy scattered throughout Freud's work (though they are less frequent than his literary references), usually in the context of some use of poetic or imaginative imagery for scientific theory. He refers to Plato, Spinoza, Schopenhauer and Nietzsche in this way. Kant also figures, though somewhat differently, in references to the generic conditions of experience. On a deeper level it has been observed that Goethe's *Fragment on Nature* exercised a truly formative influence on him, as did the 'Schellingian' biologists and essayists like Jean Paul and Lichtenberg.[8] Towards the end of his life, of course (at the time when he wrote 'I am conscious of never having been a real doctor . . .') his own speculative ambitions would become much more prominent and sweeping.

In another direction, one may discern an even deeper ambiguity in his ideas about time. The original progress of the psychoanalytical movement involved, after the discovery of its basic rules, a most radical questioning of existing temporal categories. And the culture of the time readily grasped the significance of the movement in this sense. Yet in Freud explicit reflection about time remains very limited, and for the most part identical with common attitudes of *fin de siècle* science. The latter consisted prevalently in a somewhat passive and uncritical acceptance of Kant's space–time framework, where time (like space) figures as a pure form of sensible intuition detached from any particular material content. But this is just what was challenged, implicitly, by the dream-voices and neurotic manifestations which Freud was humble enough to listen to. His 'The Interpretation of Dreams' ends with the puzzling and embarrassing idea of an 'indestructible desire' which forever models the future in the semblance of the past.

From that point onwards Freud talks more often of the absence of time, of the *atemporality* of unconscious processes, than of the time we actually experience. From beginning to end of his life's work, through all the successive strata of which it is composed, there is no more fixed point of reference than this. Understandably perhaps, the discoverer was above all concerned to chart the unknown territory which he had revealed. This is what lies behind the celebrated slogans: in the unconscious nothing ever perishes, nothing changes, nothing is ever forgotten. The urgent need to define and defend the germinal nucleus of his discovery led Freud to stress the metaphysical foundations of his concept of the unconscious, and to make statements whose very tone raised the hackles of contemporary critics; by contrast, the *clinical* problem posed by the indefinite persistence of repressed and unsatisfied impulses was underrated, or even denied. Some aspects of this imbalance have always appeared superficially to favour a 'cosmic' approach to the problem.[9]

But in that case what happens to the 'time relationship', which certainly cannot be reduced to a purely conscious intellectual act? Freud is forced to impose some limit (implicitly at least) on the atemporal character of the unconscious. Subsequent theoretical elaboration of his basic concept allowed him to locate time within the series of differentiations which bring about the development of the ego, the conscious self. Timelessness then became the province of the id, the area of impulses in perpetual search of an outlet, while in between id and ego – in a still unconscious or pre-conscious field – the temporal schemata were created.

This was not the end of his difficulties with time, unfortunately. After 'Beyond the Pleasure Principle' (1920) the death-wish joined the other life-wishes of the id, and it too had to be related to time in some way. Here, we are forced to conceive temporality as contained originally within the body of instinctive life, and so as being 'biological' or organic in nature. This was one of the principal avenues of thought opened up by the 1920 study. Even if one tries to avoid this theoretical result – departing as it does so strikingly from the evidence – what do the data behind the hypothetical death-wish suggest? The most important of them, the compulsion to repeat actions, suggests at best the existence of a primitive temporal rhythm, a kind of blind time little more than pulsation or periodic beating, far removed from the delicate modalities of ordinary temporal consciousness.

The early antithesis between conscious and unconscious with regard to time was thus progressively diminished. But Freud's conception of two systems or processes functioning according to different laws made it impossible for him to arrive at any comprehensive formulation. Nor was he particularly anxious to establish a meaningful relationship between the two, the Kantian time of the conscious mind and the primordial biological–instinctive rhythm, either by reducing one to another or by contrasting one with another. His rigid assumption of the former simply went on coexisting with his mythical account of the latter.

9. Signs of an honest recognition of this unresolved problem are not lacking in Freud's later writings. In the question of time, he maintained, there lay 'a road towards profounder understanding' along which he had not himself succeeded in travelling. His own basic preoccupation had necessarily been a different one, or so he seems to imply.

To recognize that the problem of time occupied an unexplored position outside the mainstream of Freud's researches should not be used as a pretext for the sort of infantile reproaches common in this type of argument among psychiatrists, where each 'unsolved problem' or 'manifest uncertainty' so easily generates retrospective scoldings. We now stand at some historical distance from Freud's work, and should be able to judge more coolly the actual consequences of this 'uncertainty' in it.

The most important of these was, in my opinion, that in the face of the master's own deafness to the issue, concrete description of the space–time dimension in which neurotics and psychotics actually *exist* tended to arise in opposition to psychoanalysis, or as some kind of alternative to it. In one direction, a subjective positivism reduced Freud's method to something much less than the new terrain of clinical psychiatry demanded. In another, an objective naturalism undervalued or simply ignored the meaning of the newly acquired data born – in the only way they could be – out of the neutrality of the analytic situation. The former, laying too absolute a stress on the vital preliminary phase of the process, closed its mind to the problem of the historical genesis of what was being observed; the latter, by turning suddenly deaf to the first person – the 'I' – who informs the whole analytic process, perhaps lost an even more basic dimension of it. The risk inherent in the first position was that of reducing distinct spatio-temporal experiences to closed worlds unable to communicate with each other or with their own history; in the second, neglect of space–time as subjectivity, and hence self-exclusion from the most fundamental mode of access to the real structure of that subjectivity itself.[10]

There were immediate clinical consequences too. Freud himself worried over the problem of the length of treatment, and saw its cause in the 'slowness of the profound psychical changes' induced by analysis. In this way he approached the crux of the question, the patient's temporal structure. To take the easiest clinical example: no obsessional patient can be cured until his peculiar mode of living time has been analysed and modified, and his recovery is identified with this (difficult) set of changes. Here we also see the reason behind Freud's apparently casual remarks on the differing resistance to therapy put up by the different 'traits' of the anal character: in fact, the resistance becomes more intense as analysis works through the various traits, and comes closer to the structural core of the patient's relationship with time.

10. I believe therefore that Freud's acceptance of the Kantian view of time as an innate *a priori* form prevented him (and psychoanalysis after him) from including time and temporal organization properly within the conceptual framework used for revealing the sense of neurotic and psychotic symptoms. The Kantian view is in turn, of course, only one result of a more general world-view, which one might define as the Newtonian or physicalist nucleus of Freud's cultural inheritance.

Consequently, time has been for the most part considered indirectly, as a factor at once anonymous and indifferent, something utilized for defensive purposes in the neurotic game. It has not been perceived as the end-product of an intelligible process, which both modifies it and lends it a distinct and clinically definable imprint. In the anal complex we have been examining, for instance, time appears as one of a range of unconscious substitutes, along with money. Time, defined precisely in this fashion, informs the whole course of clinical experience; we can analyse it there, and attempt to retrace its formation on the basis of given elements of personal history.

Yet it proved a dead end for Freud himself. In his thought, strangely, temporal process figures as something given once and for all: time has neither a history nor a distinct visage. This is why it is tempting to relegate it to some part of the ego 'free from conflicts' – that area dear to one sector of post-Freudian psychology which seems by some curious tropism to gather together within it all unsolved problems (as if the denial of difficulties could ever constitute the best solution for them). Freudian clinical experience, however, continued to move in the opposite direction. Let me quote a fleeting insight from the 1915 study 'Repression'. While examining different aspects of defence mechanisms, Freud writes apropos obsessional neuroses:

> At first the repression is completely successful; the ideational content is rejected and the affect made to disappear. As a substitutive formation there arises an alteration in the ego in the shape of an increased conscientiousness, and this can hardly be called a symptom. Here, substitute and symptom do not coincide.[11]

Here we find, explicitly, a mutation of the unconscious which does not seek expression through discrete episodes of symptom-formation but globally, through the appearance of a lasting attitude (conscientiousness) which – like orderliness – can easily be related to temporal organization. The so-called mechanisms of 'annulment' and 'isolation' Freud describes later on may be treated in the same way. In the first (connected significantly to reaction-formation) the subject carries out what Fenichel calls 'some real action which, in a concrete or magical sense, is the opposite of something else which he did previously, either really or in fantasy'. In the second, spatial or temporal intervals are inserted between things or actions to prevent them from coming into contact. Both patterns – so admirably described by Freud – presuppose a peculiar way of living out time founded upon a central impulse of expiation.

On such a basis it appears possible to outline a programme of work which, starting from the individual experiences which surface in the course of therapy, would establish the typical trajectories, the difficulties and internal contradictions of temporal development. We might hope in this way to reconstruct *from within* the vicissitudes of any story, so that the latter would coincide with the patient's own self-affirmation. So we might achieve subjectively what Jean Piaget succeeded in doing from outside with his testing techniques. It is more than likely that if carried in this direction the inquiry into time would be inseparable from that into space.[12]

By sticking to the specific terrain of analysis it should be possible to avoid all quasi-philosophical Heideggerian excursions into the meaning of time and death (however fascinating these may be in their own right). While the conflict–defence situation in which time is located – implying as it does an inter-subjective reality – ought also to save us from the threat of solipsism, or the reduction of temporal consciousness to that mysteriously 'private' realm where such a great deal of descriptive phenomenology has ended up.

11. I believe we have now carried internal exegesis of this Freudian text as far as it will go. On the whole the text in question has been followed and – dare I say it – mechanically applied according to the most superficially evident suggestions it contains. And this has usually involved breaking down the whole and focusing mainly upon character-traits (as Freud himself did). Hence the problem of the relationship of these traits to the whole and of their development within the articulated totality of the anal character has been eclipsed.

It is this overall, highly defined, clinically recognizable structure which I want to consider next. At the beginning of this article it was recalled how Freud mentions openly 'those whom we try to help by our psycho-analytic efforts'. But these are not simply people who wanted to find a cure for their tendencies towards excessive cleanliness or parsimony with the new therapeutic method. Freud was almost certainly referring primarily to obsessional neurotics, that is to patients in whom a complex set of symptoms was related to a very marked anal character. The two classes of subject are not at all identical, and the former may stand on its own; yet there remains in common a distinctive and quite unmistakable *ensemble*.

Let me explain the reasons for this emphasis. The argument so far has yielded a series of interconnected factors, expressing together one aspect of the clinical situation under examination. One might depict this series in linear fashion as follows, using the most evocative term to stand for each factor in it: excreta–

gift–money–time. The faeces factor is usually repressed, unconscious; the other three substitute for it on a more or less conscious level. What must be stressed is that each of these factors has a meaning within the context as a whole, consonant with the meaning of the others but irreducible to any one of them. 'Gift', linked directly to the struggle–exchange anal situation, appears closer in sense to a token or a guarantee of developing autonomy than to a 'present' in the adult sense. 'Money' appears almost as the opposite of the fluid 'visible God' of experience; hence its nature as a form of accumulation and secret enumeration to gain security is correspondingly reinforced. It is tempting to call this 'fecaloro' by analogy with (and resemblance to) 'fecaloma', the medical term for the condition in which a lump of faeces is retained until it hardens to the consistency of stone.[13] Time, lastly, also appears in this context in its most narrow and onerous sense, as the 'money-time' of obligation and calculation, good only for fragmenting and distributing life out into identical portions and sub-portions.

This range of meanings is inwardly coherent, and may be analysed also at a deeper level. Consider first the relationship between the repressed matter and the factors which substitute for it. It seems that between excreta and each of these there exists a sort of primitive comparison based on underlying equivalence. Excreta is in turn 'like' a gift, money and time. But in this transition from the first to the third substitute term, the link becomes at each stage more lax and less obvious, and the divergence between the terms becomes wider. The relationships among the three seem, broadly speaking, to be of a *pars pro toto* kind: one aspect of the antecedent form develops to the point of dominance in the form which succeeds it.

In the first case we have a relationship which might be called one of metaphor, in the second something more like metonymy. Thus we encounter a concrete example of that linguistic formulation of Freudian 'condensation' (*Verdichtung*) and 'displacement' (*Verschiebung*) associated with the work of Jacques Lacan.[14]

In this perspective, the refusal of the gift, or avarice for money and time, correspond as symptoms to a faecal metaphor; the transition from the gift through money and time, on the other hand, represents the metonymy of repressed anality, of the desire which is always, by definition, *'désir d'autre chose'*: 'For a symptom *is* a metaphor, whether or not one employs the term, just as desire *is* a metonymy, even if people make fun of the fact.'[15]

However, the complete homology of function postulated here between semantic and unconscious mechanisms appears to run up against insurmountable barriers. The 'metaphorical' relationship between the repressed material and the substitutes for it is not a transparent one of affinity of meaning, as it is in linguistic metaphors; it embraces, rather, an antithesis of sense between the two terms compared, and this contrast becomes constantly more marked in the transition from gift to time. While excreta can be rendered metaphorically as a gift without too much difficulty (we saw the historical and symbolic reasons for this), the problem increases successively with money and time. A kind of anti-metaphor, a comparison *a contrario*, takes over from the original metaphor and in the end eclipses it. In addition, the tendency of language metaphors to translate an abstract experience into concrete terms (think of the innumerable ways in which time may be said to 'flow') seems reversed here; in our case, the whole process of sublimation unfolds in between excreta on the one hand and gift, money and time on the other. Analogous observations could be made about the metonymy relationship among the three substitution factors: although some contiguity of sense is maintained, the general movement seems the opposite of what is usually attributed to linguistic metonymy. Instead of a 'thickening of meaning' there occurs a progressive thinning, an ever-greater abstraction.[16] In this sense, one might say that the metonymy tends towards metaphor, while the metaphor tends towards metonymy.

It is not difficult to see the reason for this paradoxical reversal of linguistic paradox by the unconscious. The apparatus of individual defence (repression, reaction-formation), by intervening to thrust back anality, ensures that the latter will manifest itself only in a conflict situation and through contradictory semantic forms. Direct linguistic equivalence can perhaps only be conceived in connection with pure manifestations of instinct, articulated – that is, condensed, deformed, dramatized – at an elementary level. This conception (which corresponds historically to Freud's essential insight in 'The

Interpretation of Dreams') entails a radical devaluing of the ego and its defence-mechanisms in favour of what Lacan calls 'the resistances inherent in truth's own meaningful progression'.[17] He has himself chosen to follow out the implications of this idea. But few will follow him in this direction, although many have welcomed his polemic against the dominant post-Freudian 'ego psychology' and the reduction of analysis to milk-sop 'therapy' or gooey 'counselling'.

12. It would certainly be irrelevant here to resort to the familiar objection (quite correct in itself) that we can know repressed material only through the repressive process itself, by constantly deciphering anew the inevitable compromises and ambiguities of dreams and symptomatic behaviour. This is in fact Lacan's particular concern – the witty conceptual game in which a deliberately distorted text compels the reader to interpret it between the lines. All the more so because a semantic framework – even when contorted, reversed, made *almost* unrecognizable by individual defences which can certainly not be reduced to an 'underside located in the mechanisms of the unconscious' – allows one to eliminate all arbitrary aspects from unconscious manifestations and order the latter neatly according to general laws and rules.[18]

I do not wish to embark upon still another over-general discussion of 'structuralism'. My concern here is more down-to-earth and anthropographic (if that is the right term). The linguistic chain which came to light from our study of anal character seems to have a particular consistency of its own, because it has formed itself according to a uniform syntax in which each term occupies an exact place. I say 'has formed itself' to underline the essential historicity of the process. For the linear structure of a sentence can only be the result of projecting on to one horizontal plane a series of factors whose real interconnection lies in temporal depth.[19]

In psychoanalytic work I certainly uncover another, hidden phrase behind the words the patient utters. But this procedure has to coincide with the historical reconstruction of that phrase's meaning. Both for the patient and for myself these two perspectives are inseparable, and one presupposes the other but can never take its place. That a temporal process should give rise to a semantic nexus which in turn modifies it is something of a paradox: the history in question is necessarily a specific configuration of events, while the linguistic form is to some degree schematic and predictable. Yet this paradox is always confronted by any human science at a certain stage of its development.

In this way it seems to me the terrain might be prepared for an eventual transition from the (tragically) individual to what it is we all have in common – thus transcending a classical antinomy. If it is true that the developing individual has to re-trace in his own person the essentials of the history of the species, then only when we uncover both in the ill person and in humanity at large an exactly corresponding pattern (both diachronically and synchronically) will we be able to conceive of an intelligible relationship between them. Lacking either half of this correspondence we could only remain stuck on the plane of analogies. It is only too evident that the broken history of the neurotic or psychotic personality cannot re-discover itself, once the difficult individual knot is unravelled, except in the *past* history of the species, or in whatever archaic elements survive and still live on in his own present-day history.[20]

These are methodological considerations which can only be sketched out here, and appear a necessary preliminary to any serious psychoanalytic anthropology rising above the persistent undergrowth of Freudian–Jungian sociological fiction. In relation to the anal character, they permit us to see clearly even now its anachronistic aspects. We spoke above of the refusal to give, and of its historical context in a particularly intense and prolonged infantile struggle–exchange situation. It does not appear too difficult to relate this to the semiology of the archaic gift-relationship, as described in Marcel Mauss's extremely fruitful study.[21] In the latter, the author speaks of the thing given or exchanged, which is not inert but always part of the giver ('to give something to somebody is always equivalent to giving something of one's own person'); he describes the gift as one element in a total system of obligations which are rigorously necessary and may cause war if disregarded, and which also contain a play or 'sportive' element; he mentions the 'guarantee' or token inherent in the object given, identified with the object itself and such as to constitute obligation 'in all possible societies'. He also tries to reconstruct the transition from gift to money, via for example the so-called 'money of reknown'.

In discussing anal character I referred to money that is retained like a faecal mass or lump. This is close to the figure of the 'hoarder', placed historically by Marx in the early stages of commodity circulation, when 'it is the surplus use-values alone that are converted into money. Gold and silver thus become of themselves social expressions for superfluity or wealth.' Then is born 'the *passionate* desire to hold fast the product of the first metamorphosis. This product is the transformed shape of the commodity, or its gold-chrysalis', and so the hoarder 'acts in earnest up to the Gospel of abstention . . . Hard work, saving and avarice, are, therefore, his three cardinal virtues.'[22]

Beyond the similarities of phraseology (sometimes carried to the point of literal identity) what interests me is the emergence of a *pattern* that coincides with the central part of the meaning uncovered in the anal character. Evidently the first term, excreta, although still quite clear in the individual's history, has vanished from the historical memory of the species. Freud thought that the original repression of anality went back to man's establishment of the erect posture. It survives, probably, as a shadow haunting the roots of language.

And time? If the discovery of the collective gift–money nexus has allowed us to locate the individual's character in historical context, then may one presume to discover his numerical time outside the sick individual's own personality? Clearly the central problem for the future development of psychoanalysis re-presents itself here, from another angle. At the beginning of this study, anthropological time was examined (apparently) at the moment of its birth and development. We may hope to succeed also in tracing the story of its death and dissolution.

Translated by Tom Nairn

Notes

1. Sigmund Freud, 'Character and Anal Erotism', *The Standard Edition of the Complete Psychological Works of Sigmund Freud*, ed. and trans. James Strachey, 23 vols. (London: Hogarth Press, 1953—), Vol. 9, pp. 169–70.
2. It should be noted parenthetically that this is also the inevitable barrier encountered by Melanie Klein's attempted reconstruction of the first months of life. The wealth of phantasy-life she describes can

only be *attributed* to the baby; it remains hypothetical, however much later events make it seem a necessary deduction from them.

3. Otto Fenichel, *Trattato di Psicoanalisi* (Rome: Astrolabio, 1951), p. 81. [This and subsequent quotations from Fenichel in this article are re-translated from Italian—Eds.]

4. On the basis of, in the first instance, his own subsequent study 'The Psycho-Analytic View of Psychogenic Disturbance of Vision', *Standard Edition*, Vol. 11, pp. 211–218. Other quotes below (unless referenced otherwise) are from 'Character and Anal Erotism', loc. cit.

5. Ferenczi, too, was conscious of the lacuna in Freud's argument and sought a way round it in his study 'The Ontogenesis of the Interest in Money, [this volume, pp. 264–273 – eds]. Lacking the concept of the gift relationship, however, he could only envisage the process in a quasi-chemical fashion. In later writings Freud himself came to employ the gift concept, but in the more limited sense of giving 'presents'.

6. Karl Abraham, *Selected Papers*, trans. Douglas Bryan and Alix Strachey (London: Hogarth Press, 1927), pp. 384–5. See also Ernest Jones as quoted in Abraham.

7. The fact is noted without comment in Ernest Jones, *The Life and Work of Sigmund Freud*, Vol. 1 (London: Hogarth Press; New York: Basic Books, 1953).

8. Cf. J. Schotte in *La Psychanalyse*, Vol. 5 (1959), p. 108. Also O. Andersson, *Studies in the Prehistory of Psychoanalysis* (1962).

9. This leads to a view of the unconscious as a Kantian *noumenon* or, better still, as a Sabbath of Eternity, where time itself figures as a category of repression; hence (by implication) the abolition of time and a religious reconciliation of man with his own essence. This is one conclusion, for instance, of Norman O. Brown's *Life Against Death: The Psychoanalytic Meaning of History* (London: Routledge & Kegan Paul, 1959; Sphere Books, 1968; Middletown, Conn.: Wesleyan University Press, 1959), where initially fruitful intuition is dissipated by a tide of analogy and generalization. For the time thematic in Freud, see Paul Ricoeur, *De l'interprétation* (Paris: Editions du Seuil, 1965), pp. 428–30.

10. This can unfortunately be no more than the merest outline of historical positions which obviously deserve to be clarified and distinguished at far greater length. It is certain, however, that a certain kind of *Daseins-analytic* objection to psychoanalysis is now as outmoded as psychoanalytical silence on such topics. In this sense the return to a specifically psychoanalytical approach by a whole line of phenomenologists is clearly significant: it is sufficient to recall the later Merleau-Ponty, De Waelhens, Ricoeur (the latter's evolution from *Le volontaire et l'involontaire* to *De l'interprétation* is important in this context), and in Italy the work of Enzo Paci and his group.

11. Sigmund Freud, 'Repression' (1915), *Standard Edition*, Vol. 14, pp. 156–7.

12. I am thinking especially of Jean Piaget's *The Child's Conception of Time*, trans. A. J. Pomerans (London: Routledge & Kegan Paul, 1969; New York: Basic Books, 1970), with its well-known formula: space is a snapshot of time and time is space in motion.

Anal Money-time

13. The verbal analogy is untranslatable: 'fecaloma' is common to English and Italian medical terminology, and 'fecaloro' is literally 'fecal gold'. – Trans.

14. Perhaps the most disconcerting master of modern psychoanalytic thought, little 'analysed' himself because of the difficulties of a personal language in which literary tradition (with a marked surrealist accent – Breton) and philosophical tradition (Hegel, Heidegger) are capriciously lumped together. Lacan's use of linguistics is completely different from that of, for example, Lévi-Strauss (with whom he is nevertheless always compared). For a useful approach to Lacan, see J. B. Pontalis, *Après Freud* (Paris: R. Julliard, 1965), pp. 21–81, and various articles by S. Leclaire in different psychiatric reviews.

15. Jacques Lacan, 'L'instance de la lettre dans l'inconscient ou la raison depuis Freud', *La Psychanalyse*, Vol. 3 (1957), p. 81.

16. M. Bréal, quoted in S. Ullmann, *Semantics: An Introduction to the Science of Meaning* (Oxford: Blackwell, 1962), p. 220. For the other linguistic references here employed, see ibid., pp. 211–20.

17. Lacan, 'L'instance de la lettre', p. 73.

18. ibid.

19. On the synchrony–diachrony relationship in psychoanalysis, see A. Green, 'La psychanalyse devant l'opposition de l'histoire et de la structure', *Critique* (July 1963).

20. A similar view underlies the work of the most important anthropologist–psychoanalyst Géza Róheim. See e.g. 'The Psycho-Analytical Interpretation of Culture', *International Journal of Psycho-Analysis*, Vol. 22 (1941), p. 147–69. A recent discussion is J. P. Valabrega, *La Psychanalyse*, Vol. 3 (1957), pp. 221–45.

21. Marcel Mauss, *The Gift: Forms and Functions of Exchange in Archaic Societies*, trans. Ian Cunnison (London: Cohen & West, 1954).

22. Karl Marx, *Capital* (Moscow, 1965), Vol. 1, ch. 3, sec. 3, pp. 130–3 (section 'Money', part (a) 'Hoarding').

Bibliographical Note on Fachinelli

Those who wish to follow up on Fachinelli's work can consult the following writings:

'Il desiderio dissidente', *Quaderni Piacentini*, No. 33 (February 1968).

'Gruppo chiuso o gruppo aperto', *Quaderni Piacentini*, No. 36 (November 1968).

'Nota a Benjamin', *Quaderni Piacentini*, No. 38 (July 1969), a presentation of the first Italian translation of Walter Benjamin's 'Programme for a Children's Proletarian Theatre'.

'Che cosa chiede Edipo alla sfinge?' ('What is Oedipus asking the sphinx?') *Quaderni Piacentini*, No. 40 (April 1970). Fachinelli's key text.

L'Erba Voglio: Pratica non autoritaria nella scuola, ed. Elvio Fachinelli, Luisa Muraro Vaiani and Giuseppe Sartori (Turin: Einaudi, 1971).

'Il deserto e le fortezze', *L'Erba Voglio*, Vol. 1, No. 1 (July 1971).

'Scassabambini', *L'Erba Voglio*, Vol. 1, No. 2 (September 1971).

Select Bibliography

This bibliography does not pretend to be complete: it is an attempt to suggest titles for further reading in the various categories of study which we consider to be relevant to research into the psychology of gambling. Inclusion of a text does not mean that we endorse its contents in any way. Much of the writing about gambling and gamblers is interesting and significant, though not always for the reasons which its authors pretend.

Games theory

BERNE, ERIC, *Games People Play: The Psychology of Human Relationships*, Harmondsworth, Penguin Books, 1970; New York: Grove Press, 1964.

CAILLOIS, ROGER, *Man, Play and Games*, London: Thames & Hudson, 1962.

HUIZINGA, JOHAN, *Homo Ludens*, London: Routledge, 1949.

McKINSLEY, J. C. C., *Introduction to the Theory of Games*, New York: McGraw-Hill, 1952.

VON NEUMANN, J., and MORGENSTERN, O., *The Theory of Games and Economic Behavior*, Princeton, N. J.: Princeton University Press, 1957.

History of gambling

ASHBURY, HERBERT, *Sucker's Progress*, New York: Dodd, Mead, 1938.

ASHTON, JOHN, *The History of Gambling in England*, London: Duckworth, 1898.

BARBEYRAC, J., *Traité du Jeu*, 3 vols., Amsterdam, 1737.

BLYTH, HENRY, *The Pocket Venus: A Victorian Scandal*, London: Weidenfeld & Nicolson, 1966.

CHAFTES, HENRY, *Play the Devil: A History of Gambling in the United States from 1492 to 1955*, New York: Clarkson N. Potter, 1960.

HARTMANN, CYRIL HUGHES, *Games and Gamesters of the Restoration*, London: Routledge, 1930. Containing: Cotton, Charles, *The*

Bibliography

Compleat Gamester, 1674; and Lucas, Theophilus, *Memoirs of the Lives, Intrigues and Comical Adventures of the Most Famous Gamesters and Celebrated Sharpers in the Reigns of Charles II, James II, William III and Queen Anne*, London, 1714.

HERALD, GEORGE W., and RADIN, EDWARD D., *The Big Wheel: Monte Carlo's Opulent Century*, London: Robert Hale, 1965.

HUMPHREYS, A. L., *Crockford's; or The Goddess of Chance in St James's Street: 1828–1844*, London: Hutchinson, 1953.

LAZARUS, MORITZ, *Über die Reize des Spiels*, Berlin, 1883.

LUDOVICI, L. J., *The Itch for Play*, London: Jarrolds, 1962.

NEVILLE, RALPH, *Light Come, Light Go*, London: Macmillan, 1909.

ORE, OYSTEIN, *Cardano, the Gambling Scholar*, Princeton, N.J.: Princeton University Press, 1953; Dover Publications Inc., 1965.

SCARNE, JOHN, *Complete Guide to Gambling*, London, Constable, 1967; New York: Simon & Schuster, 1961.

STEINMETZ, ANDREW, *The Gaming Table: Its Votaries and Victims*, 2 vols., London: Tinsley, 1870.

TREVELYAN, GEORGE O., *The Early History of Charles James Fox*, London: Longmans, 1899.

WYKES, ALAN, *Gambling*, London: Aldus Books, 1964.

Material produced by gamblers

ANONYMOUS, *Gamblers Anonymous*, Los Angeles: G. A. Publishing Co., 1964.

ANONYMOUS, *The Gambler's Scourge*, London, 1824.

CHESTER, S. BEACH, *Round the Green Cloth*, London: Stanley Paul & Co., 1928.

GREEN, JONATHAN, *Secret Band of Brothers*, New York, 1843.

HARCOURT, SEYMOUR, *Gaming Calendar*, London, 1820.

LONG, MASON, *The Converted Gambler Written by Himself*, Cincinnati, Ohio, 1884.

LONGRIGG, ROGER, *The Artless Gambler*, London: Pelham Books. 1964.

ROUGE ET NOIR, *The Gambling World: Anecdotic Memories and Stories of Personal Experience in the Temples of Hazard and Speculation With Some Mysteries and Iniquities of Stock Exchange Affairs*, London, Hutchinson & Co., 1898.

Money and the theory of anality

ABRAHAM, KARL, 'Contributions to the Theory of the Anal Character', *Selected Papers*, London, Hogarth Press, 1927.

BROWN, NORMAN O., *Life Against Death: The Psychoanalytic Meaning of History*, London: Routledge & Kegan Paul, 1959; Sphere Books, 1968; Middletown, Conn.: Wesleyan University Press, 1959.

FREUD, SIGMUND, 'Character and Anal Erotism' (1908), *The Standard Edition of the Complete Psychological Works of Sigmund Freud*, ed. and trans. James Strachey, 23 vols., London, Hogarth Press, Vol. 9, 1959, pp. 169–75.

— 'On Transformations of Instinct as Exemplified in Anal Erotism' (1917), *Standard Edition*, Vol. 17, 1955, pp. 127–33.

JONES, ERNEST, 'Anal Erotic Character Traits', *Papers on Psycho-Analysis*, London: Ballière, Tindall & Cox, 1948.

MAUSS, MARCEL, *The Gift: Forms and Functions of Exchange in Archaic Societies*, trans. Ian Cunnison, London: Cohen & West, 1954.

SIMMEL, GEORG, *The Sociology of Georg Simmel*, Trans. K. H. Wolff, Glencoe, Ill.: Free Press, 1950.

Moralist texts

For a selective listing of these texts see Introduction, note 86.

CHARLES, R. H., *Gambling and Betting*, Edinburgh: T. & T. Clark, 1924.

CHURCHILL, MAJOR SETON, *Betting and Gambling*, London: James Nisbett, 1894.

GLASS, REV. J., *Gambling and Religion*, London: Longman, 1924.

GREEN, PETER, *Betting and Gaming*, London: Student Christian Movement, 1924.

MOODY, REV. GORDON E., *Gambling: Hidden Dangers*, London: S.P.C.K., 1965.

PERKINS, E. BENSON, *Gambling in English Life*, rev. edn., London: Epworth Press, 1958.

Novels and fictional accounts of gambling

DOSTOYEVSKY, FYODOR, *The Gambler*. Trans. Jessie Coulson, Harmondsworth: Penguin Books, 1971.

KANDEL, ABEN, *The Strip*, New York: New American Library, 1961.

MOORE, GEORGE, *Esther Waters*, London, 1894.

PUSHKIN, A. S., 'The Queen of Spades', *Russian Short Stories*, Ed. and trans. Rochelle S. Townsend, London: Dent, 1924.

STEVENSON, ROBERT LOUIS, 'The Suicide Club', *New Arabian Nights*, London: Heinemann, 1882.

Practical literature

BINSTOCK, JUDAH, *Casino Administration: The House and the Player*, London: Bodley Head, 1969.

O'NEILL-DUNNE, PATRICK, *Roulette for the Millions*. London: Sidgwick & Jackson, 1971.

SQUIRE, NORMAN, *How to Win at Roulette*, London: Pelham Books, 1968.

Bibliography

Pools and lotteries

ASHTON, JOHN, *A History of English Lotteries*, London: Leadenhall Press, 1893.

DRAKE, ST CLAIR, and CAYTON, HORACE E., *Black Metropolis*, New York: Harcourt, 1945.

EZELL, JOHN, *Fortune's Merry Wheel: The Lottery in America*, Cambridge, Mass.: Harvard University Press, 1960.

PHILLIPS, HUBERT, *Pools and the Punter*, London: Watts & Co., 1955.

Psychoanalytical literature

BERGLER, EDMUND, 'On the Psychology of the Gambler, *Imago*, Vol. 22 (1936), pp. 409–41.

— 'The Gambler: A Misunderstood Neurotic', *Journal of Criminal Psychopathology*, Vol. 4 (1943), pp. 379–93.

— *The Basic Neurosis: Oral Regression and Psychic Masochism*, New York: Grune & Stratton, 1949.

— *The Psychology of Gambling*, London: Bernard Hanison, 1958; New York: Hill & Wang, 1958; International Universities Press, 1970.

DEVEREUX, GEORGE, 'The Psychodynamics of Mohave Gambling', *American Imago*, Vol. 7, No. 1 (1950), pp. 55–65.

FENICHEL, OTTO, *The Psychoanalytic Theory of Neurosis*, London: Kegan Paul, French, Trubner, 1946.

GALDSTON, IAGO, 'The Psychodynamics of the Triad – Alcoholism, Gambling and Superstition', *Mental Hygiene*, October, 1951.

HARRIS, HERBERT I., 'Gambling Addiction in an Adolescent Male', *Psychoanalytic Quarterly*, Vol. 33, No. 4 (1964), pp. 513–25.

HATTINGBERG, HANS VON, 'Analerotik, Angstlust und Eigensinn', *Internationale Zeitschrift für Psychoanalyse*, Vol. 2 (1914), pp. 244–58.

ISRAELI, N., 'Outlook of a Depressed Patient Interested in Planned Gambling', *American Journal of Orthopsychiatry*, Vol. 5 (1935), pp. 57–63.

KRIS, ERNST, 'Ego Development and the Comic', *International Journal of Psycho-Analysis*, Vol. 19 (1938), pp. 77–90.

LAFORGUE, RENÉ, 'On the Eroticization of Anxiety', *International Journal of Psycho-Analysis*, Vol. 11 (1930), pp. 312–21.

MENNINGER, KARL, 'Criminal Behavior as a Form of Masked Self-Destructiveness', *Bulletin of the Menninger Clinic*, Vol. 2 (1938).

OLMSTED, CHARLOTTE, *Heads I Win — Tails You Lose*, New York: Macmillan, 1962.

REIK, THEODOR, 'The Study on Dostoyevsky', *From Thirty Years With Freud*, London: Hogarth Press, 1942, pp. 142–57.

SIMMEL, ERNST, 'Zur Psychoanalyse des Spielers' ('On the Psycho-analysis of the Gambler'), lecture delivered at the sixth International Psychoanalytic Convention, September 1920; published, in précis (abstract) form, in *Internationale Zeitschrift für Psychoanalyse*, Vol. 6 (1920), p. 397.

Psychological writings, other than Freudian

AGINSKY, BURT W. and ETHEL G., 'The Pomo: A Profile of Gambling among Indians', *Annals of the American Academy of Political and Social Science*, Vol. 269 (1950), pp. 108–13.

BARKER, J. C., and MILLER, M., 'Aversion Therapy for Compulsive Gambling', *British Medical Journal*, No. 2 (1966), p. 115.

COHEN, JOHN, *Risk and Gambling: The Study of Subjective Probability*, New York: Philosophical Library, 1956.

— *Chance, Skill and Luck: The Psychology of Guessing and Gambling*, Harmondsworth: Penguin Books, 1960.

— *Behaviour in Uncertainty*, London: Allen & Unwin, 1964.

— *Psychological Probability*, London: Allen & Unwin, 1972.

EDWARDS, W. E., 'Probability Preferences in Gambling', *American Journal of Psychology*, Vol. 66 (1953), pp. 349–64.

EYSENCK, H. J., and RACHMAN, S., *Causes and Cures of Neurosis*, Oxford: Pergamon Press, 1965.

GOFFMAN, ERVING, *Where the Action Is*, London: Allen Lane The Penguin Press, 1969.

GOORNEY, A. B., 'Treatment of a Compulsive Horse-Race Gambler by Aversion Therapy', *British Journal of Psychiatry*, No. 114 (1968), pp. 329–33.

HOCHAUER, BRIGITTE, 'Decision-making in Roulette', *Acta Psychologica*, Vol. 34, Nos. 2 and 3 (1970), pp. 367–74.

HUNTER, JAMES, and BRUNNER, ARTHUR, 'Emotional Outlets of Gamblers', *Journal of Abnormal and Social Psychology*, Vol. 23, No. 1 (1928), pp. 38–9.

MORAN, E., 'Pathological Gambling', *British Journal of Hospital Medicine*, Vol. 4, No. 1 (1970), pp. 59–70.

SKINNER, B. F., *Science and Human Behavior*, New York: Macmillan, 1953.

THOMAS, W. I., 'The Gambling Instinct', *American Journal of Sociology*, Vol. 6, No. 2 (1901), pp. 750–63.

UEMATSU, TADASHI, 'Parricides in Japan', *Annals of the Hitotsubashi Academy*, Vol. 2, No. 2 (Tokyo, 1952), pp. 205–17.

Sociology and gambling

HERMAN, ROBERT D., ed., *Gambling*, New York: Harper & Row, 1967.

NEWMAN, OTTO, *Gambling: Hazard and Reward*, London: Athlone Press, 1972.

Index

Index

Domitian, Emperor, 117
Dostoyevsky, Andrei, 162
Dostoyevsky, Fyodor, 7, 18, 19, 21–4, 26, 93, 203; *Brothers Karamazov, The*, 168, 218; fear of death, 162; Freud's study, 95; neurosis, 159–61, 166; personality, 157–9; reasons for gambling, 57, 169, 172, 175, 226; relationship with father, 164, 165, 166, 167; sympathy by identification, 169
Dostoevsky and Parricide (Freud essay), 21, 157–73
Ductor Dubitantium (Taylor), 62

Edge, F. M., 245, 250, 255
Edwards, W. E., 88, 89
Effect, Law of, 83
ego, masturbation and the, 210; relationship with the super-ego, 102, 164
Egypt, 116, 244
Eliot, George, 130
Elizabeth I, Queen of England, 119
entertainment, gambling as, 202
environment, conditioning of, 143–4, 148, 149, 150
expectation, state of, 131
Eysenck, H. J., 84
Ezell, John, 71

Fachinelli, Elvio, 73, 76
faeces, first toy, 265, 266; as gift, 275, 281–2, 290, 291; relationship with money, 73–6, 268, 289–90
faith, versus fear, 151; in luck, 148, 149
fanaticism, in gambling, 176
faro, 129
fate, efficacy of, 128; as father projection, 22, 102, 164, 208, 219; gambling as question asked of, 190; need to challenge, 207, 209
father surrogate, fellow gambler as, 212
fear, contrast with luck, 143, 145, 149; courting of, 151; sexualizing of, 185, 220
Feldman, M. P., 86
fellow gamblers, relationship between, 212–13
feminine identification, unconscious, 189, 193
Fenichel, Otto, 28, 29, 30, 288; impulse neurosis, 236; on winning, 210
Ferenczi, Sandor, 73, 74, 75; childhood

omnipotence, 176, 207; Sunday neurosis, 283
Fitzpatrick, the Hon. General, 126
football pools, and capitalism, 34; and gambling dynamic, 96, 97; as lottery, 12, 41
form, in pools, 97
fortune telling, 145
Fox, Charles James, 39, 40, 120, 123
Fragment on Nature (Goethe), 284
France, 74, 252, 255; Mississippi scheme, 132
France, Clemens J., 94; The Gambling Impulse, 115–53
Francis, Sir Philip, 123
Freud, Sigmund, 2, 15, 24, 34, 43, 78, 218; anal theory, 277, 278, 279–80; anal erotism, 72, 73, 75, 76, 273–5, 278–83, 294; anal-sadistic impulses, 16, 17, 19, 98; analytical approach, 82, 83, 93, 275–6; bisexuality, 29; castration, 102; childhood omnipotence, 176; Civilization and Its Discontents, 22; Dostoyevsky's gambling, 7, 18, 25, 157–73, 203, 218; homo-sexuality, 48, 213; masturbation, 6, 23, 77, 97, 237; money, 264–5; need for punishment, 211; obsessional neurotics, 289; Obsessive Actions and Religious Practices, 52; Oedipus complex, 4, 20, 21, 91; perversion, 30; religion, 53, 56, 103; on success, 259; and time, 283–8; Traumdeutung, 251; women, 95
Fromm, Erich, 79
Future of an Illusion, The (Freud essay), 52, 53

gain, low motivational factor of, 93
Galdston, Iago, 33, 34
gambler, types of, 13–15, 188–200, 204, 220–21; characteristics of, 27–8; classical, 189–93, 220
defensive pseudo-superior, 196–7, 221
female, 198
motivated by unconscious guilt, 197–8
passive-feminine male, 193–6, 221
unexcited, 198, 221
Gambler, The (Dostoyevsky), 93, 196, 198, 226
Gamblers Anonymous organization, 3, 10, 11, 13, 59; as substitute, 92;

304

Index

Index